John Ringo

John Peters Ringo, *circa* 1881–1882

JOHN RINGO

The Gunfighter Who Never Was

Jack Burrows

The University of Arizona Press   Tucson

About the Author

JACK BURROWS, on the faculty of San Jose City College, has written many articles on various topics of western history. He has gathered carefully researched data on John Ringo for over thirty years.

First paperbound printing 1996

THE UNIVERSITY OF ARIZONA PRESS

This book was set in Caslon 540 and Caslon 3 typefaces.
⊗ This book is printed on acid-free, archival-quality paper.
Manufactured in the U.S.A.

Library of Congress Cataloging-in-Publication Data

Burrows, Jack.
  John Ringo: the gunfighter who never was.

  Bibliography: p.
  Includes Index.
  1. Ringo, John. 2. Ringo, John—Legends.
3. Outlaws—Southwest, New—Biography. 4. Folklore—
Southwest, New. 5. Southwest, New—Biography.
I. Title.
F786.R57B87 1987   979'.02'0924 [B]   87-5823
ISBN 0-8165-0975-1 (alk. paper)
ISBN 0-8165-1648-0 (pbk.: alk. paper)

British Cataloguing-in-Publication Data
A catalogue record for this book is available from the British
Library.

This book is for Helen,
with love

Contents

Acknowledgments

No HISTORY can be brought to fruition without the aid and encouragement of friends, including those one has never met in person. I am especially indebted to the late Charles R. Ringo, who provided me with the family documents without which this book could not have been written; along with these documents came "Two-Gun Charlie's" unfailing sense of humor, his encouragement, his intelligent and keen sense of history, and his belief that the record should be set straight. I am grateful to the late Eugene Cunningham, novelist, friend of old-time outlaws and lawmen, who took the time to write scores of letters in response to my questions, listened patiently to my arguments and gave his blessings to my efforts; the late Robert N. Mullin, with whom I took many trips throughout the Southwest and stood on sites of historic events, listening to him bring them to life; to Frank A. Tinker, Arizona free-lance writer and Ringo researcher, who has also written of John Ringo and who provided me with vital information along with the encouragement I so badly needed at various times; John D. Gilchriese, researcher-historian who has supplied materials important to my efforts; Glenn G. Boyer, who made valuable suggestions and granted permission to quote from his admirably edited *I Married Wyatt Earp: The Recollections of Josephine Sarah Marcus Earp;* novelist Tony Hillerman, who read the manuscript, understood precisely what I intended the book to do, and recommended its publication; Professor Harwood P. Hinton, editor of *Arizona and the West*, who long ago suggested I do something with John Ringo; the late Eve Ball, who encouraged me in my efforts; Professor C. L. Sonnichsen, whose sparkling *Ten Texas Feuds* I cited liberally, and which book headed me straight to Texas; David Cruickshanks of London, England, who supplied me with material I had not found over here and whose transatlantic research on the Earps and the Southwest is amazing; novelist and boyhood friend Ray Taylor, who listened, read, criticized, and encouraged; my patient academic colleagues, Martin Dreyfuss, Dan Epstein, Gene Costello, Leo Chávez, Charles Murry, Vince Costanza, and Eliot Wirt, who listened and listened and listened; to my wife, Helen, who also listened, eyes glazed; and to John Ringo himself, who grabbed my imagination twenty-five years ago and continues to hold it relentlessly in his grip.

I am also indebted to Carolyn Lake for her gracious permission to quote from *Wyatt Earp—Frontier Marshal*, and from her superbly edited *Under Cover for Wells, Fargo: The Unvarnished Recollections of Fred Dodge*, and to Caxton Printers, Ltd., for permission to quote from Eugene Cunningham's *Triggernometry: A Gallery of Gunfighters*.

Above all, I am indebted to Professor W. H. Hutchinson, that sagebrush sage who is equally at home in the high chaparral or the groves of academe, cow camp or classroom. "Hutch" encouraged me, gave me aid and comfort, read the manuscript and recommended it for publication. Finally, I would like to thank freelance manuscript editor Clare Spera for her assistance on this project.

J. B.

Introduction

THERE HAVE BEEN more extravagant claims made for John Ringo than for Wyatt Earp, Billy the Kid, Wild Bill Hickok, Jesse James, and Buffalo Bill combined. And although there lies buried a substratum of historical truth beneath the myths that engulf him, in a larger sense the story of John Ringo exemplifies the poverty of any considerable body of mature western history and literature that fits its characters, both fictional and real, into the epochal westering of a courageous and determined people and establishes for them a genuine western tradition, a continuity and persona that sprouts from the vast interior and soil of the American West.

John Ringo was both a part of that westering and a victim of it. His short life is the stuff of western history and of potentially intelligent western fiction. At fourteen, on a wagon train headed west, he witnessed the grotesque and useless death of his father. He helped to bear his mother's grief and to care for three little sisters and a sickly younger brother. He saw murder committed. And at nineteen, in California, he fled his filial obligations, went to Texas, and became an outlaw—and almost certainly a killer.

John Ringo was the only bad apple to fall from a well-rooted family tree. Inexplicably alienated, antisocial, unhappy, alcoholic, suicidal, and quite possibly psychotic, John Ringo knew the cold and empty reaches of a barren universe.

For thirteen of his thirty-two years he rode with outlaw gangs, one of which, the Scott Cooley Gang, was referred to by historian C. L. Sonnichsen as a "bunch of human coyotes."[1] He was not driven to outlawry. He was not the inheritor of "bad seed." He was almost certainly the architect of his own destruction.

Quite aside from the Ringo family documents that were made available to me, there were newspaper articles, records of arrest and jail breaks, inquest records, depositions and memoirs which reveal the discernible outlines of a character and personality almost completely antithetical to the paladin created by scores of writers: the champion of womanhood, friend of little children, scholar, the fastest, deadliest gunfighter in the West. One novelist referred to John Ringo over and over as "the tall rider," as if height itself were a personal achievement and virtue, and, indeed, as if he knew that John Ringo *was* tall.

There are, of course, the obvious reasons why men like John Ringo have persistently been mythicized and romanticized: there is the rather infantile notion of a life free of the restraints of civilization, lived in a romantic and illimitable landscape, which we vicariously share; the thought of the fearless man's man, who dominated society rather than being dominated by it; the image of the self-contained man, who walked tall and lived his life on his own terms. In the end we create from his shadowy outline the kind of man we would like to think existed in the Old West. The real reason, though, is that there have been no great western historical works from which to build. The West's history was too quickly seized by the dime novelists, Wild West shows and, later, by the pulps, formula western writers, and motion pictures. I am reminded of a comment made by Miss Jo James, the granddaughter of Jesse, when asked what she thought of the 1939 motion picture, "Jesse James." "Well," she said, "about the only connection it had with fact was that there once was a man named James and he did ride a horse."[2]

darkly handsome, splendidly brave, a man born for better things, who, having thrown his life recklessly away, drowned his memories in cards and drink and drifted without definite purpose or destination. . . . He was a silent man of mystery who, in bitter moods of melancholy, sometimes spoke of suicide. . . . His recklessness . . . was due to the small value he placed upon his life; if someone else killed him, he would be saved the trouble of killing himself. . . . Womanhood to him was an (icon) before which he bowed in reverence. No woman was so bad that she was ever outside the pale of his knightly chivalry. A man [chancing] a disparaging remark about any woman, be she irreproachable maid or matron or red-light siren, had to eat his words or fight. That was John Ringo's way.[2]

Ringo had three sisters who lived in San Jose, California. According to Burns, he was "devotedly attached" to them, and the endlessly repeated story has it that whenever Ringo received a letter addressed in a feminine hand (presumably by one of his sisters), he was "cast adrift" in a dangerous and drunken despond for "days thereafter." Riding with Deputy Sheriff William M. "Billy" Breakenridge one day, Ringo "shook his head sadly as he held out an envelope. 'Sweetheart?' asked Breakenridge. 'My sister,' said Ringo solemnly. 'She writes me regularly. Thinks I'm in the cattle business out here and doing fine. Doing fine. Humph! Dear little sister, I hope she never learns the truth!'"[3] A later Burns imitator, Joseph Millard, quoted Ringo, whom, he claimed, "wrote long, frequent letters to his sisters," as "crying out" in a "mood of dark bitterness, 'Thank God, they do not know the depths to which their brother has fallen'." And then, in a "cry of torment and self-loathing torn from his lips, 'I am a thief and a killer, but before God I was not raised for such a life of bitter evil as this'."[4]

Shakespearean dimensions and Oedipal-suicidal-homicidal proclivities aside, Ringo was and is to western writers the classic cowboy-gunfighter. "Ringo was born in Texas," Burns declared, with an authority that suggests a thorough check of

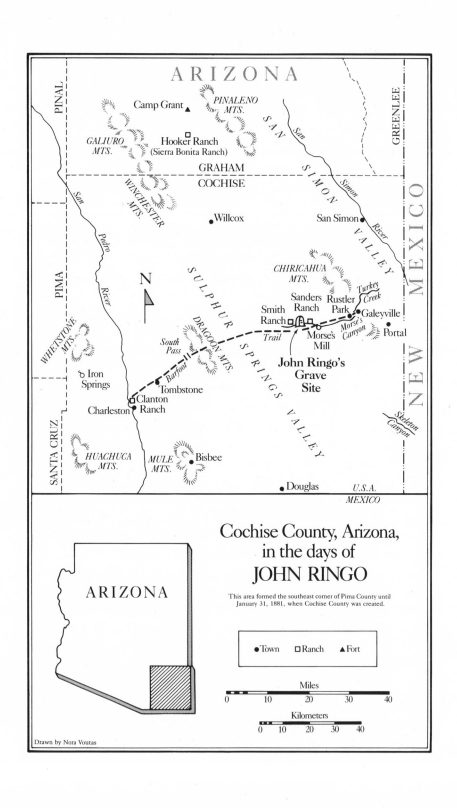

ARIZONA

PINAL

GREENLEE

Camp Grant ▲ *PINALENO MTS.*

GALIURO MTS. Hooker Ranch □ (Sierra Bonita Ranch)

S A N

S I M O N

GRAHAM
COCHISE

WINCHESTER MTS.

San *Simon* *River*

•Willcox San Simon •

CHIRICAHUA MTS.

V A L L E Y

S U L P H U R

N

Smith Ranch □ Sanders Ranch Rustler Park •Galeyville
Trail Morse's Mill Morse's Canyon •Portal

DRAGOON MTS.

Turkey Creek

San Pedro River

PIMA

WHETSTONE MTS.

South Pass

S P R I N G S

John Ringo's Grave Site

ꝋ Iron Springs

Barfoot

•Tombstone

Charleston• Clanton □ Ranch

V A L L E Y

Skeleton Canyon

SANTA CRUZ

HUACHUCA MTS.

MULE MTS. •Bisbee

•Douglas *U.S.A.*
MEXICO

N E W   M E X I C O

Cochise County, Arizona, in the days of
JOHN RINGO

This area formed the southeast corner of Pima County until
January 31, 1881, when Cochise County was created.

ARIZONA

| •Town | □ Ranch | ▲ Fort |

Miles
0   10   20   30   40

Kilometers
0   10   20   30   40

Drawn by Nora Voutas

the vital statistics. "When he was little more than a boy, he became involved in a war between sheep and cattlemen. His only brother was killed in the feud, and Ringo hunted down the three murderers and killed them."[5] Lest that seem something of an accomplishment for "little more than a boy," Burns reminds us that Ringo's tradition and antecedents were in perfect order, for he rode in the bloody nimbus of Quantrill and the James brothers, and of the Youngers, to whom he was related: "Ringo came by his reckless courage honestly. He was a second cousin of the famous Younger brothers of Missouri. . . . Col. Coleman Younger (of San Jose, California) was his grandfather."[6]

Ringo "drifted" (cowboys always "drift") west to southeastern Arizona from Mason, Texas, in 1879, where he had been a warrior in the Hoodoo War (see Chapter 8), a member of the Scott Cooley outlaw band, a probable participant in two cowardly killings, and, more lately, the occupant of a Texas jail.[7] Apparently accustomed to riding with a gang, Ringo quickly attached himself to the Curly Bill Brocius–N.H. "Old Man" Clanton rustler outfit, and as a charter leader. "He was a good shot and afraid of nothing," Deputy William Breakenridge wrote, "and a great authority with the rustling element."[8] The Curly Bill–Ringo branch of the rustler gang headquartered in Galeyville, a cluster of shacks, saloons, and privies knocked together around a defunct mine and smelter. Located at the base of the eastern escarpment of Arizona's Chiricahua Mountains and in the farthest southeastern corner of Cochise County, Galeyville had become (with at least tacit recognition by the law) a sanctuary for refugees from the Texas range wars and feuds, and from New Mexico's Lincoln County War. Hard by Galeyville was the verdant and fecund San Simon Valley, where the tall grama grass swished a man's stirrups as he rode through it and where stolen cattle, run across the Mexican border, were held, fattened, rebranded, and sold to mute and free-enterprising Arizona ranchers.

Across the Chiricahuas was another outlaw hamlet,

Charleston, a batch of adobes squatting along the banks of the San Pedro River a half-dozen miles southeast of Tombstone and in a straight line for the Mexican border, should a man have a mind or need to "cut the wind." Just up-river from Charleston was Old Man Clanton's ranch, a thick-walled and loop-holed adobe that crested a low knoll with a broad view in every direction. Below the ranch house, among the cottonwoods that grew thickly along the river flats, were holding corrals and pens for stolen Mexican steers. The Clanton ranch was headquarters for the band when it crossed the border to the south.[9] These rustler hangouts were loosely connected by the Barfoot Trail. Beginning in Charleston, the trail ran up the San Pedro to the Clanton ranch, northeast by or through Tombstone, on through South Pass of the Dragoon Mountains, and across arid Sulphur Springs Valley. It crossed the Chiricahuas through tall pine groves that came to be called Rustler Park, and dropped down the eastern slope to Galeyville. It would be the last trail John Ringo would ride.

Because so little has been and is known about Ringo, because he lived in a baffling world of lights and shadows, he has been, as I wrote some years ago, "commonly disembodied and idealized, . . . the apotheosis of the western hero, Byronic, solitary, tortured, and mysterious."[10] It would follow, then, that those who were intrigued by the brooding and abiding mystery of the man and who wished to write about him, would cling tenaciously and elaborately to two recurring and totally undocumented presumptions, along with the only two reasonably well-documented events in his life. These form the substance or nucleus of all writings about John Ringo. What is added to them are dramatic gestures of empty authority, the exemplification of just about everything that has gone wrong with western literature: shoddy research and faulty reasoning, unquestioning repetition of sensational and undocumented claims, demonstrable plagiarisms and single-source derivations, such as from Burns or Breakenridge.

The first presumption is that Ringo was a self-exiled,

black-sheep scion of a cultured, genteel, and wealthy southern family whose name was Ringgold. Corollaries of this presumption are that he shortened his name to Ringo in an effort to spare family sensibilities and to preserve its good name and that he was a college graduate, perhaps even a professor, tragically entrapped intellectually and psychically between the groves of academe and the high chaparral, a renegade professor with a gun who traded the halls of ivy for the owl-hoot trail, and whose rustication has been laid to everything from drink to a woman or to an even darker deed. Whatever it was that sent the "professor" galloping for the wide-open spaces presumably released latent furies in a brilliant but Quixotic—perhaps even psychopathic—mind. But the contentions of family gentility or a college education are supported by nothing more than what must have been a noticeably proper use of the English language. "He was plainly a man of some breeding and inherent refinement," Burns wrote. "The primitive speech of the frontier was not his language; he spoke literate English and many believed, though it is improbable, that he had been educated at college."[11]

Breakenridge is both more specific and suspiciously vague. "Ringo," he observed, "was a very mysterious man. He had a college education, but was reserved and morose. He drank heavily as if to drown his troubles; he was a perfect gentleman when sober, but inclined to be quarrelsome when drinking. He was a good shot and afraid of nothing. . . ." After cattle raids into Mexico and raids against Mexican gold smugglers,* he "generally kept by himself . . . [in] Galeyville. He read a great deal and had a small collection of standard books in his cabin."[12]

We are emphatically told that Ringo was college–educated, but we are not privy to Breakenridge's source of infor-

---

* Burns tells a blood and thunder story of the Ringo–Curly Bill Gang ambushing Mexican smugglers, killing 19 and robbing them of $70,000. The *Epitaph* sets the killing at 4 and the loot at $4,000. Tombstone *Epitaph*, August 5, 1881.

mation. He does not say "Ringo told me," nor does he mention the name or location of the college. It is possible he had no real concept of college—most frontiersmen did not—and simply made an assumption, awed, perhaps, by the presence of that "collection of standard books," which could have included anything from McGuffy's *Reader* to the latest penny dreadfuls.

The second presumption is that Ringo was one of the fastest, deadliest gunfighters in the west, a defender of womanhood and the inculcated imperatives of civilized delicacy, and, after the finest tradition of honor among thieves, a man whose word, Breakenridge wrote, "was as good as a bond,"[13] the quintessentially honorable outlaw and gunfighter. We are not given examples of Ringo's shooting ability, nor are we told whether the targets were inanimate, living, or shooting back. Breakenridge comes no closer to first person information than the casual observation that "Ringo told me enough about his family for me to know that they were not aware that he was an outlaw."[14]

Credibility deliquesces in the absence of tangible documentation. There is no record of Ringo engaging in so much as a single "classic" gunfight or of killing anyone in Arizona, although there was one brutal and clumsy attempt by Ringo to shoot a man named Louis Hancock. The shooting took place in a saloon in Safford, Arizona. The popular myth holds that Hancock had made a disparaging and unrepentant remark about a whore. But, according to the Tucson *Daily Star,* "Ringo wanted Hancock to take a drink of whiskey, and he refused, saying he preferred beer. Ringo struck him over the head with his pistol and then fired, the ball taking effect in the lower . . . left ear . . . and the fleshy part of the neck; half inch more . . . would have killed him. Ringo is under arrest."[15]

It wasn't much of a gunfight and the shooting was spectacular only for its near miss at point-blank range. But the body counters, with hurried knowingness and no discernible research, declared Hancock a "kill" and clasped him to their collective bosoms with morbid satisfaction. And though depicted as champion of both "chippie" and chaste (which, Burns said, was "John Ringo's way"), there is not even a provable suggestion of a single shot fired or punch thrown in behalf of virtue and womanhood. As for his word being "as good as a bond," we have only Breakenridge's word for that, and the facts show that Breakenridge could not always make the same claim for his own word.

In another story, Ringo was drinking and gambling in a Galeyville saloon. He lost. When no one would stake him, he left, came back with a Henry rifle, held up the game, and rode off with five hundred dollars on a stolen horse.[16] Breakenridge claimed the money was returned as soon as Ringo sobered up: "The players all got their money back and were satisfied, as they all liked Ringo."[17] (Nothing is said about the horse.) Well, almost all. Someone complained to the grand jury and Ringo was indicted for highway robbery. Deputy Sheriff Breakenridge was sent to Galeyville to fetch him in. Ringo did not wish to be arrested in front of the gang, so he asked Breakenridge to go back to Prues ranch. He would meet the deputy there in the morning. Breakenridge obediently complied, and, true to his word, ". . . Ringo was there for breakfast. He had come in the night and rather than disturb anyone he had slept in the haystack."[18]

Ringo was, Burns gushed, "an honorable outlaw. . . . His word once given was kept inviolately. Those to whom he made a promise could be sure he would fulfill it to the last letter, or die trying."[19] Doubtless Ringo was a man of his word. He might have promised Hancock that he would shoot him if he drank beer instead of whiskey. But the determination to keep one's word (however insignificant or meaningless that word or promise might have been) or "die trying" is fanatical rather than honorable, reflecting the same disordered thinking that ostensibly convinced Ringo of his right to kill a man for a disparaging remark about a woman or for preferring beer to whiskey. The effusions of Burns, Breakenridge, and others seem less a testimony to honor than to verisimilitude. Submitting to arrest on his own terms could not have placed too heavy a burden or strain on Ringo's honor, even if it did mean spending a night in a haystack.

Ringo had an unusually chummy relationship with Breakenridge and with the deputy's superior, John H. "Johnny" Behan, sheriff of Cochise County. "I met Ringo frequently . . . [in] Galeyville," Breakenridge wrote, "and was very well acquainted with him, and we had had many pleasant visits."[20]

After Ringo's arrest, the two men rode into Tombstone, where Ringo was lodged, armed and unattended, not in the jail, but in the jailer's home across the street.[21] In the morning bond was expeditiously made, Breakenridge thoughtfully brought Ringo's horse around for him, and the rustler was off to Charleston.[22] Noting the easy comaraderie between outlaws and lawmen, the Tombstone *Epitaph* complained that "there is altogether too much good feeling between the sheriff's office and the outlaws infesting this country."[23] Ringo's honor in this affair, the only recorded instance of it, appears directly equated with a complaisant sheriff's office and with the mindful attentions and respectful obsequiousness of Deputy Breakenridge himself.

2

The Tombstone Situation and the Earp-Clanton Feud

THE TWO reasonably well documented events in John Ringo's life—his near shoot-out with Wyatt Earp and John H. "Doc" Holliday on Tombstone's Allen Street, and the almost sacramental circumstances of his death, presumably by suicide (see Chapter 10)—must be considered within the context of events superficially referred to as the "Tombstone Situation" and the "Earp-Clanton Feud." Feud, in this instance, is the improper term, since it generally implies deep and abiding family hatreds which have come to bear on their own momentum and whose origins have become obscure. Doubtless the usage here derived from the family alignments in a many-faceted and complex power struggle for the political and economic domination of Tombstone and Cochise County. This struggle involved the Clanton–Ringo–Curly Bill outlaw band, the sheriff's office, the territorial governors and the Democratic and Republican parties, and pitted the three Earp brothers—Wyatt, Virgil and Morgan—along with their sidekick, John H. "Doc" Holliday, against Old Man Clanton's outlaw sons—Phineas (Phin), John Isaac (Ike), and William (Billy)—and the two McLaury brothers, Tom and Frank. The situation climaxed in the famous gunfight near the O.K. Corral* on October 26, 1881, a sanguinary tragedy (the McLaury

* The fight actually took place on a vacant lot adjacent to the O.K. Corral, near the corner of Fremont and Third Streets.

boys and Billy Clanton were killed) that begot the insouciant commission of so many related crimes, including murder, as to draw a presidential proclamation threatening martial law in Cochise County.[1]

I see no reason to indulge the usual physical description of John Ringo's bailiwick, Tombstone, to reel off the standard litany of the number and locations of whorehouses, to rhapsodize over the proliferation of saloons or the phony grave markers on an equally phony Boot Hill, or to get caught up in that weary old "man for breakfast" syndrome, or fight the O.K. Corral battle again. Except for a dual economy, mining and cattle, Tombstone was not particularly unusual among a hundred or more noted boomtowns that were born of mineral veins or raised from the offal of buffalo camps across the West. Birthed of a silver strike made in 1879 by a lone prospector, Ed Schieffelin, the town was named, presumably, after a cryptic conversation between the young prospector and a crusty old Army Chief of Scouts, Al Seiber, who came across Schieffelin pecking about in Apache country and who, according to popular legend, gruffly opined that all he would find was his tombstone. The bemused miner carried colorful place names over to three other local and rich strikes: the Lucky Cuss, the Toughnut, and the Contention. The sepulchral tone and play on names continued when future Tombstone Mayor John Clum founded his newspaper, the *Epitaph*, in 1880 in political opposition to the already established *Nugget*. Every tombstone, Clum is supposed to have said, ought to have its epitaph; and, he claimed, the name of the paper would be like free advertising.

Almost as self-consciously heroic then, with its batch of aggressive place names, as it is today, Tombstone labored mightily—and successfully—to keep its "shoot'em up" reputation alive and profitably green. And it is true that its list of sometime residents reads like a who's who in the Wild West: Wyatt Earp and his brothers, Doc Holliday, Bat Masterson, Luke Short, Charlie Storms, John Ringo, Curly Bill, the Clantons, Buckskin Frank Leslie, John Slaughter and the Mc-Laurys, along with a half-hundred lesser lights, all of whom were probably just as handy with the six-gun as their better known brethren. But it is also true that of the above-named men, only Wyatt Earp, Holliday, Masterson, and Short bore anything that might be called wider reputations. John Ringo's part in the Mason County (Hoodoo) War in Texas (see Chapter 8) is shadowy at best, and is in no sense even remotely comparable to the records of those other Texas pistoleros, John Wesley Hardin, Bill Longley, Ben Thompson, and J. King Fisher. We still know nothing of Curly Bill's origins. We are not even sure of who he was. Buckskin Frank Leslie is best known for killing a woman. John Slaughter's reputation was local and earned largely after Tombstone's wild days were over. I believe it to be more than possible that we should never have heard of any of these people, or, indeed, very much about Tombstone itself, had Wyatt Earp and Doc Holliday gone south, rather than southwest.

Tombstone was a tough enough town to sate the appetites of the most sanguinivorous, but it was by no means "the toughest mining camp in the West." Virginia City and Bannack, Montana, held in the sinister grip of the Henry Plummer Gang, were far more violent. In Tombstone the vigilantes threatened action; in Virginia City and Bannack they took it, lynching most of the Plummer Gang, including Sheriff Plummer himself. Bodie, California, had more men (and women) killed in gunfights (in her 1956 book *The Story of Bodie*, Ella M. Cain lists twelve killings on pages 28–29 alone, and observed that the list could go "on and on"). Mobeetie, Texas, may have been the toughest of them all.

No single dark and mysterious power ruled Tombstone from 1879 to 1882. But to comprehend the cross currents of animosities and ambitions, the jealousies and hatreds that flourished in the booming mining camp, of which the Earp-Clanton fight was only a single manifestation, one must consider the various law enforcement agencies that were formed, along with those other alliances that evolved symbiotically from mutual need and aspiration—even from weakness—and how they affected the individuals involved, including John Ringo.

There were actually three law enforcement agencies and one possibly quasi-legal organization functioning in Tombstone. The county sheriff held jurisdiction over all crimes in the district and county. The city marshal was elected, but in the event a vacancy occurred the mayor could appoint a replacement. His duties and responsibilities were largely confined to the city of Tombstone. The United States marshal's authority obtained when stagecoach robberies interfered with the transit of the mails. When both mail and bullion were stolen, which was usually the case, the duties of the U.S. marshal and the sheriff overlapped. Overlapping occurred, too, in Tombstone, where both the city marshal and the sheriff were responsible for enforcing such ordinances as forbade racing horses along the streets, walking them on the sidewalks, or carrying guns. In an atmosphere of mutual concern and collaboration, interlocking agencies might have been—could have been—singularly effective. In Tombstone, which was both blessed and cursed with the greatest variety of famous and infamous characters to inhabit any western bailiwick at one time,[2] mutual collaboration was more unthinkable than impossible.

Wyatt Earp rode into the raw and bustling boom camp in late 1879, a shotgun messenger for Wells, Fargo and Company. The argument over whether or not he had already been appointed a deputy sheriff for Pima County* or was appointed later, or whether he was a deputy U.S. marshal, seems unimportant and was inspired, perhaps, by Earp's biographer, Stuart N. Lake, whose treatment of his subject's arrival almost

* The Tombstone area was part of Pima County until January 31, 1881, when Cochise County was created.

as a moment of epiphany has both irritated and titillated students and scholars of western history. Earp, who was thirty-one, was somewhat known for his "lawing," as he called it, in Kansas; one could safely say only that. He was hardly famous. Revisionist historians have not thought him important enough for serious biography, but coveys of shabby hacks have swarmed, producing scores of articles so truly rotten—no other adjective suffices—as to make old Ned Buntline seem a sedulous practitioner of historical discipline and fidelity. Typical of these was the question article "Wyatt Earp—Hero or Heel?" (*Real Man* 1, No. 1 [Nov., 1957]) by one Bob Bristow, which contains neither a single completely accurate statement nor a scrap of new information, but which concludes, darkly, that "Wyatt Earp understood how treacherous a man could be. He was, after all, an authority on the subject."

Wyatt Earp's record in Wichita and Dodge City, and in Lamar, Missouri, though intermittent and unspectacular, seems solid enough. There is no demonstrable evidence that he had ever killed anyone (which is all to his credit) before coming to Tombstone. If he sought publicity at all it seems to have been in his impoverished old age when he tried to sell his story. And one could not fault him for that: he had a story to tell.

Wyatt Earp did not ride into Tombstone, face set in a grim mask, blue eyes watchfully slitted, and with a twelve-inch-barrelled "Buntline Special" Colt strapped to his leg. The big, eighteen-inch-overall "Ned" was a piece (a tumescent extension, a phallus, if one wishes to go west with young Freud and with the writers of today's "Westerns") that, according to James Serven, existed only in the imagination of Stuart Lake,[3] but which "flashes," "roars," and "buffaloes" (cracks skulls) in the pages of Lake's *Wyatt Earp: Frontier Marshall.*[4] Folks did not stop to stare. The storekeeper, who in the movies and on television seems to have nothing better to do than sweep his front boardwalk, did not pause in his labors, momentarily frozen in recognition, lean his broom cautiously against the wall, wipe his hands nervously on his apron, and hurry inside to report to the boss. Disembodied faces that bore the look of startled recognition did not float above bat-wing doors, then recede hurriedly into the interior gloom. There was no drumming of hoofbeats leaving town and no evidence, as Lake claimed, that Wyatt knew both Curly Bill and John Ringo from Wichita and Dodge City.[5]

It is enough to say that Tombstone received Wyatt Earp, if not with awe, with respect. He was, as events would establish him, a man to be reckoned with, and Lake's superlatives in no way diminish him. The Tombstone *Epitaph* did not run his name until eight months after his arrival and then, Douglas D. Martin wrote, "it spoke of him as a deputy sheriff who formed a posse and went in search of George Perine, who was wanted on a murder charge."[6] On October 20, 1880, just a year and a week before the O.K. Corral fight, the *Epitaph* congratulated Earp on his appointment as deputy sheriff: "The appointment of Wyatt Earp as deputy sheriff by Sheriff [Charles] Shibell [of Pima County], is an eminently proper one, and we, in common with citizens generally, congratulate the latter on his selection. Wyatt has filled various positions in which bravery and determination were requisites, and in every instance proved himself the right man in the right place. He is . . . shotgun messenger for Wells, Fargo and Company. . . . He will resign to accept the latter appointment. Morgan Earp succeeds his brother as shotgun messenger. . . ."[7] He was not yet celebrated in song, but Wyatt Earp was known, his achievements recognized. Fame, though, as he was to know it, would wait for the O.K. Corral.

Wyatt's brothers, the older Virgil and James and the younger Morgan, shortly joined him in Tombstone. All had reputations of sorts. Virgil was cool, deliberate, perhaps the toughest of the lot. Morgan was both hot-headed and good-natured. James did not figure in the fighting. The *Tucson Star* called them the "handsome brothers."[8] Allied with the Earps,

particularly with Wyatt and Morgan, in inexplicable friendship and loyalty was the skeletal but sartorially elegant dentist
John Henry "Doc" Holliday, whose eyes burned at once with
the fevers of tuberculosis and with the dangerous fatalism
produced by the knowledge that the disease, if not a bullet,
would kill him. Among Doc's other afflictions were alcohol, a
nasty and profane temper, and, in Western parlance if not
necessarily in reality, an "itchy trigger finger." Only the Earps
seemed to command his respect.[9] All in all, it was an awesome
quartet.

John H. Behan arrived in Tombstone early in 1880. Behan's
credentials as a peace officer were actually more impressive
than Wyatt Earp's. Headquartered in Prescott, Arizona, Behan had been deputy sheriff, under-sheriff, sheriff, assessor,
county recorder, tax collector, and deputy clerk of the District Court. He had also served as a member of the Seventh
Legislative Assembly in the House from Prescott, Yavapai
County, and the Tenth Assembly (House) from Mojave
County.[10] It seems inevitable, then, that Behan, who began
his life in Tombstone as a partner in a livery stable, would
also be appointed a deputy sheriff for Pima County.

On November 9, 1880, Wyatt Earp, ostensibly disillusioned with Sheriff Shibell's lack of concern for lawlessness in
Pima County, resigned as deputy sheriff in order to support
the candidacy of Shibell's rival for the office of sheriff, deputy
U.S. marshal Bob Paul of Tucson. Shibell handed Wyatt's
deputy badge over to Behan, and Wyatt rode shotgun for
Wells, Fargo for an unspecified length of time. It was during
this stint as a Wells, Fargo guard that Crawley P. Drake, U.S.
marshal for Arizona, appointed Wyatt deputy U.S. marshal
for the Tombstone District. (On February 11, 1984, the San
Francisco *Chronicle* reported that Wyatt Earp's letter of resignation was found in the Pima County Recorder's Office in
Tucson. Dated November 9, 1880, the letter reads: "I have

the honor herewith to resign the office of deputy sheriff of Pima County. Respectfully, Wyatt S. Earp.")

As it turned out for all concerned, including the city of Tombstone itself and what was soon to become Cochise County, Deputy Marshal Earp and Deputy Sheriff (later Sheriff) Behan were an unfortunate combination. They simply did not mesh. Behan lacked the force, the cool directness, the self-contained taciturnity and disciplined single-mindedness of Wyatt Earp. Essentially a politician, Behan was accommodating in a calculating and enterprising way, an astute middleman, a mindful and nimble go-between; in current parlance, he was an "operator," a "fixer." He was not to be one of the Old West's great lawmen. It was his destiny to scuttle back and forth between major factions and events that were far beyond his control, beyond his manipulative powers. Historical redemption, even a kind of immortality, might have been his had he coolly and determinedly interposed himself (as Cochise County sheriff) between the Earps and the cowboys at the O.K. Corral. He might have prevented a genuine tragedy. He might have been killed. He ducked, instead, to safety, like the etiolated backroom plotter in a Hopalong Cassidy movie.

Both Behan and Earp were ambitious. Both knew the territorial legislature had completed plans to lop some seven thousand square miles off the southeastern corner of Pima County, forming a new district that would bear the eponymous name of Cochise County. Both officers hoped to be appointed sheriff of Cochise County, a position which, along with certain emoluments, "paid about forty thousand dollars a year," [11] an incredible stipend when one considers it in relation even to today's salaries. And both men had reason for optimism: John P. Clum, erstwhile San Carlos Apache Agent, founder of the Tombstone *Epitaph* and later appointed postmaster, was elected mayor of Tombstone on January 4, 1881, by the votes of the Law and Order League. [12] "The *Epitaph*," wrote Douglas Martin, "became the organ of law and order in a community . . . dominated by gunmen, rustlers, and those businessmen who fattened on their trade. . . . The *Epitaph* saw in Earp an honest and fearless law officer. . . . The paper became his champion and when Clum was elected mayor he made . . . Virgil [Earp] his chief of police. Morgan [Earp] . . . served under Virgil as a special officer."[13] Moreover, Wyatt Earp and Clum were Republicans, as were the national administration and the territorial governor, John C. Frémont, the old Pathfinder, now in an inept dotage and stashed away out in the sagebrush in what was expected to be a last, uneventful sinecure. It would be Frémont who would make the appointment.

Behan was a Democrat, and the territory, in contrast to the national administration and the territorial governor, was heavily Democratic; Behan, Arizona historian Frank Lockwood declared vaguely, "had many influential backers."[14] Since Lockwood had no use for Earp, whom he considered a "cold-blooded killer,"[15] he is perhaps purposely vague. Behan's backers seem to have been those cattlemen who purchased rustled stock and those businessmen who fattened on the rustler "trade." Inexplicably, Frémont appointed Behan.[16]

Under the circumstances it would be natural, or at least predictable, for a man like Behan to seek to strengthen his position by an alliance with the outlaw element, to protect and alibi them in their later vulpine movements against the Earps, even to use them as posse members. Short of resignation from the lucrative position of sheriff, there was no other group to turn to, and he had not the stuff to stake out neutral ground and occupy and hold it. And the politicians who had secured his appointment as sheriff continued to support him. By his tacit alliance with the outlaws, Behan implicitly and perhaps subconsciously admitted to the fears and impuissance that, ironically, his outlaw associations transmuted into a personal power. A Cadmean crop of rustlers sprang up in the sanctuary that was Behan's Cochise County. Many of these rode with the Curly Bill–Ringo–Clanton band

and were doubtless told the band's leadership was beholden to the sheriff. Will Sanders, owner of the Chiricahua foothill ranch on which John Ringo is buried, told me his father remembered riding through pine-stippled Rustler Park, high in the Chiricahuas, early one morning and counting more than seventy outlaws camped among the deep pine groves. John Ringo was among them. Sanders, a small rancher, had lost no cattle to the rustlers and he, in turn, observed a strict and understood code of silence. Ringo invited Sanders to take breakfast. Sanders recalled that a thick pool of pancake batter lay in the deep sag of a tarp that was loosely suspended by its four corners to four trees. He dipped into the batter, tossed his flapjacks, ate and moved on.[17] It is of more than passing interest to note that in New Mexico's Lincoln County War the opposing sides combined never mustered such a force, or potential force.

All this, of course, is not to suggest that Behan had an outlaw army at his disposal, or that outlaw support sustained him in office by occupying the attention of the Earp brothers. It does suggest some sort of arrangement between the sheriff's office, the outlaws, and certain territorial politicians. There is a respectable body of evidence that more than circumstantially confirms Behan's outlaw connections. In *Helldorado* (pp. 131–32), Breakenridge, for example, makes quite a hero of himself for the collection of over a thousand dollars in taxes from the outlaw element in Galeyville and in the San Simon Valley with the personal aid of Curly Bill. Although Breakenridge takes credit for the unique idea of enlisting the rustler chief's help, the idea was almost certainly Behan's, since he sent Breakenridge out to collect the taxes. He must have known that collection could have been accomplished only with the aid of the rustler boss.

Johnny Behan does not seem to have been a really bad man, not in the classic sense, at least. Neither, as he demonstrated at the O.K. Corral, was he, as Breakenridge declared, "brave and fearless."[18] Sol Israel, a Tombstone old-timer, recalled in a 1928 letter to Stuart Lake, that "as to Johnny Behan, he was afraid of his own shadow. . . ."[19] Behan was an ordinary man with perhaps above-ordinary intelligence. He might have served reasonably well as sheriff of Cochise County, might have established some sort of frontier rapprochement between the outlaw element and the citizenry, with himself leaning back upon a moderately lawful and supportive citizen-backed base, had it not been for the presence (to Behan, the intrusion) of the Earp brothers and Doc Holliday. Had he not fallen back upon his outlaw supporters, the presence of the Earps would have rendered him powerless.

The Earps were aggressive and determined men. Morgan was arrogant and quarrelsome on occasion. So was Holliday, who stood for nothing more than his loyalty to the Earps. All managed to wear badges or to be deputized at one time or another. Behan could not function in such company and circumstances. There could have been no O.K. Corral fight without the Earps; Behan, on the other hand, was powerless to prevent it. The outlaws needed him and he needed them. The Earps made (and continue to make) strong friends and bitter enemies. Depending on one's proclivities or view, the Earps were town-tamers who had the guts to take on a bullying band of outlaws which dominated the sheriff and his department, or they were ruthless killers, disrupters of an amicable, look-the-other-way kind of status quo. There doubtless is truth to both positions or arguments. If one might seek analogy in nature, Tombstone was like a tankful of barracudas into which was dumped a bucketful of piranhas; around and about all these swam a jellyfish, charged with keeping the peace.

Douglas Martin seems a trifle dramatic in proclaiming Earp "a man of action, who shook the deserts and the mountains of the border when he walked."[20] But within a week of his appointment as deputy sheriff, Earp at least shook rustler chief Curly Bill's skull and his cocksure composure with a gun barrel. Curly and some of "the boys" had got themselves "roostered" and "began firing at the moon and stars on Allen Street, near Sixth." Tombstone's first city marshal, Fred White, a former army officer and a good man, responded to the shooting with Wyatt, Virgil, and Morgan Earp following. White yanked Curly Bill's gun from his hand and the weapon discharged, fatally wounding the marshal. Wyatt Earp rushed up and smashed Curly Bill over the head. "Deputy Sheriff Earp," the *Epitaph* declared proudly, "who is ever to the front when duty calls, arrived just in the nick of time. Seeing the Marshal fall, he promptly knocked his assailant down with a six-shooter, and as promptly locked him up, and with the assistance of his brothers, Virgil and Morgan, went in pursuit of the others. That he found them, an inventory of the roster of the City Prison this morning will testify."[21] There is no indication of John Ringo being among the shooters or the arrested.

White lingered several days, then died. In a deathbed statement he exonerated Curly Bill, claiming the shooting was accidental. The argument among students of western history still rages over whether Curly Bill worked the "road agent's spin" (offering the gun, butt first, dangling from the forefinger through the trigger guard, then as it is reached for spinning it up into firing position and cocking it with the momentum) on the unindoctrinated ex-soldier, who, as an officer and gentleman accustomed to rules and obedience, failed to fully gauge the depths of civilian trickery and treachery, and who perhaps did not realize what had really happened to him. This argument has obscured a significant fact: the shooting occurred just past midnight in a dark and unlighted area. Wyatt Earp could have seen only the figures of the two men, the flash of the gun, and White falling. In the circumstances, he would have been justified in killing Curly Bill on the spot. One cannot imagine Dallas Stoudenmire, Pat Garrett, Wild Bill Hickok, Frank Hamer, or any one of a dozen other Western peace officers doing anything else: Hickok shot a deputy who was rushing to his defense; Hamer killed fifty men; Stoudenmire killed a bystander in a wild and panicky shoot-out; and Pat Garrett did not try banging Billy The Kid over the head with a six-shooter in that darkened bedroom at Fort Sumner, New Mexico. Ironically, the clubbing and arrest of Curly Bill occurred one year almost to the day before the O.K. Corral fight, for which Wyatt Earp would be labeled a "cold-blooded killer" by Lockwood, Breakenridge, and scores of others.

Curly Bill was hustled off to Tucson when a vigilance committee commenced "organizing to hang the prisoner"[22] but upon Marshal White's deathbed statement he was released. Curly Bill came back to Tombstone. He did not walk stiffly down Allen Street after the finest cinematic tradition, hand hanging loosely and indolently over his low-slung gun, Stetson pulled down over slitted eyes, yelling "Wyatt Earp, c'mon out." That was not the way of Curly Bill and his "boys," with the exception, reputedly, of John Ringo.

But the rough manhandling of Curly Bill marked the beginning of declared hostilities between the Earps and Holliday and their supporters, including *Epitaph* Editor Clum and the Law and Order group, and the cowboy-outlaws led by Curly Bill and John Ringo and at least tacitly supported by Sheriff Behan's office. After the O.K. Corral fight, in which Billy Clanton and Tom and Frank McLaury were killed and in which the outlaws were forced for the first and only time into an open fight, all the actual shooting was done from ambush. On December 28, 1881, near midnight, City Marshal Virgil Earp was shotgunned in the back and crippled for life as he crossed Tombstone's Fifth and Allen streets. Three weeks later, on January 17, 1882, John Ringo did openly challenge Doc and Wyatt to a shoot-out on Allen Street.

No near-gunfight in the history of the Old West (not a single shot was fired) has been burdened with so many grossly inaccurate and personally intrusive accounts and interpretations of what happened, or what might have happened, or which reflect so much wishful thinking, as that storied encounter. Some of these approach the inane. Some accounts have Ringo snarling, cursing and yelling, and calling the Earps yellow-bellied cowards; in others, his voice is barely audible and his face bears an enigmatic smile; in still another, he "kills" Louis Hancock in Tombstone's Oriental Saloon right in front of Wyatt Earp in order to force the marshal into a fight.

Since most of these accounts suggest, or claim outright, that the Earps and Holliday were everything from *possibly* afraid to scared silly of the "educated," "genteel," but enigmatic and deadly Ringo, it is important to understand that the apotheosis of John Ringo, gunfighter *non-pareil*, was accomplished by Walter Noble Burns (*Tombstone*) and Eugene Cunningham (*Triggernometry*) out of William Breakenridge (*Helldorado*), who was bitterly jealous of Wyatt Earp. Burns was simply writing a story that was only tangentially concerned with history. Cunningham, however, seated at the avuncular Breakenridge's knee, concluded that even though Wyatt Earp and his brothers "were gunfighters; they were killers; their record in Kansas and Arizona is proof of this,"[23] they were afraid of John Ringo, the "fastest" and "deadliest" gunfighter in southeastern Arizona, whose "amazing dexterity with Colt and Winchester" completed the embodiment of the "balanced," "temperamental" and "mechanical"[24] qualities of the classic gunfighter.

I wrote Eugene Cunningham (rather presumptuously, since I was a college student at the time), challenging his claims. I pointed out that there is no record of the Earps killing anyone in Kansas; that Breakenridge apparently disliked the Earps; that there is no evidence whatever to support his belief that either Doc Holliday or Wyatt Earp was afraid of John Ringo; and that as far as the record is concerned there is not a single account of Ringo shooting it out face-to-face with *anyone* in Arizona, and so demonstrating that "amazing dexterity with Colt and Winchester."

Cunningham's response revealed his total dependence on Breakenridge as his source of information. On my comment that Breakenridge apparently disliked the Earps: "What do you MEAN 'apparently disliked' them? He THOROUGHLY disliked them. They got on his nerves, strutting like they did because they had Wyatt behind them." On Wyatt's fear of Ringo and in reference to the near-fight on Allen Street: "It *is* too bad that Ringo and Doc were kept apart—that Wyatt didn't see fit to step out and call him, ever! Not that I belittle Wyatt! My objection is to the 101% partizanry of his eulogizers." Earp's biographer, Stuart Lake, Cunningham declared, suffered from "Halo-tosis." And as for there being no record of Ringo's "triggernometry" in Arizona—not a single gunfight of record—Cunningham declared that "it's not so much what he [Ringo] did as what he MIGHT have done." [25]

It is of more than passing interest that of Breakenridge, Cunningham, and Burns, not one even mentions Ringo's attempt to kill Louis Hancock, though all three relate with satisfaction the story of his holdup of that card game in Galeyville. [26] The shooting and wounding of an unsuspecting drinking companion at point-blank range—and nearly missing him, to boot—plays hob with the image of the hollow-eyed, melancholy, pistol-packing Hamlet. Those qualities that Cunningham declared made Ringo an expert gunman are reducible to a greater respect for Ringo's irrationality and treachery than for his marksmanship. Even that splendid and solitary call-down of Holliday (or Earp, or both) seems more evocative of the disordered mind inherent in the Hancock shooting than it does of the "balanced," "temperamental," and "mechanical" qualities of the monomachist. Ringo's hands, according to Lake, Cunningham and Burns, thrust into what apparently were special pockets in an overcoat, doubtless gripped a .45 in each, and with the hammers eared back. His intent, obviously, was to shoot through his pocket bottoms, giving Doc or Wyatt little more chance than he gave Hancock. But, to repeat Cunningham, "It's not so much what he [Ringo] did as what he MIGHT have done."[27]

What Ringo might have done is the essence of his near-fight with Wyatt and Doc. Descriptions of this non-event generally feature the "three blond and blue-eyed" Earp brothers and the "cadaverous" Doc Holliday as confronted by a "looming, giant" Ringo, garbed in either a "buffalo-skin great coat" or a "canvas ulster."[28] Ringo was the self-styled "representative" of the outlaws, the Earps and Doc of law and order. The stakes were set by Ringo: the loser(s), if any remained alive or ambulatory after the battle, "would go home."[29]

At Ringo's challenge, Wyatt, a provably cool, silent, and imperturbable type, reputedly began to babble about being a peace officer and a candidate for sheriff (he was not a candidate at that time), lectured the rustler on the silliness of fighting a duel in the street, and suggested that Ringo was crazy or drunk and that he should "go sleep it off." Ringo turned contemptuously to Doc and a near "handkerchief" duel was aborted by a city cop named James Flynn, who grabbed Ringo from behind. The Earps turned into Bob Hatch's saloon and Ringo, Cunningham wrote, remained "very much 'on the prod', for John Ringo was not impressed by their numbers."[30]

The unromantic record whittles those numbers down a bit. Virgil Earp was not present. As noted before, he had been shot-gunned in the back three weeks earlier and crippled for life. He did not leave his bed for two-and-a-half months, and then he was half-carried to the side of his younger brother, Morgan, who had also been shot in the back and lay dying in Hatch's saloon.[31] It is doubtful, too, that Morgan Earp was present, or, if he was, that he was prepared to fight. A little over two months earlier, at the now famous battle at the O.K. Corral, he had taken a .44 or .45 caliber slug through the right shoulder (Morgan was righthanded) that furrowed across his back, chipped off a piece of one vertebra, and passed out the left shoulder.[32] He would not seem to have been in shape to face "the fastest gunfighter and the deadliest."

Frank Waters, whose *The Earp Brothers of Tombstone* is a bitter, inaccurate, and personally intrusive polemic (an oversized screed, really) on Wyatt Earp triggered by personal problems with Earp's widow, Josephine, describes the encounter this way: "John Ringo, the one actual and feared badman . . . came to town, walked boldly up to Holliday, and offered to shoot it out . . . in front of Wyatt Earp. . . . This was not satisfactory to Doc Holliday. Deputy Breakenridge arrived, disarmed, and took them both to the sheriff's office."[33] But, according to Breakenridge's account of the incident, Ringo was "the only man in sight"[34] when he arrived on the scene. He arrested neither Doc nor Ringo; nor did he disarm them. Ringo did accompany him to the sheriff's office, telling Breakenridge of his challenge to the Earps and Holliday as they walked. "This arrangement," Breakenridge wrote pointedly, "was not acceptable to the Earp party, and they all went into [Bob Hatch's] saloon." Sheriff Behan took Ringo's guns, put them in a desk drawer and left the office. When Ringo complained to Breakenridge that "if I go uptown without them and they [the Earps and Doc] find it out, I won't last longer than a snowball in hell," Tombstone's Deputy ostentatiously pulled the drawer open and, "forgetting to close it, I walked out also. On my return, Ringo and his guns were gone. . . ."[35] (Cunningham reported Breakenridge's little trick with relish on page 120 of *Triggernometry*, although on page 113 he had declared his belief that Breakenridge could never engage in a "shady trick.")

Burns's version of the event features Wyatt, Virgil, Morgan, and Doc, Ringo in a buffalo-skin greatcoat, pearl-handled six-shooters, and enough dialog to talk anyone out of a fight. When Wyatt declined Ringo's offer, the rustler turned to Doc: "Doc, I don't need but three feet to do my fighting. Here's my handkerchief. Take hold." He flipped the bandana over and Doc grabbed it, shouting, "I'm your huckleberry,

Ringo." But Tombstone's Mayor Thomas stopped the fight.[36] (The mayor was John Carr, not Thomas. And Carr did not stop the fight.)

Arizona author Joe Chisholm's Ringo, now possessed of the grand eminence of "Robber Baron of the Border," a confusion of cow stealing with the rapacity of the Gilded Age, stood in mid-street, motionless, "inhaling the bracing November air" (it was mid-January). Before him stood Wyatt, Virgil, and Doc. Morgan is unaccountably missing. Ringo's syntax reflected the college man: "Wyatt, if things continue as they are it is inevitable there will be a wholesale killing here someday. . . . Come out in the middle of the street with me and shoot it out." The challenge was issued even though "Ringo knew Earp wore a bullet-proof vest," a rather spectral and chilly hunk of apparel for January. Wyatt "paled" and declined.[37]

Lake's account of the incident is, of course, quite different from Burns's, even down to the wearing apparel: Ringo's buffalo-skin greatcoat becomes "a heavy ulster with slit-pockets in which he kept his hands."[38] Ringo did not brace Wyatt Earp; he braced Holliday:

> "I understand you've been talking about me, Holliday," Ringo snarled.
>
> "I have," Doc replied pleasantly. "I said—I'm sorry to see a first-class cow thief like yourself fall in with a bunch of cheap bushwhackers'."
>
> Doc's nickel-plated six-gun was slung underneath the skirt of his square-cut coat. In each of his slit pockets John Ringo had a thumb on the hammer of a Colt's forty-five, as Doc well knew.

There follows a cursing of Holliday by Ringo that would have done justice to Doc himself, and a demand for a public retraction of all the nasty things Johnny Holliday had said about Johnny Ringo. Doc's next suggestion was overheard, Lake says, by George Parsons: "Let's move into the road where no one else will get hurt," and whereas Burns's Ringo needed only three feet and a hanky with which to do his fighting, Doc asked for ten: "What I said about you goes. And, if you get what I'm driving at, all I want of you is ten feet out here in the road."

The two squared off. But Mayor Thomas (*sic*), who had sprung between them in Burns's account, was replaced by a "husky young fellow [policeman] named James Flynn," who seized Ringo from behind and held him "in a bear-like grip." (Flynn followed Virgil Earp as chief of police for Tombstone. Glenn G. Boyer to author, February 19, 1981.) "Turn him loose, Flynn," Doc Holliday called, "and you, Ringo, when you start, start shooting."

Enter now, for the first time, Wyatt Earp, who had noticed a detail that Holliday had not. "Quit this foolishness, Doc," Wyatt said, nodding at a shuttered window in the Grand Hotel, from which the muzzle of a rifle was withdrawn. . . . "That fellow would have dropped you at your first move for a gun." The incident was over, and "in each of Ringo's ulster pockets Flynn found a loaded Colt's."[39]

Lake's account, while probably more accurate than Burns's, is far more subtle and favorable to Wyatt Earp. Ringo's challenge is addressed to Holliday, rather than to Wyatt, possibly because Lake anticipated the later charges that Wyatt had backed down. And that "rifle muzzle" that was "withdrawn" from the hotel window suggests that Ringo was merely the front man for a set-up. Thus, Lake not only establishes a valid reason for Earp's not stepping in and calling Ringo, he also diminishes the rustler's vaunted and solitary courage as well, while taking note of Earp's cool watchfulness: who else would be scanning hotel windows when two of the West's "deadliest, homicidal killers" were about to shoot it out? Nor does Earp babble to Ringo about his candidacy for sheriff as he does in Burns's account. He is every inch the cool, silent, and deliberate man of the West.

Lake's claim that George W. Parsons, Tombstone

businessman and inveterate diarist, overheard the exchange between Ringo and Doc is bluntly refuted by Parson's laconic entry in his journal for January 17, 1882 (the entry does, however, confirm Lake's contention that the near-fight was, indeed, between Ringo and Doc):

> . . . Ringo and Doc Holliday came nearly having it with pistols. . . . Bad time expected with the cowboy leader and D.H. I passed both not knowing blood was up. One with a hand in breast pocket and the other probably ready. Earps just beyond. Crowded street and looked like another battle. Police vigilant for once and both disarmed.[40]

If Parsons did not even know that "blood was up," he certainly could not have overheard the threatening dialog Lake gratuitously attributes to his memory. Parsons does, however, agree that police, not Mayor Carr, broke up the near-battle. But his comment, "Earps just beyond," puzzles. Virgil could not have been there; Morgan, possibly, though Lake mentions neither. Perhaps it was Warren and James (Warren Earp was the youngest of the Earp brothers, James the oldest; neither was in the O.K. Corral fight.) And according to Breakenridge, Behan, not Flynn, took away Ringo's guns.

Lake's general reference to John Ringo parallels most accounts:

> Curly Bill and John Ringo ranked next to Old Man Clanton in outlaw councils. . . . [Brocius, Graham, and] Ringo—family name, Ringgold—were fearless gunmen of the first order, professional killers, trained in the wars of the Texas cattle barons. . . . John Ringo was tall, slender, auburn-haired, and handsome. Though he robbed, killed, and caroused with his fellows, he was . . . sullen . . . and periodically so vicious [that] even . . . friends avoided him. . . . Ringo, a week after Wyatt Earp reached Tombstone, invited a chance acquaintance in a saloon, one Louis Hancock, to have a drink and shot him through the throat when Hancock ordered beer. . . .[41]

Lake offers no source for his brief Ringo profile (one is to presume, though, that it came from the ultimate source itself—Wyatt Earp), nor does he mention the names of the saloon and town in which the shooting of Hancock occurred, nor whether or not Hancock was killed. Yet both the *Tucson Star* and the *Arizona Miner* were explicit in their December 14, 1879, coverage of the shooting: It took place in Safford, Arizona, and Hancock was only superficially wounded (and not in the throat), though Ringo's intentions were good. Lake had to have access to these accounts. From Lake's other careful omissions in *Wyatt Earp: Frontier Marshall*, one is justified in the suspicion he intended for the reader to believe the shooting took place in Tombstone and that Hancock was killed. It makes John Ringo a more formidable, more irrational protagonist.

If Lake, Burns, Cunningham, and others produced more fiction than fact, Breakenridge produced a jealous and self-serving book. While intimating, through Ringo, that the Earps and Holliday were cowards and back-shooters, he eschews comment on the probable insanity inherent in Ringo's proposition that Doc or Wyatt shoot it out with him with the understanding the loser's followers would "go home," thus ending the "feud," or "row." Breakenridge, as a peace officer, offers no thoughtful ruminations or reflections on the arrogance or absurdity of such a proposition. What, he ought to have wondered, besides a disordered mind, could have made Ringo feel he had the right to make such a proposition, and to have it taken seriously enough for a peace officer to risk his life in response; what gave him the right to usurp the functions of the duly elected or appointed peace officers—especially the County Sheriff, John Behan, and Breakenridge himself—in determining who would or would not "go home" after the fight (whatever "going home" might have meant to the Earps or to the law in Tombstone). Breakenridge offers only a one-sentence observation, which, by its brevity and content, reveals scorn and contempt for the "Earp party" and admiration for John Ringo and for his audacious offer: "This arrangement . . . was not acceptable to the Earp party, and they all went into the saloon."

So no hanky fluttered between Johnny Ringo and Johnny Holliday and no one backed down. The "police" was the cop, James Flynn, not the mayor. Flynn was the hero that day, but we do not honor him, even at this remove. We resent his interference in what might have been one honest-to-God shoot-out, face-to-face, between three bona fide Western gunfighters in the center of a Western street, and in Tombstone, to boot.

On March 18, 1882, two months to the day after Ringo called Doc and Wyatt, Morgan Earp was shot in the back and killed as he played billiards in Bob Hatch's saloon on Allen Street. Wyatt sat on a bench watching the game. The time was again near midnight and the shots were fired through the upper glassed section of a door that opened onto a dark alley. Five days later, on or about March 24, 1882, Wyatt Earp killed Curly Bill—cut him down with a sawed-off shotgun. The shooting took place in the Whetstone Mountains, thirty-five miles west of Tombstone, at Iron Springs, a cottonwood-banked water hole centered in a landscape of Manichaean potential.

The meeting with Curly Bill and seven or eight members of his gang was as accidental and ironical as the killing of him was not. Without question and understandably, Wyatt Earp set out to get the men whom he believed crippled Virgil and killed Morgan. Morgan Earp's body was to be shipped by train from Tucson to Colton, California, the home of his parents, for burial. Virgil, now helpless and a burden, would accompany the body. Wyatt, his younger brother, Warren, Doc Holliday, and three shadowy friends, "Turkey Creek" Jack Johnson, Sherman McMasters, and "Texas" Jack Vermillion, escorted Wyatt and Virgil to Contention, near Tombstone. Warren Earp, McMasters, Johnson, and Vermillion remained at Contention. Wyatt, Holliday, and Virgil took the train to

Tucson where Virgil, along with Morgan's body, was put aboard the westbound train.

As the train pulled out in the gathering dusk, Wyatt, who seems to have had confirmation that an attempt would be made to kill Virgil, himself, and Holliday at the depot, met Frank Stilwell—recognizable as he came running down the railroad track through irridescent pools of gaslight—and killed him. Stilwell, a one-time deputy sheriff under John Behan, had previously been arrested for stage robbery and, later, for the attempted murder of Virgil Earp; almost at the moment of Stilwell's death, a coroner's jury sitting in Tombstone issued a verdict charging Frank Stilwell, Pete Spence, and Florentino Cruz, alias Indian Charlie, with the murder of Morgan Earp.[42] The verdict was based on the testimony of Spence's wife, Marietta.[43] Wyatt Earp knew of Marietta Spence's testimony before his party left for Tucson. Stilwell was not shot down simply because he chanced to be loitering, armed, around the railroad yards in the dark.

Wyatt and Holliday took the train back to Contention, where they were met by vigilantes, who escorted them to Tombstone. In Tombstone, Earp learned that warrants had been issued for the arrest of Stilwell, Cruz, Spence, Hank Swilling, and a man named Freis. (No warrant was issued for John Ringo, though Wyatt believed him to be involved in both shootings.) At the same time he learned that warrants were to be issued in Tucson for the arrest of himself and certain members of his party for the killing of Stilwell.

Wyatt Earp and his party decided to leave Tombstone at once. On March 22 or 23, Wyatt and what Lake called his posse,[44] located Florentino Cruz, or Indian Charlie, in a woodcutter's camp and killed him. Lake's account of the killing, or shooting, is pulp fiction raised to high art, the penny dreadful in transition and approaching the gothic: Indian Charlie was calmly, even soothingly talked into a confession of his part in the killing of Morgan Earp. Charlie became expansive, singing like the proverbial canary and implicating, for the first

time, both Curly Bill and John Ringo, though Earp had suspected the outlaw leaders all along. Then to his dismay and
panic, the gullible Charlie was told that his confession had
earned him the privilege of shooting it out with Wyatt Earp.
Charlie was undone. "Tell him to pull himself together,"
Wyatt said to Sherman McMasters, who spoke Spanish.
Wyatt would not draw until he had counted to three in Spanish. The badly shaken Charlie could snatch for his gun at *uno*.
"*Uno*"! Wyatt counted, while Charlie fumbled. "*Dos*"! Still
fumbling. "*Tres*"! Too late: "the Buntline Special [all eighteen inches of it] flashed from the holster, and roared three
times. . . . Number two for Morg."[45] (According to Lake, that
Buntline Special had also "flashed into action" when Morgan
was killed, and again there were "three shots," blasted into
that dark alley, though the meticulous account by the *Epitaph*
of that tragic murder says nothing about Wyatt Earp shooting
back.)[46]

The *Epitaph* reported the killing of Indian Charlie somewhat differently. The Earp posse rode into a wood camp and
"inquired for Pete Spence and Indian Charlie." One of the
men there, Theodore D. Judah, told them Spence was in
Tombstone, but directed the posse to where it could find
"Florentine," alias Charlie. "A few minutes later ten or twelve
shots were heard. . . . Judah . . . found the body not far from
camp riddled with bullets."[47] A "few minutes" would not appear to allow for Charlie's detailed and dramatic confession as
described by Lake; as for the disparity between three shots
from that "flashing" Buntline and the "ten or twelve" heard
by Judah, well, perhaps Earp could not count beyond three
in Spanish. And he is presumably Lake's "source" for the
story.

With Curly Bill and John Ringo now on his list (not that
they hadn't always been there), the Earp posse (an unusually
loyal band when one considers they held no stake, really, in
the Earp fight), seems to have begun a sweep or drag of large
sections of Cochise County, hoping to bag any of the outlaws

for whom Wyatt presumably held warrants and whom he suspected of complicity in the shooting of his brothers. By this time, we are told by Lake, Earp had been informed by vigilantes that John Behan now had warrants for the arrest of himself and his posse, and had begun the swearing in of his own posse. Among the loyal citizens taking the oath to uphold the laws of Cochise County and fetch Earp and his men to justice were outlaws Ike and Phin Clanton, Pete Spence, Hank Swilling, Joe Hill, Curly Bill, and John Ringo.[48]

The Earp posse now moved to its accidental rendevous with Curly Bill at Iron Springs. Neither Earp nor Curly Bill— both, quite possibly, caught up in the quotidian monotony of barren mountains and deserts—seems to have been alert to the possibility of such a meeting, even though springs or water holes were few and far between in that arid country and were natural stopping places for outlaw and lawman alike. Perhaps Earp thought Curly Bill was with Behan's posse. Lake lays Earp's carelessness to fatigue, the heat, and no recent sign leading to the springs. We are not privy to Curly Bill's excuses. Other than to express the belief that both lawman and outlaw were guilty of the ultimate act of carelessness, conjecture serves no purpose. The Earp posse rode almost into the middle of the outlaws (Earp said the distance was ten yards), who were sprawled out like turkeys in the spring's deep cottonwood shade. With the exception of Wyatt Earp, everyone seems to have panicked and fled. Earp stood alone as Curly Bill frantically swung his shotgun up, fired wildly, and missed. In the terrible and suspended clarity of those exploding seconds and in Lake's almost fleshily tactile description, Earp saw his own double-buckshot charge blow away Curly Bill's stomach in a red sheen of bursting arteries, nearly severing his body, heard the rustler's shocked and dying scream, saw and recognized each one of the running outlaws.[49] John Ringo, to the everlasting regret of gunfighter buffs, was not among them.

It seems to have really happened that way, at least one

affirmation of the prototypical Wild West shoot-out, whose classic proportions were formed by legendary lawman and notorious outlaw, face-to-face, and at a waterhole, to boot. But the shooting of Curly Bill created its own body of mythology and spawned a debate that endures to this day: was Curly Bill really killed at Iron Springs? No body was produced to lie publicly in a glass-faced coffin for the photographers (and later postcard makers), as were the bodies of Billy Clanton and Tom and Frank McLaury. No gaudily caparisoned rustler cortege followed the slain outlaw leader to his burial place under a panoply of curses and threats, as it did when two black hearses, preceded by a brass band (whose raucous threnody seemed altogether proper), bore the McLaury brothers and Billy Clanton to Boot Hill in the "largest [funeral] ever witnessed in Tombstone."[50] Curly Bill was never seen again.

There were, of course, the later "sightings" of Curly Bill by "prominent" and "reliable" citizens, at least one of whom enjoyed (and, one imagines, was surprised by) an unexplained visit from the rustler. "A reliable merchant and rancher living at Safford," Breakenridge wrote, "told me that about two weeks after the Earp party reported killing Curly Bill, Curly himself came to his home and said he had just got back from Old Mexico." Curly was on his way to "Wyoming" and the "decent life." The friendly merchant "gave him a good saddle horse to ride away on,"[51] an inexplicable act of generosity roughly comparable to giving a visiting thief one of the two cars in the family garage, and implying, at the same time, an obligatory response to a deep and mutual friendship. Breakenridge also knew "a Mr. Vaughan," who told him that ten years after his presumed violent demise Curly Bill passed through Cochise County, entrained for Texas, stopping off in Benson "long enough to visit the postmaster, whom he had known in his earlier days in Arizona."[52] Just why this rustler and killer should be so warmly and generously welcomed to the hearths and homes of some of the more substantial citizens remains a mystery, one that receives no illumination from Breakenridge.

As in any debated historical event, there are always those garrulous old-timer, now-it-can-be-told stories. Typical is a letter to the *Epitaph* in 1929 from Judge J. C. Hancock, probably in response to solicited information. Hancock came to Arizona in 1880 and settled in Galeyville. His letter, written a half-century later, is far less a convincing defense of the outlaw element in Cochise County (as it was clearly intended to be) than it is a reflection of his own easy judicial morality. Filled with palpable absurdities, the letter declares that Curly Bill (whose last name has been variously reported as "Brocious," "Brocius," and "Graham") had a brother, Bill Graham (two Bill's in one family?), who ranched with him. Bill Graham married, but Curly Bill went to Montana, where he died of old age. Wyatt Earp, the judge wrote, "never arrested Curly Bill," let alone killed him.[53] (Apparently Hancock had no recollection of the *Epitaph's* own account of the earlier incident when Wyatt had cracked Curly Bill over the head and arrested him for shooting Marshal Fred White.) In Montana, Hancock maundered, where Curly Bill turned up, transfigured, he was affectionately known as "Old Cack," a benign and public-spirited citizen, a giver of barbecues and a lover of children who delighted in passing out candy to the kiddies.[54]

|⌇⌘⌘⌇|

Sheriff Behan and his rustler-posse galloped in and out of Tombstone in not-exactly-hot pursuit of the Earp party. Breakenridge claimed not to have ridden with the posse because he was "needed in the [Tombstone] office. He [Behan] asked me to loan my horse and rifle to John Ringo, who had left his rifle at a ranch close to town, and who with several other of the cowboys and rustlers made up the posse. He took these men knowing the Earp party would resist arrest, and, on account of the feud between them, he believed the cowboys would stay and fight."[55]

Further comment would be superfluous if Breakenridge had told the simple truth: Behan *depended* on the rustlers. No rustlers, no posse. And he had warrants to serve. Honest men obviously wanted nothing to do with him, especially when he rode at the head of an outlaw gang. And would the "cowboys" have stayed and fought? John Ringo probably would have. But Ike Clanton ran from every fight he started. He ran at the O.K. Corral and he was in full flight when he was shot and killed by a sheriff's posse in northern Arizona in 1887. Hank Swilling was a craven back-shooter, burdened, now, with the frightening knowledge that Wyatt Earp was after him, and probably haunted by recurring visions of the blasted bodies of Frank Stilwell and Indian Charlie. And with the exception of Ringo's challenge to Wyatt and Doc, all the rustlers had repeatedly demonstrated a preference for the ambush. Behan himself had never demonstrated any courage. Had a fight between the two posses occurred, leadership of Behan's posse may well have devolved upon John Ringo, a possibility that Behan, the plotter, doubtless had considered. In a fight Ringo would have been a welcome addition to any posse. Breakenridge's accounts, which Frank Lockwood (*Pioneer Days in Arizona*) held in such high esteem, were really artful deceptions, pious half-truths.

Behan and his posse trailed the Earp party to Colonel Henry C. Hooker's Sierra Bonita Ranch near Wilcox. Hooker met the posse in his ranch yard. Behan requested food for himself and his posse and demanded to know where the Earp party (which had ridden out the evening before) had gone. Hooker stared in disbelief at Behan and his rustlers. Repelled and angered by what he saw, Hooker nevertheless considered himself bound by the obligatory tradition of Western hospitality and a certain respect for the law, even when the badges that symbolized its authority glittered on the vests of a smirking band of rustlers. He would feed them, but he would tell them nothing. "Hooker," Breakenridge wrote, "who had suffered severely from the rustlers taking his cattle, was friendly with the Earps, and when Behan came with a posse composed mostly of rustlers and cowboys, with John Ringo and Phin and Ike Clanton among them, he would give him no help or information."[56]

Breakenridge, as usual, tells only part of the story. The *Epitaph* reported the event in detail: Behan accused Hooker of "upholding murderers and outlaws," whereupon Hooker exploded, "No sir, I am not. I know the Earps and I know you and I know they have always treated me like gentlemen; damn such laws and damn you, and damn your posse; they are a set of horse thieves and outlaws."[57] Abruptly the situation was dangerous. "Damn the son of a bitch," an unidentified posseman said. "Let's make him tell." One of Hooker's men then pointed his Winchester at the posseman. "You can't come into a gentleman's yard and call him a son of a bitch! Now you skin it back! If you're looking for a fight . . . you can get it before you find the Earps; you can get it right here."[58] The rustler must have complied, because there was no shooting. Hooker fed the posse (when Behan and Under-Sheriff Woods attempted verbally to disassociate themselves from the rest of the posse, Hooker pointedly seated them separately), but he told them nothing.

Behan and his posse rode on to Camp Grant, where the sheriff hoped to recruit Apache scouts and set them on Earp's trail. In the course of his negotiations for the scouts with the camp's Col. Bidwell (or Biddle), Behan rather bitterly complained that Henry Hooker had said that he did not know where the Earp party was and would not tell if he did. Bidwell, as the *Epitaph* reported it, stroked "his beard with his left hand, looked straight at the sheriff and said, 'Hooker said he didn't know and would not tell you if he did? Hooker said that, did he? Well if he did you can't get any scouts here'."[59]

Behan led his posse back to Tombstone. In late April (1882) the Earp posse rode out of the territory, on to Colorado and into legend. Wyatt Earp, in his own time, wired Sheriff Bob Paul in Tucson of his location. Extradition papers were then served by the Territory of Arizona, but Colorado Governor F. W. Pitkin, after a brief hearing, found the papers to be of questionable legal validity and refused to honor them.

ᛁᛟᛟᛟᛁ

And John Ringo: one wonders about John Ringo's thoughts during those days between the killing of Morgan Earp and the last grueling and futile posse ride in pursuit of Wyatt. He was alone. Curly Bill was dead or gone. Old Man Clanton had been killed the year before by the Mexicans whose cattle he was rustling. The lesser functionaries of the Curly Bill–Ringo–Old Man Clanton gang—Tom and Frank McLaury, the big and "loutish" but game Billy Clanton,[60] and Frank Stilwell—were also dead. Ike Clanton, who had run at the O.K. Corral, was worthless. Even Ringo's enemies, Doc Holliday and Wyatt Earp, who might have helped to keep his juices flowing, were gone. John Ringo was known as "King of the Cowboys" and "King of the Outlaws,"[61] but the titles were romantically and gratuitously bestowed. The mantle and scepter of responsibility lay unwanted and oppressively upon him. He was neither leader nor follower. He truly marched to a different drummer, and the beat was a dirge. He was too moody and withdrawn, too subject to dangerous struggles with depression, too unstable for sustained leadership. He was a loner, a participant only when it suited him to be one. In a real sense he was *of* the outlaws, not *with* them, driven by his own particular devils. The circumambient desert, with its creosote bushes, its mesquite and cacti, its thornbush and cholla, and its shimmering aridities, had become his personal Gethsemane. He was trapped in it by transcendent circumstances, of which his physical presence had probably become, to him, only a manifestation; and he would lie dead at its edge in less than three months.

This, then, was Tombstone, the town that proclaimed itself "too tough to die." Burns, Breakenridge, Lake, and Cunningham are only four of the writers whose ministrations have helped to perpetuate its lingering and heroically self-conscious existence. This, too, was the Tombstone and Cochise County of those chosen vessels for the transport of mystery, intrigue, and literary license: John Ringo and Doc Holliday. These two were bemused, sardonic onlookers, protagonists whose participation in historic events was intensely personal but without personal ambition or aspiration, whose perversities and loyalties and genteel antecedents, along with their presumed educations and intellects, rendered them near caricatures—prototypes for the later "psychological Westerns" whose themes, both textual and cinematic, projected them (or their kind) against the West as the dumping ground for misfits from a better place and a better life. They were of the scene, not a part of it. Deep down inside Ringo and Doc and their congeners there reputedly guttered a feeble flame of lineal character and the socially inculcated imperatives of decency that were regularly doused and extinguished with alcohol and bitterness. They were, presumably, destined to early deaths, knew it and accepted it, even sought it.

Of the two, Doc Holliday's is the more clearly defined personality, simply because more is known about him. In spite of advancing tuberculosis, Doc drank heavily and kept ungodly hours gambling in smoky and airless saloons. It was not a way of life calculated to recover one's health. In 1911, Pop Church, former marshal of Henrietta, Texas, explained Doc to Eugene Cunningham: "You see, Doc was different from the rest of us: *He* went into a row—or started the row—hoping he'd GIT killed *I* always 'lowed."[62] Whether Church knew Doc or merely repeated a popular belief or assumption is not explained, but it was enough for Cunningham: "I put him [Doc] into several fictions on that note—renamed of course."[63] Doc at least had a reason for his bitterness.

Ringo fulfilled the prophecy and with it, the literarily imposed obligation: he almost certainly took his own life. Because his passing from the scene was as mysterious as his arrival on it, it has been possible for bevys of assorted hacks (and even serious writers) to mold and cast him in marmoreal plaster, to make of him all the things they would like him to have been: professor, scholar, statuesque and handsome, Byronic, Shakespearean, disillusioned and cynical, a deadly gunfighter whose demonstrated mastery of the six-shooter was such that, since no one else could match him—not the Earps, not Doc Holliday—he was forced to fell himself.

I am not convinced that either Doc or Ringo nursed a death-wish. Both men might have been redeemed. But it makes a dramatic story to so depict them, a sort of awkward and shabby attempt at the morality play. We have read, heard, and seen the story over and over, in books, articles, on the radio, in the movies and on television: Doc is always hacking up his lungs in paroxysms of forced theatrical coughing while dabbing his lips with white linen against the incarnadine proof of his malady, daring someone to put him out of his misery, and Ringo is monotonously and unbelievably trying to force someone to kill him. I think Pop Church, despite his claim to contemporary status ("different from the rest of *us*"), was "'lowing" more than he had a right to. At the time of his death in 1887, Doc was in Glenwood Springs, Colorado, taking the sulphurous waters (which doubtless hastened his death) in an effort to restore his health. And Ringo, except for his effort to goad Doc, Wyatt, and possibly Morgan Earp into a fight, has no record of suicidal encounters with anyone. The attempt to kill Louis Hancock was brutal, clumsy, and one-sided; it was suicidal only on Hancock's part for preferring beer to whisky. According to a letter Ringo wrote to Sheriff Charles Shibell of Pima County explaining why he could not appear before the Pima County Grand Jury, he *had* been in some sort of gunfight and had been shot, though he does not reveal the circumstances:

I write to let you know why I can not appear—I got shot through the foot and it is impossible for me to travel for awhile.

But the letter concludes in a tone so anxious to please that only one with the most gruesome intent could read a death-wish into it:

If you get any papers for me, and will let me know, I will attend to them at once as I wish to live here. I do not wish to put you to any unnecessary trouble, nor do I wish to bring extra trouble on myself. Please let the Dist-Atty know why I do not appear, for I am very anxious that there is know [*sic*] forfeiture taken on the Bond.[64]

3
Ringo, Doc, Wyatt, and the Writers

IN MY SEARCH for the *real* John Ringo, no believable pattern emerged. Behind the protean masks of gunfighter, educator, rustler, student, psychopath, and the man "whose word was good as his bond" lurked, I suspected, something or someone of considerably less heroic proportions, perhaps even a tragic or pathetic figure, a vulnerable sufferer, or perhaps merely a homicidal drunk and thief. Intrigued, baffled in my researches and labors, I became the exegete, the seeker after isolated facts, the leisurely pursuer of stray and often absurd detail, the collector and recorder of unblushing superlatives and absurdities, the witness to astonishing liberties taken with people and with the history of the West.

There is a general symmetry to the stories and theories about John Ringo—who he really was, what he did—and all seem to point directly to Walter Noble Burns, William N. Breakenridge, and Eugene Cunningham. There are, of course, writings that antedate *Tombstone* (1927), *Helldorado* (1928), and *Triggernometry* (1947). Those early authors were on the scene and had access to information before the garrulous old ex-deputy, Breakenridge (with his ghost writer, William MacLeod Raine), commenced putting his own story down on paper. Accordingly, I have arranged a cross-section of selections from writings about, and observations on, John Ringo. These are taken from books and manuscripts, magazines, letters and depositions by contemporaries, and news-papers. Most selections include accounts of the near-gunfight between Ringo and Doc Holliday in Tombstone and, to a lesser extent, the shooting and wounding of Louis Hancock. These are the only two recorded instances of "gunplay" by the "fastest, deadliest gunfighter in the West," the quintessential outlaw. We know from his letter to Sheriff Shibell that Ringo "got shot through the foot," but we do not know the circumstances of the shooting (one story has it that he accidently shot himself). Even more interesting are the melodramatic, infantile, and self-serving variations on these two non-events and on his life in general, for the aura of mystery that envelops Ringo has made him the historic victim of the most grotesque of fictions. Often even dates, months of the year, and names of participants in historic events concerned with the enigmatic Ringo are unbelievably inaccurate. And yet, all around these writers were and are the sticks and stones of history: the newspaper accounts, the trial, court, and inquest records. In essence, the writings about John Ringo provoke more reflections on ourselves than they do on him.

ı◆ᢙᠻᢙᡃᢦ╮ı

In 1922 Frederick R. Bechdolt published a purported history titled *When the West Was Young*. Walter Noble Burns, in his source acknowledgments for *Tombstone*, wrote that "Frederick Bechdolt, as a literary pioneer in the romantic field, has done some brilliant work in *When the West Was Young*." [1] In fact the book is ludicrous. Just what Burns meant by "romantic field" is not clear, but romantic the book is. Bechdolt, of course, embraces the themes of Ringo's mysterious background and his intelligence. "He went his way, and it was a bad way," he wrote somberly, but without illumination of what that "bad way" was. "Dark deeds piled up to fill the debit pages of his life's ledger." [2] One could not find a more prosaic or banal simile. Bechdolt then launched into a melodramatic description of Ringo's last ride across the furnace-hot Sulphur Springs

Valley to his lonely death in the foothills of the Chiricahuas: his pony picks its way listlessly through creosote bushes, neck and head drooping against the shimmering aridity of the desert. Puffs of alkali dust drift up from the plodding hooves. The torpor of the desert is on horse and rider. One easily imagines the hot, mid-July sun adumbrating the shadowed hollows and canyons of the looming Chiricahua Mountains. All the scene lacks is a backdrop of the spires and mesas of Monument Valley and tumbling tumbleweeds borne thornily across the valley floor before a singing wind. Rider and horse vanish among the foothill scrub-oak.

Ringo, Bechdolt states, shot himself: "The bullet hole was fairly between his eyes, all powder marked. . . . In this manner," he declares with an unmistakable tone of regret, "it came about that the outlaws of Cochise County lost their leader; and now that the man of brain was gone it became possible for events to shape up, as they did soon afterward, toward the big Earp-Clanton gunfight. The Old-Timers are unanimous in saying that had John Ringo been alive that battle wherein the leaders of the Earp faction slew several of the biggest desperados would never have taken place as it did. . . . The chances are victory would have gone the other way."[3]

Literally nothing in this account by that "brilliant literary pioneer" is accurate. The Earp-Clanton fight at the O.K. Corral took place on October 26, 1881. Ringo died on or about July 12, 1882, eight and one-half months later. And the bullet hole was not "fairly between the eyes, all powder marked." "There was a bullet hole in the right temple," reads the report for the coroner, "the bullet coming out on the top of the head on the left side."[4] There is no mention in the report of powder marks, or burns, an omission that gives a certain credibility to the commonly held contention of murder.

One wearies of quoting Burns. Yet next to Breakenridge, and certainly on a par with Lake, Burns has kept the Tombstone story alive. I remain convinced that he spawned the

Ringo legend. I had never heard of John Ringo before reading *Tombstone,* and I doubt that I should have become enchanted with the rustler had I been obliged to take inspiration solely from Breakenridge's "blunt, unadorned" prose. I was, admittedly, seduced by such passages as the one that commences on page 261 of Burns's tale of Ringo's death, "John Ringo Cashes In": "John Ringo was drunk. For ten days he had been morosely, broodingly, tragically drunk. As straight as an Indian, he stalked about Tombstone streets, a tall, silent, sombre figure, looking a little more like Hamlet than ever, his hollow black eyes clouded and melancholy." Alongside John Ringo, Curly Bill seems merely another hoarse-voiced, border tough of Western stereotyping, while Wyatt Earp—even with his "lion's brool"—is just one of "three blond brothers."

In 1954 another "Old Tombstoner," Sarah Grace Bakarich, emerged from Tombstone's "Horse Thief Gulch" bearing her locally published book, whose title, *Gunsmoke,* I am told, she believed was purloined by the television series of the same name. Purporting to be one of those "inside" stories fashioned of local raw material, the book offers as research a list of Tombstone old-timers, who, if they knew or remembered anything at all about Tombstone's history or harbored any of that celebrated taciturn and direct Western honesty, must have left town fast when the book was published. Mrs. Bakarich wrote as though Tombstone were her private patrimony, its records, facts, and history to be twisted and perverted to her own proprietary interests, or, indeed, ignored altogether. Worse, she takes Breakenridge's pro-outlaw position. Breakenridge was on the scene. Whatever one may think of him, he had the right to a personal view. Bakarich was not a contemporary and she had no such right. The result is an amazing narrative that goes beyond the parochial to the maternal: across a span of seventy-five years Mrs. Bakarich mothers the Clantons, McLaurys, John Ringo, and others.

It is John Ringo, though, one of the especially good guys,

whom Bakarich describes in hyperbolic phrases of affection, and with motherly pride and forebearance: "John Ringo . . . was born a gentleman, in Missouri, but when a little drunk he was moody and neurotic. . . . Ringo was tall, thin-faced with dark auburn hair and warm brown eyes. Ringo was a graduate of William Jewell College at Liberty, Missouri. He was a classmate of Judge O. W. Williams, who was postmaster at Silver City, New Mexico in 1881." According to Bakarich, the people of Tombstone affectionately referred to Ringo as "John R." So great, in fact, was the warm regard for the rustler and gunman that Tombstone's cup of love ran over into an artless little ditty that was sung to the tune of "Good-bye, My Lover, Good-bye":

> *I saw John R. ride over the hill*
> *Good-bye, John R., Good-bye.*
> *We'll not meet again for many a day*
> *Good-bye, John R., Good-bye.*[5]

One envisions, weaving in and out of events in old Tombstone, a lyrical Greek chorus composed of cowboys, miners, bullwhackers, pimps, and gamblers, and all preceded by a cooing flock of "soiled doves" in lilting, if inexplicable, praise of a Homeric outlaw. Speaking of "soiled doves": "In 1879," Mrs. Bakarich wrote with motherly pride, "Ringo, always the champion of womanhood, shot and killed Louis Hancock, for whom he had just bought a drink, when Hancock made a disparaging remark about a woman." On a more sombre note, Mrs. Bakarich tells us that "Ringo was a good man gone wrong. Common gossip was that with his cousins, the Younger brothers and the James boys, he had participated in the savagely brutal Lawrenceville, Kansas, massacre under the . . . notorious guerilla Quantrell [*sic*]. . . . Quantrell himself appeared in Tombstone briefly at about this time. The tough raider had aged and wore a black beard and was lame from an old wound. . . ."[6] (Quantrill, of course, had been killed by Union Cavalry in Kentucky in 1865).

Bakarich's account of the Ringo-Doc meeting not only bears psychological overtones, it is disturbingly personal. It simply did not happen that way, so the pervasive cruelty of this concocted "act," discernible even in the ungrammatical torrent of telling it, must be laid to Bakarich, not to John Ringo: "One July* morning in 1882 Ringo met Doc Holliday on Allen Street in front of the Crystal Palace saloon. Ringo slapped the hollow chested gun-man so hard he spun half way around. Then slapped him again on the other cheek grabbed Holliday's sawed-off shotgun and smashed it over a boulder that bulked between the street and the wooden sidewalk. Ringo whirled the dentist around and said quietly, 'Just walk ahead of me down to Montgomery's stable'." At the stable Ringo ordered up his horse, mounted, and from the saddle gave the frail and "hollow chested" Doc, whose ears must have still been ringing from that slapping around, this profound bit of advice: "Doc, when you mention my name, just be careful how you mention my name."[7] Somehow the lecture does not seem to fit the bullying that preceded it; nor are we privy to the source who overheard and recorded for posterity this pungent bit of dialogue.

Even the professional writers seem to have trouble with the idiosyncratic Ringo, who easily diverts them from the logical and steady course of history. John Myers is an urbane and sophisticated writer with seven books to his credit, including the first full-length biography of Doc Holliday. Yet, if Myers's remarks on John Ringo in this witty and sometimes convincing book (*Doc Holliday*, which avoids the dogmatic heroics of Lake's *Wyatt Earp*) are at all reflective of the quality of his research, *Doc Holliday* is of questionable authority:

> "John Ringgold, more commonly called Johnny Ringo . . . left Missouri for other parts, including a series of railhead cattle towns. In Texas according to some authorities, he had taken part in the Mason County war. . . .

* This encounter actually took place in January, not July.

Johnny . . . had attended college in a day when only young men of good background normally did so. Nobody has yet lifted Ringo out of his setting of myth to allow a good look at him, so legend will have to go unchallenged. According to this he was Byronic in mood, appearance and past. Wavy auburn hair surrounded a handsome but unhappy patrician face. He was subject to alternate fits of noble generosity and savage cruelty. He drank . . . to forget other and better days. He packed the classics in his duffle bag and read them in the original Greek and Latin during breaks in his rustling . . . expeditions. He even received letters in a graceful feminine hand, and each one cast him adrift in despond for days. . . ."[8]

Though Breakenridge said Ringo "had a college education," even Burns thought that a bit doubtful. Joe Chisholm ("Tombstone's Tale") fulsomely acknowledged Ringo's academic background and transformed a meager collection of books into a library of classics; but it was Myers who decided the rustler read them in the "original Greek and Latin." It was Myers, too, who exalted Ringo into "patrician" nobility by that *amende honorable* fashioned by the popular imagination. For the most part these are simply free enhancements of Breakenridge's toneless and colorless observations, though those "letters in a graceful feminine hand" came from Burns.

Myers's account of the Hancock shooting is a simple case of accuracy sacrificed to humor. "Ringo's reputation with a gun was like everything else about him, awe-inspiring but hard to nail down. The only corpse in and around Tombstone which can be *definitely* [italics mine] assigned to him is that of one Louis Hancock. . . . Johnny encountered this fellow in an Allen Street saloon. Offended because Hancock ordered beer after he had invited him to drink whiskey, Ringo shot him while the unsuspecting Louis had his beak in the suds."[9]

Myers believes it possible that there were "two encounters" between Ringo and Doc. His reasoning, though, is carelessly based on the endless variety of descriptions of what did or did not happen, or even when, on that non-sanguinary day on Allen Street. His own account is brief and regretful of the failure of a pistolade consummation:

> According to the twice blessed tale, Ringo took his stand in the middle of Allen Street, challenging Holliday to bite on the other end of Johnny's neckerchief and shoot it out at that intimate nearness. Liking the notion, Doc was blithely striding out to accommodate Johnny when the law intervened. In terms of its own obligations the law would have been acting with propriety, but in stopping such an engagement between the two most interesting characters on the circuit it was committing a sin of its own against frontier history.[10]

In 1957 Doc Holliday popped up again, entombed and, to a certain extent, caricatured, in another relentlessly humorous biography. The book, impressively titled *The Frontier World of Doc Holliday—Faro Dealer From Dallas to Deadwood,* is by Pat Jahns, who renders us privy to Doc's most intimate thoughts, moods, and problems: his exhiliration after an earth-cleansing Tombstone rain; his black despair over his failing health; his growing sexual impotence, which exacerbated his problems with his prurient mistress, Big-Nose Kate. And Kate, as every student of the Old West knows, was a "soiled dove," a gold-camp chippie. We are generally content to accept her as quaintly such and leave the rest to our imaginations. But here we learn of her vigorous and voracious sexual urges, which seemed to come in great and raucous convulsions bordering on sadism—stimulated, one gathers, by Doc's anguished eyes and tragic vulnerability. To Kate, Doc was a hobbling and hacking aphrodisiac, even after a hard day at the crib. We bring up just short of a discussion of frontier pessaries and menstrual cramps as we follow Doc and his lubricious Kate rushing, rioting, and rutting throughout the Old West. Here is a modest example:

> Kate bounded into the room, a big Colt gun in her hand, yelling that Doc was a lousy son of a bitch for treating her the

way he did and she was going to fill him so full of holes he wouldn't float in brine. Wherewith she punctured the mattress in his vicinity with a .45 caliber slug.

Doc arose in his wrath and a long white night shirt. . . . He clobbered her one aside the head with nearly three pounds of .45 caliber Colt . . . and rather put his heart in it.

"Kate came to feeling sober and sorry and very fragile . . . and lying in Doc's bed with a wet towel on her head . . . Kate snuggled down in bed and grinned at Doc. He stood by the lamp for a long minute looking down at her and then swiftly bent over and blew out the light. . . ."[11]

Those little dots tell the story: nothing, not even a gun barrel alongside the skull, could slow down concupiscent Katie. These colorful little intimacies, by the way, along with Doc's impotence, are neither burdened with a batch of troublesome footnotes nor verified by medical or psychiatric records.

John Ringo is something less than a Hamlet to Jahns.* Her story of Ringo's meeting with Doc is, of course, funny, but no different in enlightenment and tone than Myers's:

There are many versions of this . . . one side having it that Doc was ready to perforate Ringo when he was arrested, the other claiming that Ringo invited Doc to duel on the spot and Doc declined. Actually, it appears that the police grabbed him before either had gotten beyond the brag and bluster stage. Surely Doc and Ringo were the most well-matched opponents the two factions could have picked: both educated; both alcoholics; both loyal to their friends, both totally fearless. Anything other than their killing each other on the spot is unthinkable, but like the fight between Richard I and Saladin, it never happened. . . . Ah, well! Drinks are still twelve and a half cents.[12]

In Joe Chisholm's unpublished manuscript, "Tombstone's Tale," Ringo is raised to the anachronistic eminence of "Rob-

---

* "John Ringgold," she wrote, "known as Ringo, was a well-educated souse noted for his fearlessness" (Jahns, *The Frontier World*, p. 152).

ber Baron"; his men "regarded their well-bred leader with an awe as great as their physical fear of him." He was "a Paladin among brave men," who was much-maligned by

> lazy and unscrupulous chroniclers and fakers. . . . His real name was Ringgold. This was learned from a veteran of the early American Wars [what wars does he mean?] who came to Tombstone in 1879 or 1880 and told [Sheriff] John Slaughter [and] my father, who was Justice of the Peace at Bisbee, A.T., and Robert A. Boles [Boller]—the latter . . . dug Ringo's grave—that Johnny's uncle, Captain Ringgold, had been killed in the Mexican War. . . . Ringo looms on the violent horizon of Tombstone's past, vague as King Arthur through the mist of years. . . . [The only woman he ever loved] was Lady Death.
> . . .
> Ringo was a cultured man for his day and environment, a college graduate. Between cattle raids below the Border [it was all right, please understand, to rustle *Mexican* cattle] he delved into history, archaeology, sociology, English literature, intently; continuing, no doubt, studies interrupted by some youthful misadventure. The always reliable Billy Breakenridge told me that Ringo had several shelves filled with classics in his mountain cabin.[13]

The "always reliable" Breakenridge mentioned a "small collection of standard books" in *Helldorado*, now grown to "several shelves filled with classics." In between rustling forays and pursuing interrupted studies, that "knightly fellow" shot up friends, held up friendly card games, menaced the Earps and Holliday, challenged Doc, went on Homeric binges, loomed on horizons while remaining as "vague as King Arthur," was exalted into knighthood and, presumably, seated at Tombstone's Round Table* with Breakenridge, and practiced a little archaeology on the side. He was also, Chisholm declared, a defender of womanhood, whether "soiled dove" or "chaste matron of the camp."

* Burns concocted the notion of a "Tombstone Round Table."

Late one lamplit night on the Chisholms' front porch (Ringo was a purported friend of Joe's father and a frequent visitor at their home)—during a pregnant lull in the oratorical lucubrations on the subject of archaeology and Mexican pottery—little Joe brought the discussion into prosaic and impertinent perspective: had Ringo "ever shot anybody?" Ringo "looked very serious." Justice Chisholm was angry and said that "small boys should be seen and not heard." Suddenly Ringo "indulged one of his infrequent smiles and assured me he hadn't." Then he "softened my embarrassment at being reprimanded before company by giving me a quarter to buy a package of chocolate."[14] (One is reminded of Curly Bill as "Old Cack," spending his golden years passing out candy to children in the streets of some remote Montana town, still chuckling, no doubt, over his presumed violent passing at the hands of Wyatt Earp.)

Paradoxically, Chisholm's account of the Hancock shooting comes closest of any to accuracy: "It is a matter of record Ringo never shot anyone in Tombstone. But he did have a shooting scrape with a man named Hancock at Safford, over on the Gila, on December 9, 1879, probably before he had ever gone to Tombstone. For this he was indicted; but it couldn't have been anything serious because soon afterward the charge against him was dismissed."[15]

In the 1950s a Yermo, California, couple, Louise and Fullen Artrip, discovered a rugged old man in his eighties still roaming the vast reaches of the Mojave Desert. He was not a prominent western figure, but he was a member of one of the Old West's most important families, whose name he bore: Daniel Fore Chisholm,* son of Thornton Chisholm, who blazed the Chisholm Trail north from Texas in 1866 (another member of the Chisholm family—Jesse, a Cherokee trader—marked the Chisholm Trail in 1867). Born in 1866 and nearly a prepubescent rider on the family trail, Daniel Chisholm,

---

* No apparent relation to Joe Chisholm.

alias Texas Jim, was a self-proclaimed ex-outlaw. He was, the Artrips learned, still in hiding from a wild, though certainly not misspent, youth; he was a good lad and true, but victim of the vagaries of history, listening, now, for the distant beat of posse hooves, fearful of whatever justice might catch up to an octogenarian ex-owlhooter. If the Artrips explained to the old man that any laws governing events or crimes, real or imagined, which occurred during the late nineteenth century had doubtless run their statutes of limitations, or that all witnesses were dead or incompetent and that one cannot be compelled to testify against oneself, they made no mention of it. The receptive and romantic couple believed that Dan Chisholm, or Texas Jim, was a rare discovery: a walking and talking (especially talking) repository of Western Americana, whose revelations, however brightly illuminating, they were honor-bound not to make public while he was still alive. Once he was safely in Valhalla, however, the Artrips privately published the old man's story under the pretentious title *Memoirs of (the Late) Daniel Fore (Jim) Chisholm and the Chisholm Trail.*

The amazing yarns spun by Chisholm, or Texas Jim, probably explain why the book was privately published, but the Artrips were true believers. They gave themselves over to the romance of the old man's presence and to his colorful ruminations, which they often shared in the heady and persuasive ambience of desert campfires. Their "Foreward" [*sic*] to this small volume seriously promises that

> unsolved murders, killings, and robberies which have baffled historians all these years are herein, for the first time, brought to light.
>
> In disclosing these facts, the writers . . . make no attempt to assess blame, to condemn, or to praise; instead, we will impartially set down the events, as they were told to us by Daniel Fore (Jim) Chisholm, and let he who is qualified to judge, set (sic) in judgment.
>
> In revealing the facts . . . a soul was laid bare, . . . a life . . . beset by conflicting crosscurrents was stripped naked and

held up for final judgment; a life through whose fabric FATE had woven a pattern of blazing guns, bloodshed and violent death; seemingly an . . . inescapable pattern, destined to repeat itself over and over again. . . .[16]

But if what follows in the text is even partly true, the authors' "Foreward" is more or less an understatement. Chisholm was the personification of ubiquity. He was in every eddy and current of western history: he was a child of the Sutton-Taylor Feud in Texas; a cowboy for John Slaughter; a friend of Doc Holliday, who once saved his life; a member of the Curly Bill–Ringo–Old Man Clanton gang, who was with them when they ambushed a Mexican pack train in Skeleton Canyon;[17] he held Wyatt Earp's guns after John Ringo had disarmed the marshal in Tombstone's Oriental Saloon, though his is the only account of such an encounter; he just happened to be putting his horse up at the O.K. Corral when that famous fight occurred. He saw it all, and fixed blame on the Earps, though he does not appear at any time as a witness, either in person or in print. He participated in the deadly Tewksbury-Graham blood feud in Arizona's Pleasant Valley, an action in which he could not possibly have had any business and where history, again, has no record of him. In 1896 he visited his "old friend" Curly Bill at his rancho in Mexico, some fourteen years after Curly had been killed by Wyatt Earp[18] (could "Old Cack" have tired of passing out candy to the kids in Montana?).

Chisholm, though, was more than a mere participant. He was a picaresque confidante to John Ringo and Curly Bill, both mature (for those days, practically middle-aged) men who unfathomably—and certainly not after the close-mouthed tradition of the Old West—unburdened their souls and bared their secrets to this callow youth. On the morning of March 27, 1882, a day or so after Wyatt Earp had killed Curly Bill at Iron Springs, Arizona, Chisholm was jogging across the San Pedro valley. Presently he noticed that he was being followed by a lone horseman. Texas Jim waited.

> The horseman was John Ringgold, better known in the southwest country as "Johnny Ringo. . . ." "Howdy, Kid, . . . What's your hurry?" "Any particular reason for wanting to catch up with me?" Texas Jim asked, his hand . . . in easy reach of his six-shooter.
> Ringo laughed and said, "Come off the 'high horse,' Kid, and forget about that gun. I have a message . . . from a friend." [19]

The friend turned out to be Curly Bill. Texas Jim was surprised. He thought Curly Bill had been killed at Iron Springs (that encounter seems to have been one of the few historic events Jim missed).

> "Killed, hell!" Ringo laughed and said: "That old 'curly lobo' wasn't even within a day's ride of Wyatt Earp and his GANG when that fight was supposed to have taken place." [20]

Curly Bill, it seems, was getting ready to leave the country and wanted to sell Jim some stock. Jim was a known purchaser for a "Freight and Stage" line (unnamed). Jim and Ringo headed for Galeyville and the still very much alive Curly Bill. As they rode, Jim puzzled over Ringo:

> "As they made their way along the trail, Texas Jim studied the grim, silent figure there in front of him; he wondered what manner of trouble could have turned a mild natured, intelligent man like Johnny Ringo into such a ruthless, cold-blooded killer. It was common knowledge that Ringo was, at one time, a respected college professor; for a number of years he had been associated with one of the larger eastern colleges. Some said it was DRINK that had caused his downfall; others claimed a WOMAN was back of it all. . . . In his darker moods he was shunned by all; no man who knew him, not even those who called him FRIEND dared to approach him,

> . . . even killers like Curly Bill, Jim Hughes, Doc Holliday, and the Earps, trod lightly in Ringo's presence.[21]

At Galeyville, there was Curly Bill, sure enough. Ringo told Curly of his presumed death and showed him the *Epitaph* story. Curly read the story and said, "Either old man Clum, or the party who gave him this story, seem to have been doing a lot of wishful thinking. However, they may have unintentionally done me a BIG favor."[22] Texas Jim and Curly Bill struck a deal for Curly's livestock and equipment, including a heavy freight wagon, though why a horseback rustler would have had such a cumbersome piece of equipment on hand is a mystery Texas Jim does not explain. Curly Bill accepted three thousand dollars cash from Jim, who just happened to be packing that amount around with him. Curly then announced his intention of quitting the country: "Anyway," he grinned, "the Earps pulling out, together with the fact that people believe I am DEAD makes it an ideal time for me to CHANGE my stomping grounds."[23]

Ringo and Texas Jim headed for Silver City, New Mexico, with the stock and equipment. Curly Bill was off to Mexico. The secret of Curly's passing would be kept: "Even after William Brockus (sic) Graham had long since passed on," the Artrips intoned, "Jim's lips were of necessity STILL sealed until the time of telling his COMPLETE story, when he too was 'beyond the reaches' of the law."[24] Just what law or who would have been "reaching" for Jim in the 1950s, or even in 1896, for his associations with Curly Bill (which were never a matter of record, anyway) evokes no wonder or curiosity in the Artrips.

On the way to Silver City Ringo confessed to Jim that he, Curly Bill, and Jim Hughes had "AMBUSHED" Morgan and Virgil Earp in retaliation for the "cold blooded" killing of Billy Clanton and the McLaury brothers. "We decided since they wanted to play it dirty, we would give them a dose of their own medicine—WHITTLE them down one at a time, at our own discretion."[25] Indian Charlie and Frank Stilwell had been murdered in vain. Ringo also revealed how Wyatt Earp had tried to "cut him in" on a deal to rob the Tombstone-Benson stage.* Ringo withdrew from the plot when he learned that Doc Holliday would be present. He "didn't want to be IN on any DEAL with a 'trigger happy', 'fore-flusher [*sic*]', such as Holliday was. Ringo said he figured that Holliday would probably go out on the JOB drunk and would BALL things up!" In between such confessions Ringo sermonized self-pityingly on his fall from grace to evil ways. "The only peace I'll ever know is in the fantasy of a DRINK befogged brain. I was ONCE a respected human being, with a philosophy of life to live by: but all that seems so vague and far away now, like a half-remembered dream of long ago!"[26] It is, of course, impossible to tell where Texas Jim leaves off and the Artrips take over. It should be remembered, though, that at the time of his peregrinations with Ringo, his wheeling and dealing with Curly Bill, Daniel Fore Chisholm was sixteen years old.

In some respects this little memoir, set in dramatic, nineteenth-century type, is rather remarkable. Dates, places, and events are generally accurate. The little drama during which Curly Bill takes his leave for Mexico after Jim buys him out reveals some thought given to the argument over whether Wyatt Earp killed Curly Bill at Iron Springs, or whether Curly used this publicized exit as the means to a real one; and it is no less plausible than William Breakenridge's story of the benevolent rancher who gave Curly a "good saddle horse" on which to head for Wyoming. Someone, clearly, did a bit of research, and I strongly suspect that the someone was Chisholm himself, who probably spent those golden and watchful years reading Burns's *Tombstone* and Breakenridge's *Helldorado*.

Eugene Cunningham's dramatic sketch of Ringo in

---

* In *The Earp Brothers of Tombstone* (p. 186), Frank Waters actually cited Jim Chisholm as authority for his contention that Wyatt Earp was a stage robber.

Triggernometry is based almost entirely on what Breakenridge told him (although Breakenridge obviously did not tell him about Louis Hancock, the near victim of Ringo's "amazing dexterity" with "Colt or Winchester"):

> John Ringo, even more than Curly Bill, was a leading spirit among the rustlers of Galeyville and Charleston. Curly Bill more often led the rustlers than did Ringo, but that was because of Ringo's frequent withdrawals from his kind. John Ringo—Ringgold was the family name in California Breakenridge learned in later years—was the "black sheep" of an aristocratic family and well educated. Liquor was his weakness. . . . Men who knew him observed that he was more likely to go upon one of his wild sprees after receiving a letter from California addressed . . . in feminine handwriting. But what the rustlers knew of him—besides his amazing dexterity with Colt or Winchester—was that no man could safely forecast John Ringo's next movement [Hancock might have said Amen to that]. . . . But erratic as he was, John Ringo was a man with whom everyone in that part of Arizona must reckon, the fastest gunfighter and the deadliest, a man who courted trouble with the thoughtless courage of a bulldog.[27]

Ringo does fire the imagination, and he elicits an uncommon number of bewildering observations. Obviously, "everyone in that part of Arizona" did not have to "reckon" with Ringo. The statement is meaningless, a space-filler. Even those who did have to reckon with him did not really know him. Cunningham offers a slight variation on the near-fight with Holliday: "The story persists to this day, despite frantic pro-Earp recorders' denials, of his proposal to Doc Holliday and others of the Earp crowd that he and any or all of them 'shoot out' the feud between the Earps and the rustlers. . . . But John Ringo was one gunfighter none of the Earps wanted any part of. The belligerent little Holliday *might* have swapped shots with him, but Wyatt Earp led his party inside Hatch's Saloon and left Ringo walking up and down the street, hands on the guns in his overcoat pocket, very much on the prod."[28] Ringo challenged *everyone!* Cunningham was obviously unaware that Virgil Earp could not have been present.

I wrote Cunningham about some of his comments on Ringo. I wanted to know *whom* he had shot. In defense of Earp and Holliday, and, not incidentally, history, I referred to George Parson's diary: Doc was obviously *ready* to fight. Could Cunningham name even one gunfight in which Ringo had participated? What evidence did he have of Ringo's "amazing dexterity with Colt or Winchester?" He had, of course, been asked the questions before. His response was long and unconcerned with the minutiae of careful research:

> John X. Jones joins the Los Angeles Corral, THE WESTERNERS. He buys him [*Wild Bill Hickok*] *Prince of Pistoleers* [by Frank Wilstach] and *Frontier Marshal* and reads them carefully. Then he gets *Triggernometry* and BOIL! goes his blood; . . . a few are doing good spadework in extent no professional writer can afford. . . . They put in hours and . . . dozens of dollars to get two lines from a faded diary which—well! which maybe just confuse an already roiled incident. . . . [An] acquaintance of mine believes I credit Ringo with too much influence. "Where did Ringo get such a rep? Whom did he kill . . . ? I have an account of how he backed down right quick from [Buckskin] Frank Leslie. . . . In Tucson Public Library is a copy of a diary by George Parsons . . . January 17, 1882. HE states that 'Ringo and Doc came nearly having it with pistols . . . Police vigilant for once. . . .'"

I have talked by the hour with Billy Breakenridge, who had a steel trap mind, and others about Ringo and Curly Bill and the Clantons—back and forth—in and out—trying to get them into Human Being status. For at that very moment I was planning a novel in which Ringo was the villain and I did not want him a paper doll; and I wanted to shadow out the basis for his influence on simpler minds, such as Curly's. . . .

Ringo. . . . Every Tombstoner-of-his-time I've met has recalled his FORCE. We've all met that type—good and bad men whose personality came out at others. Not whom he *had* shot but whom he might shoot, seems to me, is the question men asked. As for that "diarized" remark, I don't know whether Parsons is setting down what he saw or what was told him. The way I have learned it—Ringo and Holliday stood with a group and were snarling at each other; might have done more (Ringo seems always to have been trying to start a row with the Earp faction), only a husky cop grabbed Ringo from behind and pinned his arms, while Wyatt came along and took Holliday off. There are various accounts of this, some highly embroidered, some which seem to me to have got themselves entangled with other incidents to make just any sort of yarn the teller wanted told. . . .

You spoke of Ringo. Some of the California branch—Ringgold—hired Billy Breakenridge to dig up Tombstone—angles on John, in 20's I think. I am vague on this because at the time of his death Billy and I were planning more Tombstone and he told me we'd do a Ringo-as'd-BE-a-Ringo and he had lots of stuff but we didn't have time to discuss it then. When he died I am told that a nephew or equivalent vandal dumped his leavings-and-gatherings in the fire. Billy was sold on John! As for me—I do' no'—I doubt that I could have stayed with him for a book-length of value; I might have achieved some sort of dispassionate appraisal interesting only to a psychologist. He was a drunk and a wastrel and I saw so many of those Up and Down in my very young days that their charm wore off soon. I have to take old Tombstoner's verdict that he was hell-on-wheels with the belt-guns and so completely (insanely?) unafraid of man or beast that not merely the Earps wanted no part of him. Doc Holliday was of course off the same bolt—because of TB. . . .[29]

In synthesis, this long, elliptical, and colorful reply suggests that: researchers are obsessed with trivia; George Parsons might not have been on the scene at all, and, indeed, "diarized" remarks often merely add to the confusion; what Ringo *might* have done was more important than what he did; one has to accept every old Tombstoner's word that Ringo had "force" and that he was "hell-on-wheels with the belt-guns," unless, of course, that old Tombstoner happened to have kept a diary. And Breakenridge is the only old Tombstoner cited.

This description, of course, is the novelist's view, freely admitted, not the historian's. Cunningham heard what he wanted to hear. If he had been truly interested in the real Ringo, those "back and forth—in and out" conversations would have elicited far more facts and information than he committed to book and letter—most especially so if Breakenridge had actually had "lots of stuff" (later destroyed by a "nephew or equivalent vandal"). I am not in any way suggesting that Cunningham did not tell me the truth as he knew it. He was simply more interested in the mystery of Ringo than in his reality. Some of that lost "stuff" would have come up had it existed and been systematically sought. But Cunningham, who contemplated putting Ringo in a novel as a "villain," did not want a "paper doll."

George Parsons is regarded by historians as a competent, even nosy and persistent, diarist. His account of the shooting of Virgil Earp, for example, is especially detailed and accurate. It would be far safer to believe his concise and impartial entries than the later claims of the jealous and petulant Breakenridge. Parsons recorded in his private journal that he was on the Ringo-Doc scene. I believe him; he had no reason to fabricate, or embroider. Breakenridge, on the other hand, was not only "sold on John," but also thoroughly disliked the Earps: "They got on my nerves—you know how it is—strutting because they had Wyatt behind them—nobody else amounted to a thing."[30]

When a persistent "WESTERNER" continued to plague Cunningham on the precise details of the dialogue between Ringo and Doc, he wrote me: "Last week I told that solemn WESTERNER I think what Ringo said to Doc Holliday was: Physician! Heel* thyself!"[31]

The shooting of Louis Hancock was well reported (see

---

* Meaning "Arm yourself," or "Grab your gun."

the newspaper accounts of this event, quoted in Chapter 1). It is fitting and instructive, though, to review a fictional account of the Hancock shooting (the one which follows is from Ray Hogan's novel, *The Life and Death of Johnny Ringo*) because it emphasizes the desperate need to chalk up at least one shooting and killing to John Ringo. Hogan's novel is generally a dialogue distillation of Lake's *Wyatt Earp: Frontier Marshal* and Burns's *Tombstone;* its main theme is the presumed "fact" of Ringo's personal and irreparable agony and the appalling singularity of his reputedly deadly obsession with the holiness of the barroom drinking-ritual. The "killing" of Hancock takes place in Tombstone (as most accounts do, rather than in Safford where the shooting actually occurred), where Ringo pushed up to a bar lined with standing men, ordered a whiskey, and drank off the straight shot without pause. Glancing to his left he saw Hancock, whom he knew slightly, and asked him to have a drink with him. When the bartender put out a second glass,

Ringo filled it and pushed it at Hancock. The man shook his head, waggled the mug in his hand. "Thanks. I'm drinking beer. Reckon I'll just stick with it." The room hushed suddenly . . .

"I'm asking you to drink with me," Ringo said softly. "One gentleman to another."

Hancock shifted his weight from the left to the right foot . . . "Man's got a right to drink what he wants . . ."

"Take it," Ringo said, quietly insistent.

"You drink it," Hancock said flatly. "I'll do as I damn please . . ."

Ringo's ivory handled Colts came up in a swift, smooth blur. The crash of the gunshot was a deafening explosion in the saloon. Hancock slammed back against the bar, setting off a bright tinkle of glassware. The man hung there momentarily and then slipped to the floor, dead.

[Ringo slowly finished his second drink, then lectured the hushed crowd:] "I offer a man a drink I expect him to ac-

cept. . . . Little rule of mine I'd like you all to remember"—
and walked out into the night. There would be no repercussions. Hancock should not have refused the . . . drink. . . .
It was a rule studiously observed throughout the frontier. And
Hancock was armed, therefore it could not be termed murder.[32]

There was, of course, no such "rule studiously observed
throughout the frontier." Nor was it acceptable to shoot another man simply because he was armed. If all the men who
were armed and refused drinks had been shot for breeching a
muscular kind of protocol, the Old West would have been
littered with corpses from Jackson Hole to the Big Bend. And,
as the contemporary newspapers noted, Ringo *was* arrested.

⟨✦⟩

Bad as most of the books on the Old West are, both fact and
fiction, the worst of them seem historically and literarily pure
when compared to popular magazines published from the
1950s through the 1980s. These go beyond vulgarity to a disgusting and uniform dishonesty, to a mean and nasty anti-intellectual attitude toward history and toward historical figures. Alongside them, the old dime-novels and the later pulps
possess *sui generis* qualities that reflect a blythe and insular
kind of innocence and honesty. The pulps were melodramatic, bigoted, often outrageous, even macabre, but they
were never pretentious and they never laid serious claim to
historical parallels and accuracy. As Tony Goodstone points
out in his admirable compilation and study *The Pulps*, many
of these works had redeeming features: the central character
of pulp-author Max Brand's "The Ghost" (*All-Story Weekly*,
1919), for example, was the Greek god Pan incarnate, and
J. E. Grinstead's "Old Pard" (*All Western Magazine*, 1933) "has
a straight-forward quality which suggests a more realistic 'Old
West'. . . . Characterization is developed through action, and
the ending has all the poetry one associates with the West."
"Butler's Nag" by Frank Richardson Pierce, (*Western Story*,

1925), Goodstone continues, "has a gentle, homespun humor which is native to the western image," and "A Ticket Outside," by Robert Ormond Case, (*Western Story,* 1933), "derives its power from his gripping portrayal of the numbing Yukon elements." Goodstone concludes his selected Western pulp quintet with Luke Short's, "Tough Enough" (*Argosy,* 1937), which, he believes, "demonstrates his [Short's] ability to create mood and tension within a framework of minimum action. Perhaps the most outstanding facet of Short's style is his ability to bring life to his characters through his simple description of minor—but revealing—gestures and dialog."[33]

It seems most unlikely that future editors and compilers will find any such redeeming features in popular magazines, whose article-stories on real Western figures are often neither fiction nor history, but grotesque caricatures—clumsy attempts to use the techniques of the former to obfuscate ignorance of the latter. Gary Roberts described them well, and with the measured charity and dignity of the professional:

> As usual, the most blatant excesses came in the popular magazines, rushing to cash in on the new trend with loud claims to authenticity. What the careful used with restraint, if not objectivity, a new generation of "rocking chair historians" seized with vigor, producing prose as purple as any produced a generation earlier. Not content with the arguments that could be supported with evidence, the magazine hacks created "evidence." Past writers, particularly [Stuart N.] Lake and [William E.] Connelley, were bitterly attacked by men who had neither the talent nor the research ability nor the understanding of the West's history of those earlier writers.

Again charitably, Roberts dignified this crew of literary vandals as "debunkers":

> In this form, debunking permitted no departure from the objective—the exposé of Western heroes. Nothing that might reflect credit, however slight, could be tolerated. Instead of the handsome courageous heroes of the past, the debunkers

offered a set of cowardly backshooters devoid of any vestige of moral character, courage, or marksmanship. . . . Earp was no longer the mustachioed "Lion of Tombstone" but a "cadaverous" and sniveling weakling. Hickok was now "effeminate" . . . and Billy the Kid was a hideous cretin. . . .[34]

John Ringo, though, has been the perfect foil for many of those popular magazine writers whose work lacks genuine research or good fictional characterizations; indeed, they depend on the shadowy outlines of such men as John Ringo. The *lack* of documentation is important, because it enables them to "flesh out," in their own ways, a character for whose development they need take no responsibility; and, since such a character has already been vaguely established as a historical entity, he makes no real demands on their meager talents. Then, as in the case of John Ringo, they borrow, often word for word, from such writers as Eugene Cunningham, Walter Noble Burns, and Stuart Lake. Since Ringo and Wyatt Earp were known to be enemies, the popular writer is also absolved of the creative intricacies of adversary development. He need only choose "his" winner.

One of the worst of these fiction articles appeared in *Men— True Adventure*. It is titled simply "Ringo" (there's magic in that name!) and authored by Dave Markson. I say one of the worst because Markson so flagrantly and arrogantly thought himself a very earthy and clever writer. The article can be adequately described only in its own words. But first, note should be taken of the puzzling and bizarre illustration that accompanies the article: Ringo stands atop a small hummock, arms outstretched and face raised to the heavens in supplication. A Colt .45 dangles from the forefinger of his right hand. Unaccountably, there are great rents in his trousers and his shirt has been torn to shreds. His chest is bare and remnants of the sleeves hang from his arms. He is hatless. In the foreground are, one assumes, three of his rustler companions. Two stand mesmerized with fear. One, his animal teeth bared in terror, has begun to run. Possibly the illustration is intended to symbolize one of Ringo's celebrated periods of despond when he became so drunkenly vicious and depressed that even his friends cleared out. The tattered shirt is probably supposed to symbolize self-destruction. The illustration bears a caption that would have awed old Ned Buntline: "He came out of nowhere with dirt on his hands and dirt in his soul—and he was washed in the blood of the West."[35]

The story opens with tough, he-man talk that occasionally lapses into a stereotyped concept of the vernacular:

> You talk about gunfighters, there weren't but one: John Ringo by name.
>
> Rode into the West out of nowhere with blood on his hands and the memory of it in his soul—a man apart with something haunting him, something big. But no man asked what: John Ringo rode his own trail and none crossed it.
>
> A big man. You can safely disregard the others."[36]

The "others" included Billy the Kid, "a buck-toothed juvenile delinquent from the slums of New York," Wild Bill Hickok, Jesse James, Bill Longley, John Wesley Hardin, and, of course,

> Wyatt Berry Stapp Earp, the self-styled "Lion of Tombstone," who used his lawman's badge as license for a sequence of outrageous, cold-blooded. . . .
>
> Never mind. These and all the rest—too long a look at their reputations and they fizzle and die. But Ringo looms!
>
> Large. Ridden by furies like a man under a curse—the one among all others to be truly reckoned with.[37]

Arrayed against that formidable pantheon of gunmen, all of whom have documented records, Markson's Ringo "looms"—precisely because he *has* no record of note. Ringo's "looming" is attributable only to those mysterious "furies" which "rode" him and which "furies," in turn, are ridden for all *they* are worth, and then some, by Dave Markson. One recalls also that Joe Chisholm's Ringo "loomed on horizons" and Markson's declaration that Ringo was "the one . . . to be truly reckoned with" is straight from Cunningham's "John Ringo was a man with whom everyone in that part of Arizona must reckon." And Earp was not the "self-styled" Lion of Tombstone. That title was gratuitously conferred upon him by Walter Noble Burns.

Throughout his article Markson makes use of a number of mechanical devices: one is the sentence that raises a provocative question, then trails off suggestively and mysteriously into an unenlightening burst of dots and dashes. A heap of ignorance can be covered up under a batch of these mechanical squiggles. Another is the one- or two-word sentence, paragraphically juxtaposed for dramatic visual effect. Still another is Ringo's repetitious and insistent public plea: "Wyatt, whyn't you an me fight?"[38] Markson's Ringo literally follows Earp all over Tombstone with his embarrassing importunities, which, one might add, do not seem to reflect the syntax of the college man, the "amateur archaeologist," the learned discourser on Judge Chisholm's front porch. Another device exploits Earp's middle initials, B.S. (Berry Stapp).

Markson swaggers on: "Ringo was a man playing a boy's game, and even against the 'invincible' Earp it was no contest. He threw down the gauntlet before Earp not once, not twice, but three times, and each time he put his challenge into plain English: 'Earp, let's me an' you fight.' One time Earp was backed by no less than seven men. Ringo, as was his way, was alone." According to Markson, Ringo's determination to make Earp fight began "one night when Wyatt took it into his head to arrest Curly Bill for 'disturbing the peace.' Wyatt caught him drunk in a dark alley and bent the barrel of his Buntline Special over the rustler's skull—this being one of the few uses to which history records he ever put the outrageously cumbersome weapon."[39]

Never mind, of course, that Markson chose to describe Curly Bill's killing of Marshal Fred White as "disturbing the peace." Never mind that there never *was* a Buntline Special—

Never Mind.

Shortly after the publication of my article "Ringo," in *The American West*, a friend sent me a xeroxed copy of an article titled "General Jo Shelby and Johnny Ringo," by someone named Howard N. Monnett. Neither the name of the magazine or journal from which the four-page article was excerpted nor the date of publication was included. The article centers around a photograph taken of Confederate General Jo[seph] Shelby in October of 1864, some two weeks before the Battle of Westport, Missouri, was joined. The photo was last seen in 1897 and, according to Monnett, historians have sought it ever since.

> Now, after 107 years [which would seem to date publication of his article in 1971], the Boonville [Missouri] picture of General Shelby has turned up in Tombstone, Arizona! . . . The picture was found in a box of old receipts and legal papers salvaged from a decrepit building in Tombstone, Arizona's fabulous ghost town "too tough to die". . . . But what is written on the reverse side of the photograph is even more important than the picture. In faint and faded ink script is the following:
> General Jo Shelby—
> My general, I rode with him
> in Missouri in 1864.
>   John Ringo[40]

The rest of Monnett's article is a rehash of the usual stuff (for want of a better word) written about John Ringo, but it is worthy of repetition for future reference. "Who was John Ringo?" Monnett asks. Well, he is "tall," "brooding," and "inscrutable," just as old Joe Chisholm and Walter Noble Burns had said he was, "a legendary character whose fierce loyalties were matched only by his blazing guns. . . ."[41] It is difficult enough to imagine such phraseology committed to paper in the 1970s (one is reminded of Mel Brooks's movie satire "Blazing Saddles"), but we are not even told who was on the receiving end of those "blazing guns," unless, of course, we "kill" poor old Louis Hancock once more. "Johnny Ringo was the terror of old Tombstone. . . . That he was well-educated, a most chivalrous gentleman of unquestioned loyalty and courage, and a deadly killer are *known facts* [italics mine]. Other than that, the rest is pure legend. Some believe he was born in Missouri—Texas—Maryland. Most think Ringo was not his real name, that he was the scion of a prominent, wealthy family [shades of Eugene Cunningham] and he changed it to protect that family from his odorous reputation. It is said he . . . rode with Quantrill . . . was kin to . . . the Younger brothers . . . friend of Frank and Jesse James. But that is all speculation. . . ."[42]

Monnett goes on to tell us we may still hear the story in the "brooding Chiricahua Mountains" of how a mysterious and beautiful woman, accompanied by two boys, came to Ringo's grave of a moonlit night, "removed the body and took it back to Missouri where it is buried in the cemetery of a little . . . river town. But that is all legend."[43]

It shore is, podner. I heard no such story during the number of visits I made to the grave, a big-bouldered cairn hard by the five-armed blackjack oak where Ringo's body was found and directly, if unromantically, behind Will Sanders's chicken coop. In 1973 a group of well-meaning Arizona highway department employees and Ringo buffs raised a six-foot marker over the grave[44] and disturbed the eloquently organic tranquility of the site; it is enough to scare away that "ghost" who stalks about the old oak of windy, moonlit nights.

But, Monnett concludes, "what is not legend is that a man, later known as Johnny Ringo, rode with General Jo Shelby in the Missouri Raid of 1864, fought in the Battle of Westport, and for sentiment clung to an old picture of a most notable Missouri gentleman and soldier. Perhaps that was the only thing remaining to Johnny Ringo of a happier and more honorable life."[45]

John Ringo and General Shelby will be considered in a more revealing context later (see Chapter 7). But even on the surface the article is absurd: the October, 1864, photo of General Shelby accompanies the article, but there is no photo of the reverse side of the Shelby portrait bearing the handwritten inscription and signature of John Ringo. We are apparently expected to take Monnett's word that it is there.

⊱⊰

The depositions concerning John Ringo speak eloquently for themselves. Often they are personally intrusive, boastful, and demonstrably inaccurate. They are always colorful. Here is Robert M. Boller, teamster:

> [I] read some of the books making heroes of the Earps, . . . it makes me mad. . . . In Dodge I knew the Earps, Doc Holliday, Bat Masterson . . . and the rest of that lowdown gang before they came to Tombstone. . . . I have never allowed anyone to call me a liar not even in my teens. [I know more] about law in Cochise County than any other man living today, Breakenridge not excepted. . . .
>
> [I] came to Arizona January 1, 1881, age 18, . . . came by way of San Simon . . . heard shooting . . . 35 rustlers celebrating New Year. They asked us where we were going and were very nice to us.
>
> [I] drove team in [the] Chiricahuas to Tombstone . . . met "Billy the Kid" [Claiborne], Curly Bill. . . . I helped bury Ringo and found the body. . . . Ringo was a suicide . . . had the D.T.'s and imagined there were snakes in his boots. [His] pistol had one empty shell. [I] signed [the] sworn statement [as to how I] found things.
>
> Later Ringo's sister came down from California and took the body back with her.
>
> [Buckskin] Frank Leslie was [a] would-be bad man.
>
> Ringo was a pretty nice fellow and came from a good fam-

ily but he was wild, used to get on some drunks and became very despondent.[46]

It is highly doubtful that Boller knew the Earps, Holliday, or Masterson in Dodge City. If he were eighteen in 1881, he would have been sixteen in 1879, the year the Earps and Holliday came to Tombstone. Earp's heyday in Dodge was during 1876–1878. It is most unlikely that a thirteen- or fourteen-year-old child would have known a group of gamblers, saloon keepers, frequenters of whore houses, and peace officers nearly twice his age.

Boller was never a peace officer, so his boast of knowing more about the law in Cochise than Breakenridge seems to be just that. He did sign the affidavit for the coroner's and sheriff's inquest into Ringo's death, and he helped to bury the body; but the affidavit declared John Yoast to be the one who found the body.[47] His theories of how Ringo died are his own and no more or less authoritative than anyone else's. His most serious error is the claim that Ringo's sister removed his body to California.

A cattleman named A. M. Franklin left a brief, undated, penciled account (deposited at the Arizona Pioneers Historical Society) of two experiences with Ringo:

> [I] remember a fellow had it in for me and when I went into a saloon he began to cuss me out. He tried in every way he could to make me answer back. Of course he was armed and all he wanted was an excuse. About that time Ringo came in. He heard enough to catch the drift then he sauntered to the bar . . . slapped down his money and announced, "All of Franklin['s] and my friends have a drink." No one dared insult him by refusing and all had a drink—the obnoxious fellow included. At another time a crowd was trying to start something in the store. . . . Ringo took in the situation at a glance. Stepping up beside me and slamming his gun on the counter he remarked, "If there is going to be a row I think I would like to be in on it." Everyone suddenly decided they had business elsewhere.[48]

Franklin's statement can be neither proved nor refuted. But if true it would appear to verify Ringo's dual personality: the good and the bad. Here he is a veritable Paladin, the defender of the defenseless, who uses his fearsome reputation for the good of others and who might easily have been the prototype for the leading character in Jack Schaefer's novel *Shane.* Yet one also observes in the Franklin episode the irrationality of the man who shot Louis Hancock for refusing whiskey: when he ordered drinks all around, "no one dared insult him by refusing." Still, he had, in effect, defused one dangerous situation by palpably creating, or threatening to create, a new one, though in view of his reputation and of Hancock's experience, one much less likely to occur. The validity of this account, if written years after the events, is questionable—especially if it was "penciled" after the publication of Burns's *Tombstone.*

An unnamed stage driver whose route ran from Clifton, Arizona, to Lordsburg, New Mexico, in the 1880s remembered John Ringo in a brief reminiscence:

> John Ringo [was] tall, good looking, [and] well educated. [He was] mean when drinking [and] gambling. [He] kept [his] horse at Smyth's [livery stable in] Lordsburg, [and] often went off without paying for [the] feed. [The] corral man complained to Smyth who said, "That's all right. Take good care of the horse when it comes in. I'd rather have Ringo's friendship than his hatred—besides when he has the money he'll come in and pay."
>
> [I] heard [there] was a fude [*sic*] in Texas called the "Ringo War" and that he killed 22 men. I never heard of Ringo killing an American in this part of the country.[49]

Here again is the theme of Ringo's dual personality and the fearful, almost unctuous, deference accorded him. It was better to have his friendship than his hatred. If he rode off without paying the hostler, let him go: the other side of him—the good side—would bring him back sooner or later to pay. His height and good looks are repeated here, ostensibly as the stage driver saw and remembered him. I suspect, though, the stage driver later read something about Ringo's education which reminded him of the rustler's presumably distinctive speech. There was no "Ringo War" and no record of his killing twenty-two men. One should not miss the meaning, though, behind the laconic statement that Ringo was not known to have killed "an American" in Arizona–New Mexico: Mexicans, of course, did not count. It should also be noted that the date of this reminiscence, 1927, coincides with that of the publication of Burns's *Tombstone*.

Judge J. C. Hancock, who transformed Curly Bill into "Old Cack" (see Chapter 2, note 54) and who was one of Frank Waters's oft-quoted sources in *The Earp Brothers of Tombstone*, hated Wyatt Earp and admired John Ringo:

Wyatt Earp was not the brave man or the Lion of Tombstone. [The] real lion was [John] Ringo, and the bravest man I ever knew. [He] never courted notoriety or wore long hair or a ten gallon hat, [he was] smooth shaved, used good language and did not have [a] "soft Southern drawl" or use the words "heah" or "aboot."

[He was a] fine looking man—[I] saw him sober and under the influence, but I never saw him abuse or "shoot 'em up."

[He] was not a two gun man. [He carried a] Colt .45 single action, blued six shooter. [He] dared them [presumably the Earps and Holliday] one at a time. John had nerve all right.

[He was] born in California. [The] Earps [were] afraid of three men—Curly Bill, Ringo, and John Behan.

Wyatt [Earp] never arrested Curly Bill; [nor, Hancock declared, did he kill the outlaw at Iron Springs].[50]

It is doubtful that Hancock was as free with his praise of the outlaw element in Cochise County when he was a jurist as he was in his apparent dotage. There is no other way to explain him. No one ever seriously suggested Wyatt Earp was "not the brave man," not even Breakenridge. The claim that the Earps were afraid of John Behan, of all people, is absurd. Earp did arrest Curly Bill, and there is extensive documentation of the arrest and pistol whipping. That would seem to refute the judge's assertion that the "Earps were afraid of Curly Bill." As for Ringo being the "real Lion of Tombstone," well, there is absolutely no proof of that. Hancock is correct in his description of Ringo's weaponry, and he affirms the outlaw's good looks and proper use of language. As for never seeing Ringo "abuse, or shoot 'em up," he could have got a powerful argument to the contrary from another chap, name of Louis Hancock. Ironically, J. C. Hancock's letter was published in the *Epitaph* just a month and a half before the ailing Wyatt Earp died. Had he written the letter a year or so earlier, he would almost certainly have been forced by Earp into a retraction. According to Glenn Boyer, Earp invariably took action against slanderous stories. I am told by historian John D. Gilchriese that shortly after Wyatt Earp came to California he heard that former Texas Ranger and Arizona lawman Jeff Milton had been loudly disparaging his courage. Earp sent Milton a telegram offering to meet Big Jeff any place, any time. Milton did not reply.[51]

⊱⋅☙❦☙⋅⊰

When John Ringo died, on July 14, 1882, the newspapers were unexpectedly kind, considering the fact that he was a well-known rustler and gunman. The report in the *Tucson Star* made it obvious that he had commanded respect, for all his quixotic, antisocial behavior:

> John Ringgold, one of the best known men in southeastern Arizona, was found dead in Morse's Canyon, in the Chiricahua Mountains, last Friday. He evidently committed suicide. He was known in this section as "King of the Cowboys," and was fearless in the extreme. He had many staunch friends and bitter enemies. The pistol, with one chamber emptied, was found in his clenched fist. [He] shot himself in the head, [the] bullet entering the right side, between eye and ear, and com-

ing out on top of the head. Some members of his family reside at San Jose, California.[52]

The *Epitaph* account treated Ringo's passing as though Tombstone and Cochise County had lost a model citizen:

DEATH OF JOHN RINGO

. . . few men in Cochise County or southern Arizona were better known. He was recognized by friends and foes as a recklessly brave man, one who would go any distance, or undergo any hardship to serve a friend or punish an enemy. While undoubtedly reckless, he was far from being a desperado, and we know of no murder being laid to his charge. Friends and foes are unanimous in the opinion that he was a strictly honorable man in all his dealings, and that his word was as good as his bond. Many people who were intimately acquainted with him in life have serious doubts that he took his own life, while an equally large number say he frequently threatened to commit suicide, and the event was expected at any time. The circumstances of the case hardly leave any room for doubt as to his self-destruction.

He was subject to frequent fits of melancholy and had an abnormal fear of being killed. Two weeks ago last Sunday in conversing with the writer, he said he was as certain of being killed, as he was of living then. He said he might run along for a couple of years more, and may not last two days.[53]

This brief article by an unknown reporter (the *Epitaph*, unfortunately, did not byline its reporters) is one of the most important pieces ever written about John Ringo. First, it embodies in him and emphasizes those virtues so traditionally valued in the Old West: trust, honor, loyalty, and courage. It is easy to see this bit of subjective reportage as father to unnumbered hero-worshiping articles, stories, and books about John Ringo. Second, it appears to reaffirm the acute melancholia of a man who presumably had irretrievably squandered the good life, the "scion," the gloomy and prescient academic. But one also detects a certain self-pity, and it is a bit difficult to reconcile "reckless courage" with an "abnormal fear of being killed." Third, it really offers nothing more than the assertion of "reckless courage" to those who believe—or want to believe—Ringo to be a deadly gunfighter. There are no examples of such courage. There is no murder (or presumably any killings) "laid to his charge"—not even Louis Hancock.

The most puzzling aspect of the article is the inexplicable declaration that Ringo was "far from being a desperado." Just what would one call a gunman, rustler chief, and probable killer of Mexicans who tried to provoke a gunfight in the streets of Tombstone with Doc Holliday or with Wyatt Earp, a deputy U.S. marshal, and who reputedly was so periodically vicious that even his own kind withdrew from him? The answer to this question probably lies in at least the partial truth to the reporter's effusions, which, nevertheless, establish an image that can take any direction or position a writer chooses. Possibly the reporter was young and awed by the romance of Ringo and by his melancholy presence. It is possible, too, that the passing of the last of the great gunmen and outlaw leaders had produced a mild form of nostalgia. More probably it simply reflected a new and less knowledgeable editorial policy, since John Clum had sold the *Epitaph* the preceding May and left Tombstone.

The passage of time, however, saw the development of a decidedly unromantic and cynical view of the Old West's reckless and courageous gunmen and of the tough reputation of the Old West itself. In a sarcastic editorial on June 7, 1938, the *Tucson Star* helped to kill plans by the Arizona Forest Service to place a marker on Ringo's grave describing him as "King of the Outlaws in Old Tombstone Days." Speaking of Ranger Fred Winn, who was to have been the speaker at the dedication ceremony, the *Star* declared:

> We can't imagine what the orator can say about John Ringo that would be both complimentary and truthful [except] two

minutes of silence. He was probably less bold and valiant than the title "King of the Outlaws" indicated.

If Johnny were alive today and should come truculently into this office, we who have waded through the dragon's blood of two depressions, should sieze him by the collar and waistband and throw him down the stairs.[54]

And that, quite likely, would have been that particular editor's last editorial.

Now, in the mid-1980s, the marker is there (it was put in place in 1973).

And here is that Galeyville card game—so dear to the hearts of such Western writers as Cunningham, Breakenridge, Burns, and too many of their plagiarizers to mention—as it was reported in the Tombstone *Nugget:*

A SOCIAL GAME

One of the Galeyville's festive cowboys named Ringold [*sic*] last Friday entered into a game of poker, and not being as expert with the "Keards" as he was with his "gun" he soon "went broke." [Ringo apparently left the game, brooding over his loss.] But he returned with a companion named David Estes, one . . . armed with a Henry rifle and the other with a six-shooter. The players were promptly ordered to "hold up their hands," and the cowboys proceeded to "go through" the party, securing in the neighborhood of $500. Some of the party were so frightened that they broke for the woods, where they remained concealed until daylight. A well known saloon keeper . . . had $500 on his person. He dodged the Henry rifle and six-shooter and escaped into the darkness, returning shortly with a shotgun, but the bold desperados had vamoosed. When the robbers left town they took a horse belonging to one of the citizens.[55]

This was the incident that brought Billy Breakenridge to Galeyville with a warrant for Ringo's arrest, which warrant Ringo "honored" by coming in to Tombstone on his own terms.

4
A Summary and
That Magic Name

OVER THE YEARS I watched and read with something approaching amazement as John Ringo's awesome reputation grew, as his Dionysiac excesses and reputed self-loathing merged more palpably with unreality than with reality, as historians, contemporaries, and fiction writers contradicted each other in their discussions of him, often with an unusual degree of unprofessional and professional hubris. "It has," Ray Hogan wrote, "been a matter of clothing a skeleton with flesh, placing muscle and skin on the stark bones of scattered truths."[1] I have no wish to enter a caveat against a little "fleshing out," but it seems to me the "truths" have become a bit too "scattered" and the "stark bones" fattened to obesity. I am reminded of Hogan's own account of the shooting of Louis Hancock (pp. 27–28 of *The Life and Death of Johnny Ringo*), which involved the "swift, smooth blur" of Ringo's "ivory-handled Colts," the "crack of the gunshot," a "deafening explosion," Hancock "slammed back against the bar," a "bright tinkle of glassware," the body "hung there momentarily," then "slipped to the floor, dead." Now *that* is "clothing a skeleton" with "*flesh*"!

Hogan had experimented tentatively with John Ringo's name four years before the publication of *The Life and Death of Johnny Ringo*. In *Marshal Without a Badge*, a novel, Marshal Mark Kennicott kills a Billy Ringo[2] in what seems to have been a set-up. Ringo here is a coarse, bloodshot-eyed bad man who, after being forced to turn over his pistol to the lightning-fast Kennicott, is killed by the marshal when he appears to go for a hide-out gun. He turns out to have been unarmed and Kennicott loses his badge, temporarily, and the bad guys take over the town, temporarily. All this, of course, was before the great "fleshing out."

At this point, the admixture that I observed of documented history and polemic, the personal rages and intrusions of certain authors, and the blatant fictions, along with the imperative of this narrative, now demand synthesis—a summing up of all the claims made for and about John Ringo: He was born in Texas, in Missouri, in California, in Maryland. His real name was Ringgold and he was the black-sheep scion of a wealthy and genteel southern family. He was related to the Younger family, to the Daltons, and possibly to the Jameses. Colonel Coleman Younger of San Jose, California, was his grandfather. He was a college graduate, possibly a college professor. He graduated from William Jewell College in Missouri and later was associated with one of the larger eastern colleges. He read the classics in the original Latin and Greek. There is no photo of him. He was tall, thin-faced, and with a wistful or sad expression, auburn-haired, and handsome. His eyes were warm blue, baby blue, china blue, warm brown, sombre gray. He was depressed, tenebrous, a vicious drunk, and a sober gentleman.

He carried ivory-handled guns and he rode with Quantrill, the Jameses and the Youngers. He fought in the Civil War in the battle of Westport with General Jo Shelby. He killed the killers of his brother in Texas, where he was also a respected school official. He was a warrior in the Hoodoo War (the Mason County Range War) and the Sutton-Taylor Feud, both in Texas. He revered womanhood and would, in fact, kill a man who insulted a woman, as in the case of Louis Hancock. He worshiped his "dear little sisters," who wrote to him in a "graceful, feminine hand," in such a manner as to suggest

Freudian overtones. His sisters, in turn, loved him dearly. His family in San Jose, California, thought him to be in the cattle business.

Ringo was an amateur archaeologist.

He committed suicide.

He was killed by Buckskin Frank Leslie, by Johnny-Behind-the-Deuce, by Doc Holliday, by Wyatt Earp, by a cowboy called Lou Cooley, and by an unnamed cowboy. And, finally, he was the deadliest gunfighter in the West, feared alike by his own kind and by the Earps and Doc Holliday.

⊱✦⊰

I found these blatantly conflicting claims both intriguing and offensive—intriguing simply because they were made; offensive because not one of them, with the exception of John Ringo's participation in the Hoodoo War, could be proved. Neither, apparently, could they be disproved. And so, after years of gathering and sifting, of running down leads, of traveling and writing letters, I found myself with bulging files of what I had facetiously begun to dignify as "Ringo-ana." But I was no closer to the man himself than when I first met him, a grim and melancholy "Hamlet," "stalking" the pages of Walter Noble Burns's *Tombstone*.

I began my labors with presumptuous visions of writing the first psychobiography of a western character, one who chanced also to have been an eastern academic gone sour, both blessed and cursed with superb coordination of mind and body, and beset by Oedipal rages that manifested themselves in vicious personality changes upon receipt of those letters penned in a "graceful, feminine hand." With some background in psychology, I knew psychobiography to be a risky and worrisome enterprise.[3] But I had some notion that the faint mother-sister theme and the veneration of women in general that runs tantalizingly through the writings about John Ringo, if confirmed by research and discovery, would enable me to drag him within Freudian clutches, to lug him to the couch in absentia. I found, instead, that I could not even draw him inside the periphery of history, let alone psychology. He was relegated to the anecdotal view, and even continuity and a reconciliation of theme were impossible. Indeed, the only perceivable psychology to be found in the writings about John Ringo is in the writers themselves. All too often Ringo is a personal extension of what a given author fancies himself to be, or what he would like to be, or to have been.

Discernible, too, in writings about Ringo is the subconscious or conscious unease of the authors with the imperfection of man, and the opportunity the shadowy Ringo offers them to make up for those deficiencies. Outlaw and killer or not, John Ringo is so heavily endowed with virtues as to constitute a near composite of the perfect man. Recall, for example, that Joe Chisholm's Ringo was a "Robber Baron of the Desert" who "looms" on borders, an archaeologist and discourser, as well as the reverent champion of "chaste matron" and "soiled dove" alike. Dave Markson's Ringo, "ridden by furies," also "looms—large." Sara Bakarich's Ringo was celebrated in song, John Myer's Ringo read the classics in the "original Latin and Greek," and Walter Noble Burns's Ringo was a "Hamlet." Eugene Cunningham's Ringo was one with whom "everyone in Southeastern Arizona must reckon." A careful student of that era will note that Doc Holliday is far more often maligned and denounced as a psychopathic killer than is John Ringo. Yet Holliday is *known* to have fought in the open, *known* to have been loyal to friends, and *known* to have had some education; in addition, he was never a proven outlaw or even much of killer, as far as the record goes. Our preoccupation with this "tragic hero" aspect in the writings about Ringo tells us more about ourselves than the writings tell us about the outlaw and probable killer himself.

But one does not make a book of such stuff, or even a decent article. Nor can one fashion a book around anecdotes—most particularly when even those are in short supply and probably ninety percent spurious at that. Frustration, though, and all that time spent in research impelled me to a continued quest for a theme. Why, I kept asking myself, aside from his near fight with Doc Holliday (and perhaps with Wyatt Earp), have we even *heard* of John Ringo? We know he was involved in the Hoodoo War in Texas (see Chapter 8), during which he was *probably* involved in two treacherous, not to say cowardly, killings; but here one detects no vestige of Burns's Hamlet or of Breakenridge's honorable outlaw, gentleman, and college graduate, whose guns the deputy returned after the near shoot-out with Doc Holliday.

Sketchy as it is, I concluded that the Texas story is probably the correct one—i.e., John Ringo was a treacherous, back-shooting murderer and thief, whose perverted sense of honor doubtless was refracted through the minds first of men who both admired and feared him and then of later writers who, consciously or subconsciously, sought to create a near perfect hero-type, one flawed only by personal trauma. But John Ringo blazed no trails, raised no ranch from desert or plain, ramrodded no big outfit; the only cattle he drove were stolen. The question returned: why is John Ringo even considered among the great figures of the Old West? The West was full of men just like him. Eugene Cunningham, at a loss for a tangible record beyond Breakenridge, wrote me that the answer was probably the mystery of the man—not what he had done, but what he *might* have done. History, however, judges men and women by what they have done, and not all documented figures are famous. "Mysterious" Dave Mather, for example, *was* mysterious—a dangerous gunman, sometime lawman, reputedly educated and descended from the Puritan theologians Increase and Cotten Mather—yet he is hardly a footnote to western history or legend.

I do not recall when it occurred to me that Ringo's immortality probably lies in the tonal quality of his name, but I was much excited by the idea. I decided to write an article in which I would concentrate on the tonality and the literary and cinematic adaptability of the name Ringo, and to see what, if anything, would happen.[4]

In the article, published in *The American West*, I wrote: "One suspects that Ringo's immortality lies in the tonal quality of his name, [which] . . . is eloquent of outlawry, dark, mysterious. It has the ring of heroism, a name without origin or identification. . . . Ringo is a name that lends itself well to book titles, articles, songs, theatre marquees."[5] I cited Dixon Wecter's pithy essay on Paul Revere in *The Hero In America*, in which he points out that Revere's "nationwide fame [is owed] solely to [Henry Wadsworth] Longfellow. Prior to Longfellow's poem ["Paul Revere's Ride," published in *Tales of a Wayside Inn*, 1863], Revere's name was not included in a single dictionary of American biography."[6] Longfellow was inspired to write "Paul Revere's Ride" after a visit to the old North Church, and he was obviously not one to let history interfere with his vital rhyme-scheme. The historical Revere was captured by the British and his "fellow courier," William Dawes, carried the news of the British approach to Concord. "Revere," Wecter wrote, "was a name which had the ring of heroism."[7] Not unreasonably or unesthetically, if somewhat unethically, Longfellow must have concluded that not much could be done with

> *Listen my children, and you shall hear*
> *Of the midnight ride of Bill Dawes.*

The unfortunate Dawes, as Wecter writes, galloped from Concord on "into oblivion." In her poem "What's in a Name?", Helen F. Moore imagines a posthumous discussion with the deserving Dawes, during which it seems to have been suggested that he ask why he was lost to history, and to which Dawes replies,

> *"Why should I ask? The reason is clear*
> *My name was Dawes and his Revere."*[8]

Following is a sampling of motion pictures, television shows, songs, and advertisements that have capitalized on Ringo's name: a 1966 movie was titled "A Pistol for Ringo"; another, the same year, was "Ringo and his Golden Pistol." The six sons of a prominent California family were all given tough-guy nicknames; the sixth chose his own: "Ringo." In the television show "Hondo," in 1967 Ringo was shot down by Jesse and Frank James, Bob Ford and his brother, and Cole Younger and his brothers, when it was learned that Ringo had shot and killed Quantrill during the Civil War (it took a heap of shooting to kill Ringo). The westering outlaw in the motion picture "Stagecoach" (with John Wayne) was the "Ringo Kid."* The aging pistolero in an early 1950s movie called "The Gunfighter" was Gregory Peck as "Jimmie" Ringo, a weary outlaw trying to go home, but unable to escape his reputation (evoking the endlessly repeated myth that gunfighters sought out other gunfighters in primal efforts to build reputations).

In a barroom scene of the television series "High Chaparral," "Uncle Buck" Cannon points across the room to a stolid, grim, and brooding fellow: "'At there's Johnny Ringo, Blue Boy." Blue Boy Cannon stares, stupefied. "Hi ya, Ringo," Uncle Buck yells, obsequiously. Ringo stares back, in brooding contemplation. Finally he nods: "Buck." In another episode of "High Chaparral," Ringo is hired to kill an Apache chief.

Another television show was called "The Guns of Johnny Rondo." The use of the same first name and the similarity of surnames are too close to be debated. And the theme was a Ringo theme: Rondo was a gunfighter who was also trying to hang up his guns; unlike "Jimmie" Ringo, he was successful. And no wonder. According to the little ditty that was sung before, during, and after the show, he had plumb run out of opposition:

* A 1986 re-make of this film—made for television this time—had country-music star Kris Kristofferson in the Ringo part.

Sixteen tried
And sixteen died
by the guns of Jooooohnie Rondo.

Even Hopalong Cassidy got a crack at John Ringo in an old movie. Hoppy and John were getting along quite well, though somewhat warily, when John suddenly rose above his reverence for women and up and plugged Belle Star. That was a little too rich for Hoppy's blood, so he acceded to the Code of the West and killed John Ringo. In the movie version of the "Gunfight at O.K. Corral," Doc Holliday (Kirk Douglas) killed John Ringo (John Ireland), who, of course, was not in that fight at all.

Ringo even had his own television series, in which he finally got to be the good guy—a sheriff, if you will, of the town of Velardi, which sounds like the setting for one of those "spaghetti Westerns." Actor Don Durrant was a square-jawed, clean-cut Sheriff Ringo who, between enforcing the law and plugging reputation hunters, invented the French-patented LeMat revolver, an over–and–under rig—a .45 above and a .410 shotgun below—that was used in the Civil War, mostly by southern officers (Jeb Stuart carried one). The "Johnny Ringo Show" opened and closed with a song:

Ringo, Johnny Ringo
His fears were never shown
The fastest gun in all the West
The quickest ever known.

A bit redundant, perhaps, but it made its point. And speaking of songs, Lorne Greene of the popular television series "Bonanza" made a record titled "Ringo"; old Pappy Cartwright almost had a hit on his hands by the time the youth of America discovered he wasn't singing about one of the Beatles.* The words, in Greene's stentorian and sibilant chant, were resonant and heroic indeed:

* Ringo Starr

Then come dawn to setting sun
He practiced with that deadly gun.
And hour on hour I watched in awe—
No human being could match the draw of Rrrringo.

On his stone they can't explain
the tarnished star above the name of Rrrringo.[9]

Ringo even made it to England. A cartoon strip, "Rick Martin" by John Diamond, running in the London *Evening News* in 1966, featured Ringo shooting up Tombstone. "Hurrahing the town," Diamond explains, "almost a ritual prelude to real trouble, Johnny Ringo and his gang tear through Tombstone like a tornado." Inside a building, two British types head for the woodwork in an exploding shower of glass shards. Says one, clutching his bowler, "It's that Ringo mob. Knew there was gonna be trouble moment Ringo showed up." Says the other, "Reckon what we need around here is some real peace officers."[10] Righto, Old Chap—send for Wyatt Earp (reckon Scotland Yard won't do).

The evocation of Ringo even occurs in the advertisements for a male after-shave lotion or cologne called "Rango." It can be argued, of course, that everything that begins with the letter "R" and ends with the letter "o" is not intended to be an association with the Old West's "most deadly" gunman. It can also be argued that the substitution of the letter "a" for the letter "i" is merely a legal precaution. Either way, the theme of the advertisement for "Rango" as portrayed on television is as overwhelmingly Western as the lotion itself apparently is. One whiff of that macho stuff, hanging in the clear desert air around the movie set known as "Old Tucson," sends a voluptuous young thing on a frenzied and bouncy gallop through a saguaro forest, hot on the scent. Just as she is about to round the bend, a muscular arm holding a rifle pointing skyward, is thrust before the camera. *Bang!* The hardriding lass drags her nag to a lathered halt and comes tearing back. We see him, then, sitting his horse in booted and sombreroed splendor, irresistably reeking of "Rango." Rango, Ringo. The association, along with the motif, is inescapable. Even the rather prosaic title of this book is enlivened by the magic of the name—*Ringo*.

When I wrote the article on Ringo, I was concerned with more than just the tonal quality of the name: I hoped to smoke out someone with more information. I had heard rumors and I nursed visions of someone sitting on a bundle of raw material, poised to ship it to just the right writer, who, naturally, would be myself. I even slipped a subtle hint into the article at the end of the discussion of Ringo's death. "It makes little difference who killed Ringo," I observed, "or if he killed himself. If new material turns up we shall be grateful for someone's scholarly serendipity."[11] This time, my vision materialized.

Book II
THE MAN

If the character of the West was spectacular, romantic and lawless, its reputation for being so outran the facts.

Walter Prescott Webb

5
"Two-Gun Charlie" Ringo

IT SEEMS to me now that "Ringo" had hardly appeared in print when I received a thick envelope in the mail bearing the return address of Charles R. Ringo, C.P.A., Oakland, California. In it was a long, complimentary, and chatty letter that subtly and obliquely let me know that, although I had written an interesting article and one with a provocative point of view, I did not have the real story of John Ringo. I responded to the letter, and Charles Ringo and I began a warm correspondence over the next two years that was interrupted in part by his incipient illness, in part by his greater preoccupation with the genealogy of his own side of the Ringo family (which was, indeed, generally distinguished, and which included a number of pioneers who had absolutely nothing to do with John Ringo).

To go back a bit: the late Charles R. Ringo, Certified Public Accountant and tax attorney, was, in the early 1970s, an eminent and distinguished septuagenarian and citizen. He held degrees from the University of California, Columbia University, and a law degree from San Francisco Law School. He was a teacher and a successful businessman. He belonged to numerous groups and organizations, including The California Historical Society, and he was a descendant of a pioneer California family. Charlie, as he began signing his name early in our correspondence (sometimes "Two-Gun Charlie"), did not exactly fulfill my vision of a box or bundle of records and documents arriving in the mails with no strings attached. He dribbled material to me in the form of letters, mostly hand-written and often in a near indecipherable scrawl. Handwritten letters and documents sent to him by members of the Ringo family and by others were photocopied and passed on to me. As Charles tentatively doled out material, it quickly became obvious, as I had always suspected, that virtually everything that has been written about John Ringo is blatantly incorrect or downright spurious. For the sake of conciseness, clarity, and chronology, I think it is best to discuss the immediate Ringo family in some sort of order, and through it to let the story of John Ringo unfold. It is imperative to understand the Ringo family before one can even begin to comprehend the myths that have grown up around John Ringo.

The family name *is* Ringo, not Ringgold, and it is a very old American family of Dutch lineage. Dutch variations on the name have been Ringout, Reingout, Ryngo, Reyngout, Ringot, Ringoot, Ringoet, and Ringois.[1] The use of Ringgold, or Ringold, began, for unexplained reasons, with members of the family who lived in Maryland, and to a certain extent it was used by Ringos in Texas.[2] On the use of "Ringgold" in the Texas newspapers that covered the exploits and depredations of John Ringo and the Cooley Gang, David Lear Ringo wrote, "It was, of course, our John. And I suppose John Ringo didn't go around correcting their spelling."[3]

According to a Ringo genealogy chart, the first Ringo in America was Philip Jansen Ringo, who was born in Holland, married in New Amsterdam, and died in the "Atlantic Ocean" (no explanation) in 1662,[4] two years before New Amsterdam became New York. Philip Jansen Ringo had five children, four of whom are listed on the chart, but of whom only one— Albertus Ringo, 1656–1679—had issue (seven children).[5] The Ringos, then, descend directly from Albertus.

The Ringos were wanderers, pioneers, which doubtless accounts for some of John's restless peregrinations (that, along with various sheriffs' posses). Ringos followed Daniel Boone into Kentucky, spread out to Indiana, Missouri, Arkansas, Texas, Nevada, and California. The closest living relatives of John Ringo in the 1970s were Frank Myrl Cushing and Zana Cushing Batchelder, John's nephew and niece (the son and daughter of John Ringo's youngest sister, Mattie Bell Ringo, who married William LeBaron Cushing on April 22, 1890, in San Jose, California).[6] Cushing, I learned from Charles, lived in Tustin, California, and was a retired printer who owned and operated his own printing outfit; a life-long bachelor, he was in possession of all memorabilia and mementos relating to John Ringo, with the exception of John Ringo's pistol, a Revolutionary-War cooking pot, and the original diary, or journal, of Mary Peters Ringo, John Ringo's mother. These had all been given by a Ringo descendant to a writer named Allen Erwin; Cushing, however, must have had temporary access to the journal, as he printed forty-five copies of it in 1954.[7]

Charles wrote me that there was a good photograph of John Ringo in the family's possession. He also wrote that John Ringo was the eldest of a family of two boys and three girls; the other children (oldest to youngest) were Martin Albert, Fanny Fern, Mary Enna, and Mattie Bell.[8] Charles evidently had sent Frank Cushing a photocopied copy of my article. He now suggested that I write Cushing. He thought that if I handled correspondence with Cushing with appropriate delicacy, the correspondence, if it materialized, could lead to collaboration. "I think," Charles wrote, "you are the one to write the story of Johnny Ringo."[9]

I wrote Cushing, telling him that Charles had suggested I do so, and expressed my interest in doing further work on John Ringo. I received a prompt and courteous reply, but he was completely noncommittal and the letter bore the tone of finality, of an obligation tended to and done. I wrote him again, this time detailing my background in research and writing, my academic credentials, and expressing my long and abiding interest in John Ringo. I think my error was in asking him if it were possible to see the picture of Ringo. I enclosed a copy of the magazine with the "Ringo" article. He did not reply. Charles now urged me to go to Tustin, California, to meet and talk with Cushing; but as a college instructor with family obligations I could not take the time that would obviously have been necessary to win the old man's (he was seventy-seven) confidence. Clearly he was a suspicious man and jealous of the family secrets. I declined to write him again.[10]

Charles now sent me copies of three of Cushing's letters, two of which had been sent to Dr. William K. Hall (another Ringo descendant) and one to Charles. And here, in three or four short paragraphs, one finally confronts the source of the mystery and the myths that have enshrouded and, to a considerable extent, created John Ringo. To be concise, John's immediate family—those "dear little sisters"—felt bitterly shamed and disgraced by their gunman-outlaw brother, and they labored with an unswerving single-mindedness and no little success to suppress all information and facts about him; in so doing, they perverted the natural course of history. They corrected none of the myths that sprang up around John Ringo. Indeed, they appear to have taken refuge in them, doubtless hoping that the further writers and historians strayed from the facts the less likely they were to connect the sedate Ringo family of San Jose, California, to John Ringo, Arizona outlaw. Their hopes were probably bolstered by the fact that everyone believed that John's last name was Ringgold and that Ringo was merely a protective *nom de gun*, assumed by this "black-sheep scion" out of some vestigial decency that still flowed through the bloodlines of that "genteel Southern family." The persistent stories, though, of "loving" sisters living in California with Grandpa Coleman Younger must have been unnerving. Here is the way John Ringo's nephew explained it:

My grandmother, Mary Peters Ringo, kept a diary during her trip West in 1864. My mother [Mattie Bell Ringo] was only two years old at the time. I printed the diary some years ago and had it copyrighted. I intended to add a couple of chapters about the family after they settled in San Jose including some true facts of the adventures of Johnny Ringo. . . . Only 45 copies of the diary were printed for private distribution to historical libraries. . . . During my mother's lifetime she was very much opposed to having anything printed about Johnny and I have respected her wishes. Now that all the family have passed away I feel that some of the facts should be published to clear up some of the fantastic tales that have been circulated.[11]

Ironically, the Ringos and Cushing had helped to create those "fantastic tales" about John Ringo. Had they permitted the facts to come out, indeed, had they corrected the myths that appeared in print, it is likely we should never have heard very much of John Ringo. What they labored to conceal, the writers, intrigued, made up tenfold.

Even by the standards of the late nineteenth and early twentieth centuries, the Ringos fear of disgrace, particularly at the remove of more than a half century, seems obsessive. As of 1986, I have heard of nothing published by Frank Cushing. I doubt that he would ever have published the story. Whether or not anything can be read into his feeling that *some* of the "facts" should be published and *some* of the "fantastic tales" should be cleared up, the uncertainty of his terminology and the lack of an expression of firmness or resolution leave one with the conviction that he would have at least been selective with his "facts."

I suspect Cushing was smoked out, really, by the indefatigable Allen Erwin, a writer and the owner of John Ringo's six-gun* and the original copy of Mary Peters Ringo's journal. Obviously, Erwin was close to the true story of John Ringo, having made contact with a less secretive and

---

* After Erwin's death in 1979, John Ringo's pistol was sold at auction by Sotheby, Parke, Bernet to an unknown purchaser for thirteen thousand dollars. *California Art and Antiques Monthly* 4, No. 10 (mid-October, 1980), p. 13.

disgrace-conscious San Francisco branch of the Ringo family. Cushing, to say the least—and perhaps understandably—was angry.

> My Aunt Enna, had the Simms stew pot carried by the Revolutionary War veteran who lived to be 100 years old. She left it to Fanny (Ringo) Jackson's son, Frank, and on his death his daughter gave the pot to a Mr. Allen Erwin, together with Johnny Ringo's revolver and the original copy of Mary Peters Ringo's diary. This Erwin claimed to be a writer of American Western history and she must have fallen for him. . . . I have tried to locate him but the letter was returned. . . . My sister and I have all the Martin [John Ringo's father] and Mary love letters and personal stuff.[12]

Cushing's references to "a Mr. Erwin" and his statement that "this Erwin claimed to be a writer of American Western history" would justify an assumption that Cushing did not know Erwin or anything much about him. Yet, slightly more than six months later Cushing revealed something quite different in a letter to Charles:

> You will be surprised to learn that I received a phone call from Erwin a few weeks ago. . . . I have known him for twelve or more years and he has visited me several times in connection with his research on Johnny Ringo. He first contacted Frank Jackson about writing a book and television story on Johnny but was seeking information as to the early life and history of Johnny. His research covered the same things as other writers. Frank Jackson became too ill to be bothered with the matter and turned it over to me. I had my nephew (he is connected with Warner Brothers) to investigate Erwin but he was completely unknown by any of the motion picture companies. . . .
>
> He promised to get in touch with me the first time he comes over this way. I have a proposition to offer him which I feel he will be impressed.
>
> I am particularly interested in getting him to put the pistol

and diary in the Arizona Museum or Library or selling them
to me. He has considerable research material so I might be
able to have him collaborate with me in preparing the story.
By inflating his ego I might accomplish my purpose. Wish me
luck.[13]

Any way one chooses to view it, this is an unappealing letter.
On the one hand, Cushing dismisses Erwin's research; on the
other, he refers to his "considerable research material." Most
distasteful, though, is the obvious intent to use or exploit
Erwin. The "proposition" is not articulated or stated, but one
considers it suspect since it is followed by, "By inflating his
ego I might accomplish my purpose." We do not know
whether the "purpose" in "collaboration" was sincere. If it
was, why would it be necessary to "inflate" Erwin's "ego"? As
for the pistol and the diary, it seems to me they did belong in
a museum; one suspects, though, that collaboration was a
hoped-for step towards acquisition of the pistol and diary. I
do not know whether the Cushing-Erwin collaboration was
ever begun.

At the end of the letter, Charles appended a handwritten
note:

"Dear Jack:
    You are too sensitive. You should follow up on Frank Cush-
ing. He is looking for a collaborator."[14]

I resisted the impulse to write that I had no pistol and diary
to offer as the collateral that collaboration would have demanded. (The pistol, authenticated as John Ringo's and with
its unusually low serial number—222, would have been worth
more than ten thousand dollars, even in 1970.)

Elsewhere in the letter, Cushing wrote Charles that "your
letters and Ringo correspondence have been most interesting
and will be a great help in working on my Johnny Ringo history. I am gathering material and doing some research. . . .
My sister [Zana Cushing Batchelder] is still too ill to locate

the Ringo material she has which is of most importance as it contains considerable correspondence between Martin and Mary Ringo and letters between Mary and her sisters."[15] I have not seen this correspondence, though I suspect Erwin has. These letters would certainly have been helpful, but I do not consider it likely that they are vital to the understanding of John Ringo.

The historical lacunae created by Frank Cushing's observance of his mother's wish for silence on anything pertaining to John Ringo, or at least for a decent interval of it, was annoying to Charles, who was avuncularly anxious to see a book of some sort on the Ringos in print. Charles bore none of the obsessive secrecy or shame over an outlaw forbear that afflicted the more immediate members of the Ringo family. He did, however, seem somewhat ambivalent—or perhaps he simply observed a lawyer's caution. To Will (Ringo?) he wrote: "He [John Ringo] brought terrible disgrace on the family name and honor and they have never forgiven him."[16] One feels that Charles had no difficulty in forgiving the erring John, and that he had, in fact, grown quite fond of him. Charles was something of the bemused dilettante, who felt it rather interesting to be a secure, solid, successful, and respected citizen with a Western outlaw hanging on an otherwise nearly perfectly formed family tree. It was like a slight cheek wound that merely accentuated and added a rakish touch to a handsome face. His relationship to John Ringo was sufficiently removed to permit affection rather than affliction. "Because we did know the Ringo sisters of San Jose," he wrote May King, "I have become quite interested in Johnny Ringo. His grandfather, Peter Ringo, was a first cousin of my great-grandfather, Samuel Ringo. This makes him a sixth cousin of mine—as Frank Cushing was the son of Mattie Bell Ringo—sister of Johnny—he is my seventh cousin—quite close!"[17]

Charles loved the family anecdote. When a client's inter-

ests coincidentally brought him to acquaintance with Ken
Earp, a land developer and professed kin of Wyatt, Earp com-
mented: "In the old days when a Ringo and [an] Earp got
together they did so with guns, not pencils." "Yes," riposted
Charlie, "they both used lead but in a different capacity."[18] It
is difficult to imagine such a riposte coming from Cushing. To
Will (probably a nephew), with whom he might have felt a
certain kind of approach was necessary, Charles concluded
that John Ringo "may have been brave and a good shot, but
it looks like he was nothing more but a drunk, murderer,
cattle thief and crook,"[19] an observation that adds spice to the
legend; a seventh cousin may consider any bad blood that
might have flowed his way to be sufficiently diluted.

I always thought—and think—that Charles, while whim-
sically interested in John Ringo, saw the outlaw largely as the
key or lead-in to a book about the Ringo family. Always the
indefatigable genealogist, Charles wrote endlessly and often
repetitiously of the distinguished and opulent branches on the
Ringo family tree. "They [the Ringos] did not produce a president of the United States or [a] great lawmaker," he wrote
May King. "However there were judges—such as Daniel
Ringo—Chief Justice of Arkansas. There were numerous
doctors, clergymen, and professional people."[20]

In 1972 Charles received a pamphlet titled *John Ringo and
His Gold* from the Hunterdon County [New Jersey] *Democrat*.
The John Ringo (1655–1731) of the pamphlet was the son of
the first Ringo in America (Philip Jansen Ringo). The pamphlet tells a rather childish story of piracy, with John (Jan) Ringo
as victim. He escapes the pirates with the aid of "two ne-
groes," taking the pirate ship with him. When he disposes of
the ship, he discovers that a chest he has kept is filled with
gold. Honest soul that he was (and obviously no kin to "our
John") he buried the chest. He could not bring himself to use
blood money.[21] To his cousin David Lear Ringo, Charles en-
thused, "It would make a good drama starting with him and
the pirates and ending up with Johnny Ringo of Tombstone,

Arizona."[22] Over one hundred fifty years gaped between John the Pirate and John the Rustler. One wonders how those doctors, lawyers, merchants, clergymen and seminarians could have generated enough interest and "drama" to carry anyone but the most genealogically concerned Ringo across such a historical rictus.

At any rate, in 1970 Charles wrote me that "I have an idea that the present generation would like the truth to come out. I doubt that they know much about his [John Ringo's] exploits after he left home. I don't think they want to believe them. He is too close! and they consider him a disgrace to the family name." He also told me that I could "certainly . . . use what you found out from me."[23] A short time earlier Charles had given me the photograph of John Ringo, along with a copy of *The Journal of Mrs. Mary Ringo*, a thirty-six page account of the family's wagon train journey from Liberty, Missouri, to California in 1864. In December of 1972, after a serious operation, Charles wrote that "we are now in the process of writing a book about the Ringo family. I think it is about time that an authoritative [and] unbiased book be written about Johnny and his family connections."[24] I do not know if the book was ever written. Charles's recurring illness and his subsequent death might have deprived the family of its motive force. But I do not believe Charles fully understood that John Ringo's radical departure from family patterns necessitated extensive research outside family records, or that it was necessary to place him in historical perspective against the West and the myths and stories that only feebly illuminated him.

Charles confused genealogy with history. He was neither well enough nor equipped for such an undertaking. And Frank Cushing, burdened by a century-old "disgrace" and by unreal and imposed family loyalties, cat-and-mousing it with potential collaborators and jealously releasing "some" of the "facts," possessed neither a sense of history nor, apparently, a respect for it. He was obsessed with secrecy and with clearing the family name. And how would the family name be cleared? By a book one supposes, an apologia, really, not a history, presumably featuring a parade of distinguished Ringos—lawyers, doctors, merchants, clergymen, and seminarians—whose august presence marching facelessly through the pages and climbing up and down the family trees of genealogy charts would doubtless, in the mind of anyone who cared to read the book, reduce the lone black sheep to a little lost lamb. "Any writing by Cushing," Charles wrote to Will, "would be inclined to soft-peddle [sic] Johnny's actions to clear their name. This is human nature."[25] In a letter to me outlining a possible book, Charles said, "I do feel enough facts exist to write a dramatic story." And then: "You will not be able to accomplish this if you stick too close to Cushing."[26]

6

The Journal of Mary Peters Ringo

JOHN RINGO descends directly from Henry Ringo, 1724–1803, his great, great grandfather; through his great grandfather, Major Ringo, 1755–1836 (Major apparently was a name, not a military rank); and through Peter Ringo, 1797–?, his grandfather.[1] John's father, Martin Ringo, was born October 1, 1819, in Kentucky.[2] On June 7, 1846, Martin enlisted in the Army at Liberty, Missouri, to fight in the War with Mexico. He was stationed for some time in Sacramento, California, where he contracted tuberculosis. He was honorably discharged at New Orleans on June 23, 1847.[3] On September 5, 1848, Martin Ringo married Mary Peters in Clay County, Missouri, the place of her birth on November 23, 1826.[4] From Missouri (no date available) the young couple moved to Wayne County, Indiana.

John Peters Ringo, named for his mother, was born May 3, 1850, in Greenfork, Wayne County, Indiana. Martin Albert was born September(?) 28, 1854; Fanny Fern, July 7, 1857; Mary Enna, May 2, 1860; and Mattie Bell, April 18, 1862.[5] Thus the positive assertions that John Ringo was born in Texas, Missouri, California, and Maryland were merely guesswork, as were most of the extravagant claims made for him.

John Ringo was not widely known in either his early or later lifetime, as were the Jameses, the Youngers, the Daltons, and Billy the Kid, and so, unlike them, he escaped the attention of the "dime novelists," who might have created a "youth" for him. One recalls Prentiss Ingraham's little William Frederick Cody manifesting all the heroics later conferred upon Buffalo Bill by capturing four outlaws at the age of eight—and killing one of them; of J. W. Buel's Jesse James portending a future of cruelty and violence by skulking about and burying small animals alive. Billy the Kid, at thirteen, reputedly stabbed to death the man who insulted his mother. John Ringo did not really become a "western character" until forty-five years after his death, when he appeared, transfigured, in Burns's *Tombstone*,[6] as a gaunt, handsome, and brooding Hamlet with a gun, whose reverence for women fell just short of "get thee to a nunnery."

A year later, in *Helldorado* (1928), Breakenridge anointed Ringo a fearless outlaw, a man of his word, and a dead shot, intimating then—and later—that even Wyatt Earp, his brothers, and Doc Holliday were afraid of him. Too late in history to dub him a Robin Hood—a great proletarian hero who, like Jesse James, robbed the robber barons and the bankers or, like Billy the Kid, took on the land barons—Breakenridge simply conferred a college degree on John Ringo. And unlike Jesse James and Buffalo Bill, the only song sung about him in his day was "Goodbye, John R., Goodbye," (see Chapter 3) courtesy of Sara Grace Bakarich, who seems also to be the only one to have heard it.

For the record, though, John Ringo's life began at fourteen when he, along with the rest of his family, joined a wagon train west from Liberty, Missouri, in 1864. Even so, we do not know if the family was living in Liberty at the time it joined the wagon train, or if it moved from Indiana specifically to pick up a wagon train, since Liberty was a "jump-off" point. From Mattie Bell (Ringo) Cushing's seventeen-line Forward (*sic*) to Mary's *Journal*, which Mattie copied when she was eighty, the family simply materialized on the date and place of departure:

On the eighteenth of May eighteen hundred sixty-four, a party of adventurous people started on the hazardous trip across the continent to California. Among them was my father Martin Ringo, age 45 years, his wife Mary Ringo, age 38 years, brother John, age 14 years, Albert, age 11 years, sister Fanny, age 7 years, Enna, age 4 years, Mattie (myself), age 2 years.

We had two large covered wagons, one drawn by oxen and one by mules. . . . My father had been in the Mexican War, was stationed at Sacramento for some time where he contracted tuberculosis and he thought it would be better for him in a milder climate, but he didn't live to get there.

Other people joined our party until at last there was (*sic*) 70 wagons.[7]

We are not told the family's destination in California, nor are we told what Martin Ringo planned to do upon arrival. We do not know what his occupation was in Missouri and Indiana nor how or how well he supported his family. Presumably the family was in reasonably sound financial circumstances in order to have purchased "two large covered wagons" along with a span of mules and a span of oxen. Beyond these meager facts we know only that the family began the journey to California for reasons of the father's health.

It is possible that Mary Ringo's correspondence with her sisters, which Frank Cushing deemed important, contained insightful references to John's early years during his Indiana and Missouri boyhood, revealing, perhaps, behavior that portended future trouble. But if one can draw any conclusions at all from her *Journal*, Mary Ringo was not given to thoughtful observations and effusions. Writing was obviously a labor for her and she lacked the structural and grammatical skills for clear elucidation and the separation of her thoughts. Her journal, covering a nearly five-month odyssey, consists of slightly more than thirty-six pages. She takes note of such landmarks as Ash Hollow, Courthouse Rock, Chimney Rock, Independence Rock, Split Rock, Devil's Gate, Fort Bridger, and Indian Wells, worries about being "attacted" by Indians, wishes for a "good sermon," and frets about traveling on the Sabbath. A deeply religious woman, she was given to faith rather than to introspection, to prayer rather than to analysis. Only when stark, unbelievable tragedy occurred in the depths of that immutable Western landscape are we able to read between the lines and to feel her heartbreak, her desperation, and to be thankful for the therapeutic torrent of words that helped to relieve her. Nowhere else in her *Journal* are insights offered. Everyone is impersonalized, cogs in the wheels rolling West. We catch no glimpse of the man in the boy. If "Johnny" was a problem, or if Mary Ringo had any forebodings, she kept them to herself. John is mentioned only six times in the *Journal*. Here, in her own words and structure, are excerpts from relevant sections of Mary Ringo's *Journal,* including all references to "Johnny," with intrusions on my part only for clarification and emphasis:

May 19—Thursday

[The Ringo family had crossed the Missouri River at Leavenworth, Kansas.] ". . . A gentleman by the name of Owen drives the mules in the city for me while Mr. Ringo helps Johnny* with the Oxen here."[8]

June 7—Tuesday

". . . Today Johnnie got his foot hurt quite badly by the wheels running over it, it seems to have been a day of accidents, a little boy was run over by a wagon and killed and a wagon master by the name of Hase killed one of his teamsters, shot him through the head. The murdered man leaves a wife and children."[9] [This may or may not have been John Ringo's first brush with sudden and violent death.]

---

* Mary Ringo's *Journal* refers to her elder son as "Johnny," "Johnnie," and "John," in various entries.

June 8—Wednesday

"We lay by for the gentlemen to go buffalo hunting, they stay all day and until one o'clock at night, they came back much elated having killed a nice buffalo, the meat is very tender. Johnnie goes along notwithstanding his foot is very sore, he says they saw a great many Elk and Antelopes."[10]

June 14—Tuesday

"It is still raining. . . . Johnnie has a chill when we stop and now seems quite sick I hope it may not be anything serious. Johnnie remains quite sick tonight."[11]

June 21—Tuesday

"We lay by here so as to lay in a supply of wood. Mr. Ringo, John and Allie [John's brother, Martin Albert] take the wagon and go up a canyon some 2½ mi. and get plenty of good dry Cedar, they tell me it is a most beautiful place in those mountains, every variety of flowers."[12]

[Although she kept a day-to-day account of her journey, Mary Ringo made no reference to John's illness after the entry on June 14. His casual appearance on the wood-gathering expedition seven days later is, of course, proof of his recovery. One wonders, though, about the nature, symptoms, and seriousness of his illness.]

June 26—Sunday

"We are still in camp, I was in hopes we would have a sermon but Mr. Hodges [identification unknown] was helping to cross over the boat. . . ."[13]

June 29—Wednesday

"I walked with Mr. Ringo down to the river [possibly the Platte?], the water does look so swift, they are crossing wagons quite fast. Several Indians came to camp this morning, one of them had a saber, we asked him where he got it, he said he killed a soldier and took it. I have cut myself a dress

and am going to try and make it this week." [14] [Transition from
killing to dress-making posed no problem for Mary Ringo!]

July 15—Friday

[On this date, somewhere between Chimney Rock and Scotts
Bluff, the train had an Indian scare. By the mid-1860s settlements and military posts had begun to spring up along the
Oregon Trail. Wagon trains had passed through relatively un-
molested ten to fifteen years earlier, but by 1864 the Indians
had caught a glimpse of the future—settlements strung out
in the wake of the "prairie schooners"—and their harrass-
ment of wagon trains was heightened, often dramatically.
The Ringo train had more than its share of afrights and
alarms. At a telegraph office (?) ten miles west of Chimney
Rock, the train was warned of Indian depredations], ". . . but
we did not think much of it and had gone on some 2 miles
when they attacted two of our wagons. Mr. Gouly and one
other gentleman had turned out at the wrong road and we
drove on knowing they could see us and would cross the prairie and come to us, whilst we were looking at them we saw
the Indians manouvering around them and then rode close
enough to shoot the arrows through their wagon sheets just
missing their heads, they fired at them and the Indians ran as
fast as their horses could go, they crossed the river and attacted another emigrant train killing one man and wounding
another. As soon as they attacted we went back to the ranch,
correlled [*sic*], and prepared for a fight but they will not fight
if they think you are prepared for them. I do not think I ever
spent such a night for I could not sleep a wink. All the families in the train stayed in the telegraph office and anxiously
waited for the morning." [15]

[One could wish to know how young John Ringo com-
ported himself during that long night. Did he show signs of
the fearlessness later attributed to him, that "bulldog" courage? Did he take his position with the men among the cor-
ralled wagons, or did he remain in the telegraph office? It

should be remembered that he was fourteen years old at the time, old enough, on the Western frontier, to pick up and use a gun. Alas! Mary Ringo is mute.]

July 19—Tuesday

". . . we have quite an exciting time, correlled [*sic*] twice thinking the Indians were going to attack us but we mistook friendly Indians and one of our train fired at them. . . ."[16]

July 25—Monday

"This morning early some emigrants came to camp who had a man killed by the Indians last night, they report sad times ahead. I pray God we may get along safely. . . ."[17]

July 27—Wednesday

". . . We find posted on a tree a notice that the Indians have killed six men near here. We hear they have had a fight ahead of us. I do hope and pray God that we may get through safely, it keeps me so uneasy and anxious."[18]

July 28—Thursday

[Inexplicably, almost in refutation of her expressed fears of the day before she writes, insouciantly, on this date:] ". . . Nothing of importance transpires today, above here 3 miles the Indians killed some men and took the ladies prisoners."[19] [One is not prepared for the July 30 entry in her *Journal*. A prefatory note would be both superfluous and presumptuous.]

July 30—Saturday

"And now Oh God comes the saddest record of my life for this day my husband accidentally shot himself and was buried by the wayside and oh, my heart is breaking, if I had no children how gladly would I lay me down with my dead—but now Oh God I pray for strength to raise our precious children and oh—may no one ever suffer the anguish that is breaking my heart, my little children are crying all the time and I—oh what am I to do. Every one in camp is kind to us but God alone can heal the breaking heart. After burying my darling husband we hitch up and drive some 5 miles. Mr. Davenport drove my mules for me and Oh, the agony of parting from that grave, to go and leave him on that hillside where I shall never see it more but thank God 'tis only the body lying there and may we meet in Heaven where there is no more death but only life eternally." [20]

An eyewitness account of Martin Ringo's death carried in the *Liberty* [Missouri] *Tribune* reveals it to have been an especially horrible one for the family. The account, from "W--- Davidson" addressed to "Mr. R. H. Will-----," reads as follows:

> Just after daylight on the morning of the 30th July Mr. Ringo stepped out . . . of the wagons as, I suppose, for the purpose of looking around to see if Indians were in sight and his shotgun went off accidentally in his own hands, the load entering at his right eye and coming out at the top of his head. At the report of his gun I saw his hat blown up 20 feet in the air and his brains were scattered in all directions. I never saw a more heartrending sight, and to see the distress and agony of his wife and children was painful in the extreme. Mr. Ringo's death cast a gloom over the whole company. . . . [21]

Martin Ringo's death was the more horrible because it was accidental, unexpected. Had he been killed in an Indian attack while defending the train and his family his death could at least have been put in perspective. He would have fulfilled the function of husband, father, and protector.

So profound was Mary's grief that one hesitates, even at the distance of more than a century, to intrude questions, but one wonders how John responded to the death of his father. Did he assume, or was he forced to assume, leadership as head of the family? Did Martin's death by his own gun reflect a clumsiness that fourteen-year-old John, in his anguish, resented, and which led to his own storied "dexterity" with pistol and rifle? Are there extensions here, symbolism? Was it Martin Ringo's senseless death refracted, years later, through that shimmering veil of desert heat and the haze of alcohol that finally put the gun to John Ringo's head? Did the futility of his father's death leave him with conscious or unconscious feelings of betrayal which, along with his mother's enduring faith, set up conflicts in the boy that remained unresolved in the man? And, although one would conclude the opposite from her *Journal,* was Mary Ringo's dependence on John too great after Martin's death? Was there a dependence the boy came to resent and which caused him, as Charles Ringo learned from Frank Cushing, to later "[leave] the family in the lurch?"[22]

If these questions seem no more than labored or awkward psychological fumblings, it must be remembered that neither Mary Ringo nor her family later offered any insights. They observed a bitter and conspiratorial silence. Yet John Ringo seems to have been the only member of a pious and respected family to have made a radical departure from family traditions and behavior. It was like John-Boy Walton of television's *The Waltons* popping up as John Dillinger. One can only guess at what possible psychic trauma John suffered, what conflicts troubled his thoughts. Neither a child nor yet a man, he was at an impressionable and vulnerable age. Albert, at eleven, and as we shall see, a sickly youngster, was doubtless also affected. But the difference between eleven and fourteen is the difference between adolescence and puberty. At seven, Fanny probably remembered certain aspects of the tragedy, most particularly her mother's grief. But that is the age of a protective resiliency, of a disconnected, dreamlike quality to events that rarely settle into the pattern of tragedy. Enna, at four, and Mattie, at two, probably remembered nothing. The burden, then, of seeing and feeling and coping with the tragedy of his family fell upon John Ringo.]

July 31—Sunday

"We are up and start early. I could not sleep but rested tolerably well. I and Allie drive our mules they are gentle and go so nicely. This has been the longest day I have ever spent. We travel about 14 miles and camp—we keep out a strong guard but I was uneasy and afraid all night." [23] [This was the day after Martin's death. One can only try to imagine Mary's thoughts and feelings of the night before and on leaving her husband's grave, the awful and growing comprehension of her loss, of the fatherless children, and now the uncertain future, while marveling at the courage and resolution that found her driving her mules west in the morning. But why was Albert helping to drive the wagon? Where was John?]

August 2—Tuesday

". . . Several ladies called to see me and every one is very kind but I am so lonely and tonight Fanny has an attack of cholremorbus and after she gets easy I rest better than I have any night since the death of my dear husband. Oh God help me bear this hard trial." [24]

August 6—Saturday

". . . Today we make some 14 miles and camp at Willow Spring. . . . I feel so sad and lonely." [25]

August 11—Thursday

"We travel 13 miles and camp near three crossing a beautiful place but everything seems lonely to me. I hate to see night coming and do hope we will soon get through to Salt Lake" [26]

August 15—Monday

". . . Mr. Davis comes to see me and I am always glad to see him for he is the last one Mr. Ringo ever talked to. Oh God thou hast sorely afflicted me—give me strength to bear this heart tryal." [27]

August 21—Sunday

". . . I have not spent my Sabbath as I would like to. . . ."[28]

August 28—Sunday

"We lay over today as it is the Sabbath. I am glad that we do. I do not think it right to travel on the Sabbath."[29]

September 2—Friday

"We start late and have come 4 or 5 miles, have passed Huffs ranch where I see the first corn growing I have seen this year. I sent Johnny to see if he could buy some potatoes and he has not caught up with us yet, he does not get any potatoes but gets some nice turnips."[30] [This is the last time Johnny's name is mentioned in the journal.]

September 8—Thursday

[In Salt Lake City, Mary had hoped to dispose of her mules, oxen and wagons and take a coach to California. She was not one to complain or condemn (she did not like the Mormons), but the Major Barrow (referred to in an earlier entry as Major Barron) whom she had hoped would assist her in selling her outfit seemed to think it worth so little that she elected to take it through to Austin, Nevada.] ". . . I thought I had better not try to sell them and have hired a Mr. John Donly to drive my oxen and am going to try to go through in my wagons."[31] [The John Ringo who was supposed to have fought in the Civil War, which in 1864 was in its last year, was too young, apparently, to drive his mother's wagons.]

Friday—October 7

[On this date Mary and her children reached Austin, Nevada] ". . . where I have the pleasure of seeing cousin Charley Peters and my old acquaintance Mr. Ford from Liberty, Mo. They are very kind to me and assist me to dispose of my oxen and wagon."[32]

October 8—Saturday
"We remain in Austin, Nev."[33]

The appended "In *Conclusion*" by Mary's daughter Mattie, though less than two small pages in length, is very revealing, because it clarifies certain parts of the journal. Referring to her mother's October 8 entry, Mattie wrote:

> That is the last Mother wrote in her diary so I will have to finish the best I can from things she told us at different times. . . . In Austin she had a son born, fortunately it was still-born for he was terribly disfigured from mother seeing father after he was shot. Even my brother who was fourteen years old noticed it and said he looked just like father did. On the way out when we reached Fort Laramie, Wyoming, the government offered her an escort of soldiers to go back to Missouri but she said . . . it wouldn't seem like home without father.
>
> I don't know how long we stayed in Austin, probably a week or ten days and I don't know how we made the rest of the trip. We took the mules and one wagon to San Jose and she told of stopping in San Francisco. . . .
>
> We finally reached San Jose where Mother's sister lived. My aunt and her husband had a very large place and Mr. Younger raised blooded cattle. They had a small house on the place that had formerly been a carriage house and had been made into a house. We lived there a year as mother was not able to do anything for some time but she paid our living expenses as of course she had some money but it was confederate money and she lost 36 dollars on the hundred.
>
> We moved to San Jose and lived on Second Street where mother began the task of providing for her little family, the way was rough but with sheer determination she raised her family unaided.
>
> M.B.C.[34]

We learn here, for the first time, that Mary Ringo had been pregnant, a further indication of how little of a personal nature she confided to her *Journal*. She complained, occasionally, of not feeling well but she suggested nothing that could not have been laid to torpor, fatigue, tragedy and responsibility, or to any one of these. More interesting was the belief, obviously shared by the family even in old age, that the stillborn child was "terribly disfigured" as a result of Mary's having seen her husband's mutilated face. Not only does such a belief suggest adherence to a totally unfounded superstition—the classic "old wive's tale"—it suggests a family subsumed in the belief of some sort of divine retribution or intervention; and beyond that, it portended a later and irrevocable determination not to forgive John his sins. And Johnny—he saw his father, too, though one would never have known it from reading Mary's *Journal*, and he saw the disfigured child. He had seen and experienced quite enough, really, to set him on a different and troubled course. He learned of violence from the wagon master who killed a teamster, who was a husband and a father; he experienced Indian frights; he helped to bury the shattered remains of his father in the Wyoming wilderness; he bore the instability of the loss of his father under conditions and circumstances in which there was no respite from his mother's grief, no retreat from adult agony and responsibility, no chance for the regenerative and quick-healing powers of youth to work; he saw the mutilated child, perhaps saw it as a fatal flaw. The sisters, so unforgiving later, experienced none of his trauma. We can, I think, begin to understand what made Johnny run.

Mary Ringo's refusal to return to Missouri because "it wouldn't seem like home without father" seems to justify an assumption that the family had lived in Missouri some time before the removal to California. And the reference to "Confederate money" would presume a move from free-soil Indiana to pro-slavery Missouri before the commencement of the Civil War. The Ringos, as Charles claimed, supported the Confederacy: "At least one or two were slave-holders."[35]

What is most interesting here, though, is the shattering of two of the major myths that helped to create the legend of John Ringo. One was the belief that Colonel Coleman Younger was John's grandfather. Younger, a distinguished citizen who was never an outlaw himself, was, nevertheless, uncle to the notorious Younger gang,* thus assuring the bloodline impeccability of John's outlaw credentials. And since the Youngers were related to the Daltons, Ringo was twice blessed. In reality, Coleman Younger was married to Mary Ringo's older sister, Augusta. John's uncle by marriage, he was not related to Ringo by blood in any way. Augusta Peters had married a Presbyterian pastor, a Reverend James M. Inskeep (or Inskip), in St. Joseph, Missouri, in 1842. In 1849 Inskeep died, and in 1853 Augusta married Colonel Younger in Clay County, Missouri.[36] Younger had established a blooded horse ranch in San Jose, California, in 1851 (Younger's ranch has been referred to alternately as a horse ranch and a cattle ranch; perhaps it was both). He took Augusta back to California, and his ranch seems to have been the destination of the Martin Ringo family.

The other shattered myth was that of John Ringo as the embittered black sheep "scion" of a genteel and wealthy southern family. John Ringo was, indeed, a black sheep, and the family was both genteel and of southern antecedents. "Scion," however, as the term has been used to describe John Ringo, is evocative not only of an heir to land and money—perhaps even to a plantation—but to a tradition of education and aristocracy as well, a privileged young blade gone sour, an Ashley Wilkes with a drinking problem and a gun. The writers never envisioned the sad and bewildered family that straggled into San Jose in late October or early November of 1864 and took up residence in a carriage house on the Younger

* The outlaw, Cole Younger, was named for his uncle, Colonel Coleman Younger.

ranch. According to Mattie Ringo, they paid their own way and after a year moved to a home on Second Street. "The way was rough," she had declared, but the family survived. "When Mary Ringo got to California," Frank Cushing later told Charles Ringo, "she was in serious condition, financially and otherwise."[37] Young Johnny, the "scion" of mythic landed gentry, the loving son and devoted brother of western mythology, would not make her life any easier.

7
The Graduate

MARY RINGO'S *Journal* is an enormously important document, not, of course, for its insights and personal revelations, but because it fixes John Ringo so precisely in time and place as to indisputably demolish all the major myths that were created about him. We know he did not fight in the Civil War because he was too young; he was only fourteen years old when the war ended and he was living in California. We know he did not, as a thirteen-year-old child, ride with Quantrill in the sacking of Lawrence, Kansas, in 1863. One recalls Howard Monnett's article, "General Jo Shelby and Johnny Ringo," which not only repeats just about every myth ever written about John Ringo, while allowing that it could all be a matter of legend, but concludes with this declaration, which surely must establish some sort of record for irresponsible fatuity: "What is not legend is that a man, later known as Johnny Ringo, rode with General Jo Shelby in the Missouri Raid of 1864, fought in the Battle of Westport, and for sentiment clung to an old picture of a most noted Missouri gentleman and soldier. Perhaps that was the only thing remaining to Johnny Ringo of a happier and more honorable life."[1] What actually is not legend is that the Battle of Westport, Missouri, was fought on October 23, 1864, exactly fifteen days *after* John Ringo and his family arrived in Austin, Nevada.

One of the most intriguing of all the stories about John

Ringo—the one, certainly, that set me on his trail—is that he was a college graduate and had, perhaps, even been a professor in an eastern college. The story began with William Breakenridge, or at least the positive claim appeared in print for the first time in his *Helldorado*. Walter Noble Burns, as we saw earlier, had first referred to the claim, but even he, who accepted just about any yarn as gospel (and then generally improved on it), thought the story "doubtful." Joe Chisholm, who more or less plagiarized *Helldorado* right down to partial use of the title and who claimed to have known John Ringo, simply took Breakenridge's declaration and created a historical farrago. "Ringo was a cultured man," he wrote, "a college graduate [who was] careful never to flaunt . . . his superior education before his illiterate followers [who] nevertheless regarded their well-bred leader with an awe as great as their physical fear of him. They were respectful and loyal to Johnny, but there was a cultural wall . . . that was a ban to real intimacy."[2] That "cultural wall," along with Ringo's seemingly compulsive and monomaniacal preoccupation with death, have become the endlessly repeated *leitmotifs* of television and motion-picture westerns. We have seen him or his kind dozens of times. He is usually sombre, brooding, drinking, and well-dressed. He exudes self-pity. His speech is sardonic and stilted, shot through with pseudo-academic remarks that dumbfound the local peasantry. He cynically awaits his death and he often performs a last good deed on the way out, like plugging the rotten mayor or banker, and so freeing the town of bondage. When finally he lies dead he is at least partially redeemed.

According to Louise and Fullen Artrip, Daniel Fore (Texas Jim) Chisholm (the sixteen-year-old lad to whom Ringo bared his soul) stated that the real name was John Ringgold, but he was better known as Johnny Ringo. It was also, Chisholm declared, "common knowledge" that he had once been a "respected college professor [who had been] associated with one of the larger eastern colleges."[3]

Charles Ringo, himself a university man and one-time professor, was, like myself, intrigued by the persistent story of John's education. If you are going to have an outlaw in the family, it would be nice if he also possessed some special or redeeming distinction. The possibility did not seem altogether unreasonable, considering the history of other distinguished Ringos. But at the conclusion of his long and informative letter to Will, Charles referred to John's education almost as if it were an afterthought: "There is one thing I forgot," he wrote. "On page 134 of *Helldorado* Breakenridge states that Ringo had a college education and in many ways was refined. He liked to read a great deal. I asked Mr. Cushing about this. He said that Ringo did not finish grammar school. The family was great [on] reading the classics and Ringo probably carried on this tradition."[4] While Joe Chisholm's "cultural wall" collapses and Daniel Chisholm's rusticated professor dissolves into a grammar school dropout, and while both men stand as naked frauds, let us not forget that even if John Ringo did "carry on the family tradition" of reading the classics, he did not read them, as John Myers declared, in the original Greek and Latin.

Questions, however, remain. How did the story of John Ringo as college graduate get started in the first place? Was the brooding, inscrutable, enigmatic, refined, gentlemanly, taciturn Ringo—all adjectives used to describe him—something of a braggart when in his cups? Did he claim to be a college graduate? Breakenridge's flat assertion would suggest as much. It is possible, though, as indicated in Chapter 1, that Breakenridge simply made the assumption from Ringo's "refined" use of the English language. It is also possible that Ringo let Breakenridge believe what he chose to believe. It is my belief that William Breakenridge was every bit the "suave and crafty dissimulator" that historian Frank Lockwood thought Wyatt Earp to be. More bluntly, I suspect him of making up most of the stories he told about John Ringo, including that "college education," in an effort to create a life-sized adversary to Wyatt Earp, of whom, as Eugene Cunningham wrote me, Breakenridge was inordinately jealous. Cunningham also wrote me that "some of the California branch—Ringgold—hired Billy Breakenridge to dig up . . . angles on John, in the 20's I think," that Breakenridge "had lots of stuff" on Ringo, that Breakenridge and Cunningham had planned a "Ringo-as'd-BE-a-Ringo," but that the plan had aborted on Breakenridge's death, at which time his nephew had allegedly burnt all his "stuff."[5]

I believe Cunningham. I do not believe Breakenridge. In the first place, if Breakenridge had known as much about John Ringo as he claimed to know, he would not have referred to the California Ringos as "Ringgold." At no time did the California family go by any name other than Ringo. Enna Ringo, for example, a spinster who taught elementary school for fifty years in San Jose, California, was listed in the city Directory of 1897 as "Ringo, M. Enna Miss, teacher Horace Mann School, 97 S. 1st."[6] If the family had "hired" Breakenridge in any such endeavor, it most certainly would not have hired him under the name of Ringgold. Why give the detective in your employ a phony surname when he is charged with the task of "digging up angles" on a family member? Besides, the Ringo family had more "angles" on John than they wanted, and they had had them for nearly fifty years before the "hiring" of Breakenridge. And just why would the family be interested in "new angles" while laboring indefatigably to cover up the old ones? Breakenridge was, I think, about as honest with Cunningham as he was with Frank Lockwood, to whom he proved "conclusively" that Wyatt Earp did not kill Curly Bill (see Chapter 10, note 42).

One can understand how a writer more concerned with a dramatic story than with historical accuracy might, in exasperation, conclude that it did not make much difference whether John Ringo was born in Missouri, Texas, Maryland, or California. There were Ringos in all four states. One can also understand the conviction that the Ringos were related to the Youngers. One can even concede that Ringo as college graduate was not such a far-fetched assumption—particularly if one wanted to believe it—since Ringos lived in Liberty, Missouri, and a man named Charles S. Ringo did, indeed, graduate from William and Jewell College there.[7] But the yarn that has John bloodily avenging his brother (who would have to be Martin Albert, the "Allie" referred to in Mary Ringo's *Journal*), who had been "killed" in a Texas range war is totally without source, derivation, or even suggestion. Albert never left California; he died in San Jose on August 29, 1873, of what appears to have been tuberculosis.[8] I suspect this yarn was deliberately concocted in keeping with some romantic notion of western revenge (*The Vengeance Trail, Red Vengeance, Bloody Vengeance* are, for example, titles of western stories) and as justification for whatever blood and thunder activities its inventor had in mind for John Ringo. But if Walter Noble Burns is to be believed at all, Ringo himself is responsible for the story. After claiming with the certainty of the true believer that "Ringo hunted down the three murderers [of his brother] and killed them," Burns declared this to be ". . . Ringo's own story of how he came to drift into outlawry. It was told in a rare mood of confidence to William Fyffe, a Mormon rancher on Five Mile Creek in the Chiricahuas, at whose home he often stopped overnight on his trips between Tombstone and Galeyville."[9]

So the question is raised: did John Ringo create himself, the college graduate, the avenger of his brother? It is possible he did, at least in part. Josephine Earp, calling John Ringo "the exception" to the general untidiness of the gang around him, found him "reserved and gentlemanly. . . . I doubt, on my own observation, that Ringo was as wantonly murderous as some have tried to portray him, though he was *admittedly* a killer [Italics mine]. Wyatt was mortally certain he was one of the men who ambushed both Virge and Morg."[10] What seems to emerge is a man whose reserve, whose mystery gave credibility and authority to his occasional, perhaps rare, talk or even brag. He seems to have created a convincing aura of combined refinement and menace about himself. And while I have no doubt that he *was* a dangerous man, his was the dangerousness of treachery as far as the historical record is concerned: two cowardly Texas killings in which he was a probable, though not provable, participant (see Chapter 8), and his senseless attack on Louis Hancock. That celebrated Allen Street challenge to Doc Holliday and Wyatt Earp, which is all that the Ringo romanticizers and Earp detractors have, really, to make a legitimate gunfighter of their man, is put in proper perspective by Josephine Earp: Ringo, she believed, chose his time for a challenge very carefully, when Wyatt and Doc were in enough trouble over the O.K. Corral shooting (although Wyatt did not let his O.K. Corral troubles interfere with the killing of Frank Stilwell and Indian Charlie.) And her claim that Ringo had the "whiskey shakes" is likely also true, since Breakenridge himself said Ringo was "quarrelsome when drinking." Neither Wyatt nor Doc intended to compound their problems by indulging a meaningless challenge to a shoot-out and perhaps being charged by Sheriff Behan with murdering a helpless drunk.[11] Josie, of course, was not precisely the disinterested observer, but there was nothing to limit John Ringo to a *single challenge*. He could have called Wyatt Earp at any time or any place, had he been as serious about a fight with the marshal or with Doc as so many writers have claimed he was. That "husky" cop, James Flynn, who seized Ringo from behind on Allen Street, could not always have been on hand. The most interesting fact of all about John Ringo, the man of "bulldog" courage, the one "real gunfighter," the "fastest and deadliest" of them all, the "college graduate," the man driven by "dark furies" who "killed with a ferret's ferocity" (the last two claims were made by Clayton Matthews in "Ringo—Champion of the Outlaws," *Mankind*, 4, No. 10 [December 1974], pp. 65–69), the one man whom "everyone feared," is that there is no record whatever—neither written nor oral—of his ever having actually engaged in a single face-to-face violent confrontation with anyone.

Just as those three mythic killers of his brother were necessary to the writers to give John Ringo purpose and reason, to rasie him above the status of mere frontier thug, so, too, has it been important to them that no photograph of him was known to exist. Virtually every western character who was ever caught with a gun in his hand was photographed at one time or another, including a score or more of dead men who were yanked erect by smirking bystanders to stand in frozen and bizarre "authenticity" before the camera, sometimes with rifles rammed grotesquely between stiffened arms.[12] But no photo of John Ringo appeared to give him a flesh and blood *persona*, to hold the writers to the limitations of known and familiar features (and to the impressions such features create), to a tactile presence that would not have admitted of the soaring physical descriptions that created a Shakespearean abstraction with a lean, "patrician face" surrounded by "wavy Auburn hair," a brooding Adonis with eyes of a half-dozen different colors and hues that gazed wistfully inward upon a different and better past life. "The *persona* created by the writers of popular fiction," Henry Nash Smith wrote in reference to Buffalo Bill, "was so accurate an expression of the demands of the popular imagination that it proved powerful enough to shape an actual man in its own image."[13]

Published as the frontispiece in this book is an excellent photograph of John Ringo, probably taken in 1881 and suppressed by the family for ninety years. It was given to me by Charles Ringo, who felt it should accompany the history I was writing. The first thing one notices is that the formidable face in the photo does not invite the intimate and diminutive "Johnny." It also bears no resemblance whatever to that handsome dude spread across the September 13, 1974, issue of the *Tombstone Epitaph*, which one Ben Traywick "believed to be a photograph of Johnny Ringo." It bears no resemblance to any of the descriptions of him. The face is broad and square rather than "thin." The chin is especially strong, as is the nose, but the mouth is almost entirely covered by the richly sweeping handlebar moustache. What surprises the most, however, is the absence of that halo of auburn hair. John Ringo had very little hair, and what there was of it lay pancake-flat and thin against his skull.

But if the hairline is receding and the face is not exactly "patrician," the eyes—the dominant feature—are light and cold enough to satisfy every stereotype or to justify any banality ever uttered or written about "steely-eyed" gunmen of the Old West. The eyes, in combination with the strong features, create an impression of intense resolution, the feeling that he was, indeed, a man of headlong and bulldog courage. It is a cold and remote face, yet incongruously youthful, even beneath that sweep of moustache. It is so unlike the Byronic descriptions of him it is difficult to affix it visually to events he was supposed to have participated in. Burns's brooding, hollow-eyed Hamlet and six-shooter ascetic has taken too firm a hold. The "darkly handsome" John Ringo in his "cowboy rig" who held up the card game in Galeyville, the quiet, brooding rustler who rode into Tombstone with Breakenridge, the bear-coated "giant" who stalked the Earps and Holliday on Allen Street, the halo-haired, classics-reading patrician is not the John Ringo in the photo. In a case of art *not* imitating life, he remains peculiarly the creation of the writers.

8

The Hoodoo War and Those Dear Little Sisters

JOHN RINGO seems to have "gone bad" in San Jose, where he remained, presumably with his mother and sisters, for five years. But except for what Frank Cushing told Charles Ringo—that "John became quite a drunkard and left home at 19 in 1869 . . . [leaving] the family in the lurch,"[1] I know nothing of what happened to John in San Jose. Perhaps, as I suggested, John suffered genuine trauma from the five-month exodus west, which must have seemed to him more like a hegira after the death of his father. Perhaps he was expected to assume the mantle of family responsibility at too early an age and simply rebelled. Perhaps, too, the long and tragic wagon trek left him restless, unsettled, and uncertain. Quite possibly his own emotional needs were unfulfilled at an uncertain and vulnerable time in his life while his mother, herself "in a serious condition, financially and otherwise," was preoccupied with her own grief, ministering to the sickly "Allie," and tending to three growing little girls. He may actually have come to hate his family. Cushing told Charles that "they [the family] wrote numerous letters to him but he did not even write back."[2] It is possible, too, that, beset by incomprehensible and conflicting emotions, he bore an enormous burden of youthful guilt (those "dear-little-sister" letters were supposed to have cast him into states of dangerous despond) that was later transmuted into those celebrated feelings of self-loathing.

Cushing, as I noted earlier, considered Ringo material—including the correspondence between Martin and Mary and between Mary and her sister (this correspondence was then in the possession of Cushing's sister, Zana, who was too ill to locate it)—to be important. While this correspondence might be helpful, I cannot believe it to be vital to the story of John Ringo. The Martin-Mary correspondence would have been of no consequence whatever to the *legend* of John Ringo because of Martin's tragic death when John was only fourteen. (Just when that correspondence passed between Martin and Mary remains a mystery; it could have occurred during the Mexican War and before John was born, or when and *if* Martin was later absent from his family for protracted periods, during which their letters might have made reference to the young John.) Mary's correspondence with her sisters[3] may well have contained expressions of anxiety over John's behavior in San Jose, where he became "quite a drunkard"; and it is certainly possible that, after he left home and failed to respond to letters, Mary's worries were intensified and amplified in her letters to her sister. It is possible, too, that Mary had learned something of John's activities in Texas, since his membership in the Cooley Gang was mentioned at least twice in Texas newspapers in 1875, and again in January of 1876. Yet, if one can draw any conclusions at all from her *Journal*, Mary probably wrote very little about John that did not reflect mostly upon her personal grief and sense of loss. One recalls her excruciating agonies over Martin's death, but she mentioned not one word of how fourteen-year-old John personally reacted to the death of his father.

Whatever his reason or reasons for leaving San Jose and his family—trauma, neglect, too much responsibility (the latter manifested, perhaps, in his later refusal to lead or follow, except as he chose to do so), or because the Ringo family tree had simply produced a rotten apple—nineteen-year-old John

Ringo headed for Texas in 1869. Texas was not just a romantic choice. By the end of the Civil War there was a "goodly contingent" of Ringos in Texas, from Palo Pinto County to San Saba.[4] Peter Ringo, Martin's uncle (?), had obtained a Texas land grant as early as 1840; Peter, David Ringo wrote Charles, "may have been the one John Ringo ostensibly went to Texas to visit when he got caught up in the Hoodoo War."[5]

The Hoodoo War, an appellation used to describe the vigilantism and night-rider characteristics of what was really the Mason County Range War, was both complex and confusing. Essentially, it was a kind of war within a war that bore the ugly stamp—brand, I suppose one should say—of bigotry, along with the commission of rampant thefts and unspeakably brutal and cowardly murders. On one side were the Germans, first and second generation settlers, derisively called "Dutchmen" by the opposing side, the "Americans."[6] The Germans had committed the unpardonable sin of supporting the Union during the Civil War, both morally and sometimes by enlistment,[7] and, observed C. L. Sonnichsen, ". . . between the Home Guard and the Comanche Indians they had about all they could handle."[8] When the Civil War ended, German-American animosities endured. Except for the family blood-feud, one finds a parallel with Arizona's Pleasant Valley War: just as gangs of outlaws moved easily back and forth between the Hashknife Range War and the Tewksbury-Graham feud, so did "organized bands of these human coyotes"[9] take advantage of the German-American feud.

The Germans were hardest hit by the outlaws and they fought back. The "Americans," according to the Austin *Daily Statesman*, "though in perfect accord with the Germans in opposing the doings of the outlaws . . .[take] no open action against them lest they, too, should fall before the bullet of the concealed or midnight assassin. . . . The Germans are left alone to combat these malign scourges of civilization."[10] In addition, declared Sonnichsen, "some of the local ranchers were not much better than the thieves. Trail herds were made

up every spring, and many times the trail bosses were completely indifferent as to whose cows they drove. Even reputable ranchers [picked] up strays and mavericks."[11] The Germans, though, tried to reach a peaceful and legal solution to
their problems, while at the same time groping to put the
uneven, three-way struggle into perspective. They elected
Sheriff John Clark and Cattle Inspector Dan Hoerster "to office,"[12] both of whom were regarded as honest men, unafraid
of potential enemies and their threats, immune to the pres-
sures of cliques and even to the seductive possibility of
bribes.[13] Unfortunately, as it turned out, they were not immune to taking the law into their own hands.

The year 1875, Sonnichsen wrote, saw ". . . a tidal wave
of rustling which made all previous outbreaks seem puny."[14]
Clark and Hoerster now gathered posses and began a sweep
of the areas west and southwest of Mason, on Brady Creek
and the James River, where trail herds were being rounded
up and held. The James River posse found the rustled cattle,
but the rustlers had "high-tailed it." Clark was successful: on
Brady Creek his posse caught the notorious Backus brothers
and eight of their riders "readying a herd," Sonnichsen observed dryly, "belonging to almost everybody in Mason
County but themselves. It is said that only three of the cows
they had gathered belonged to them."[15] Three of the Backus
riders escaped; the other five, including the Backus brothers,
were taken to Mason and jailed.

Just what turned the two posses into a lynch mob cannot
be ascribed to any one thing, or to some sudden volatility;
there were lingering animosities, no doubt, and inchoate
rages, of course, but above all, it would appear, there was
flawed leadership. Tom Gamel, a posse member, claimed that
both Clark and Hoerster urged getting rid of the jailed rustlers
by taking the law into their own hands.[16] Gamel objected and
left the posses. "From this time on," Sonnichsen wrote, "Gamel was a supporter of the American side, and his accusations
may be taken for whatever they are worth."[17] However one

wishes to view it, a masked mob broke into the jail the night of February 18, 1875, and forcibly removed the five rustlers. Sheriff Clark, after enlisting the help of Texas Ranger Lieutenant Dan W. Roberts (who was on business in Mason), threatened to open fire on the mob, then meekly surrendered. The question of whether Clark and Roberts were merely playing a pre-arranged role is moot. Certainly they revealed no knowledge of mob psychology, none of the determined coolness in the face of mob fury that creates contrast and confusion, a breech into which a professional and courageous lawman would step, along with a sawed-off shotgun, widening it further by picking out the leaders as his first victims. One cannot imagine a mob taking the prisoners from Wyatt Earp. The mob succeeded in lynching the Backus brothers and shooting a third rustler to death before Clark began a half-hearted pursuit. The last two of the rustlers were rescued.

Gamel now considered himself a marked man and gathered his own followers about him.[18] In late March of 1875, Gamel and his "party" met Sheriff Clark at the head of some sixty Germans in Mason, but there was no fight. After a shaky day or so, some sort of "peace was proclaimed,"[19] and it appeared as though the trouble were over. But the peace lasted only for the moment: Tim Williamson, a well-known and well-liked American, was arrested in May of 1875 on an old charge of having stolen a yearling. The arresting officer, Deputy John Wohrle, seems to have deliberately led Williamson into a nest of bushwhackers, where he was murdered by Peter Bader, a German farmer.[20]

The killing of Williamson brought the Scott Cooley gang—and with it, John Ringo—into the Hoodoo War. Cooley, the story goes, had been an Indian captive whose parents had been massacred in Palo Pinto County. Williamson, while on a cattle drive to Kansas, had brought the psychologically scarred youngster back to Texas and raised him.[21] Fanatically loyal to Williamson and perhaps a bit of a psychopath, Cooley now murdered and scalped Wohrle,[22] and the war was on again. According to San Antonio and Austin newspapers, Sheriff Clark and the Germans decided to break up the Cooley gang by what had become the usual method: an ambush. For pay, a Mason gambler named Cheyney rode down to Loyal Valley, where the Cooley gang had gathered, and told Mose Beard and George Gladden they were wanted in Mason. Cheyney then lit out at a dead run for Mason. It is not clear just why Beard and Gladden were selected for the ambush, what they were told that was compelling enough to fetch them, or why they did not become suspicious at Cheyney's guilty flight. But come they did and they were ambushed.[23] Mose Beard was killed and Gladden wounded, although his life was spared as a result of his pathetic begging. Gladden returned to the Cooley gang, recovered, and once again took up the fight.

It was at this point that John Ringo put in an appearance as one of the killers of Cheyney. Tom Gamel wrote that

Ringoe [*sic*] and [a man named] Williams, rode up to Cheyney's house early one morning and hollowed [*sic*] "hello." Cheyney came out and they asked him if they could get some breakfast. Cheyney asked Ringo and Williams down and they stepped upon the porch and washed their faces. Cheyney washed and was drying his face and while he had his face covered with the towel, Ringo and Williams shot him down and rode back to where their friends were awaiting them [in Mason]. . . . They went on to Bridges Hotel and ate breakfast with their guns across their laps. When [Scott] Cooley's gang rode up to the hotel, Wilson Hey, Sr. [a roomer at the hotel] . . . asked Cooley to get down and eat breakfast and Cooley replied, "You go inside and tell Mrs. Bridges there is some fresh meat up the creek," at the same time making a gesture in the direction where Cheyney was killed a few minutes before.[24]

Two newspapers, The San Antonio *Express* of October 6, 1875, and the Austin *Daily Statesman* of October 17, 1875, carried the same general story. About a year later a Texas grand jury indicted John Ringo and George Gladden for the murder of "James Chaney" (*sic*); Williams was not mentioned in the indictment.[25]

Shortly after the killing of Cheyney, Ringo and Cooley killed Charley Bader, the innocent brother of Peter, by mistake. They were jailed in Lampassas County near Burnet, but were "busted" loose by friends. On November 7, 1876, John Ringo and George Gladden were arrested by Texas Rangers and jailed. Gladden was sentenced to ninety-nine years in the penitentiary. There is no apparent record of the length of Ringo's sentence. Sonnichsen believes he beat the rap and hightailed it for Arizona.[26] He was, however, in the Travis County, Texas, jail in 1877, along with the gunman John Wesley Hardin and a number of well-known outlaws,[27] where he seems to have been considered as desperate and as dangerous as the famous Hardin himself, who reputedly and incongruously complained about being cast into the lock-up with the likes of anyone as mean and vicious as John Ringo. Historian Wayne Gard claims that Ringo broke jail and fled Texas[28] (John Wesley Hardin may have declined to go along). Later evidence, however, discovered by Arizona freelance writer Frank A. Tinker, indicated that John Ringo served briefly as a constable in Loyal Valley, Texas, in 1878;[29] Tombstone historian Alford Turner confirmed Ringo's constabulary in Mason County Precinct #4 in the year 1878.[30] The following year Ringo made his first appearance of record in Arizona, when he tried to kill Louis Hancock in Safford on December 14, 1879.

We shall probably never know for sure what, or who, or perhaps what combination of events drew John Ringo into the Hoodoo War. Certainly it was nothing so noble as the avenging of a slain younger brother,* nor was it anything so respectable as a legitimate stake in a range war. He was not fighting against a fenced-off water hole or barbed wire strung across

---

* John Ringo's only brother, Martin Albert, had died years earlier (1873) of an illness—probably tuberculosis—in San Jose, California (see Chapter 7, note 8).

open range. He was simply one of those "human coyotes," a willing and ruthless follower of the psychotic Scott Cooley who, incidentally, carried Deputy Wohrle's scalp around in his pocket.[31] Nor was John Ringo a wide-eyed youth during the Hoodoo War, caught up in the romance and freedom of the owlhoot trail. He was twenty-nine when held in the Travis County Jail. By western standards he was an experienced, mature, and hardened outlaw—but he wasn't too "mean" or too "vicious," apparently, for the tastes of Old Man Clanton and Curly Bill.

Questions, to which there appear to be no answers, persist. By what mode or method of transportation had John Ringo traveled to Texas? Not by rail, of course, since the Southern Pacific did not push its rails out of California until 1877, eight years after John left San Jose. It must have been by stage-coach, then, or by horseback. But how did he pay for his transportation? Did his mother give him the money? Did she suggest he visit Texas relatives? Did she purchase a horse for him? Did Colonel Younger supply him with a mount? Did he steal one? Did he ever visit the Ringos in Palo Pinto County and San Saba? If so, how long did he remain with them? Did he have trouble with them, too, and move on? Or did he become an outlaw before he reached his relatives? What did he do between 1869 and 1875 when he first appeared in news-print?

I have talked and corresponded with many historians and "buffs" who were and are interested in John Ringo, some of whom alluded, more coyly than convincingly, to detailed knowledge of what one referred to rather grandiloquently as "John Ringo's Texas Period." But my own research and that of others who have assisted me in Texas has unearthed nothing more than I have recounted of the Hoodoo War. Charles Ringo referred to a "courthouse [that] burned down,"[32] whose records might have implicated John in a killing. But, as a

Texan told me, "*most* courthouses were burned during Reconstruction to destroy records," and Charles did not know the date of the burning or even the name of the town or county in which the courthouse was located. It is possible, though, to draw certain assumptions about John Ringo's "Texas Period." First, Frank Cushing made no mention to Charles of any Ringo correspondence other than that between Martin and Mary and between Mary and her sister(s). That is to say, unless Cushing held back on Charles, or Charles held back on me—and I do not believe he did—there is no known correspondence between Mary and her Texas relatives. Yet one recalls Cushing's reference to "numerous letters" written to John by his mother and sisters and to which he did not respond ("he did not even write back"). To what address or addresses were those letters sent? Logic would point to the Palo Pinto County and San Saba Ringos. But did these relatives respond, assuring mother and sisters that the letters had been handed over to John, who simply had not bothered to answer them, or were the letters returned after a time with covering letters informing Mary and her daughters that John had not turned up? Ringo obviously received *some* letters from his sisters. According to the Tucson *Weekly Citizen* of July 30, 1882, John Ringo's horse was found "about two miles from where the deceased was found," still saddled and with "Ringo's coat upon the back of it." In the coat's pockets were some photos(?) and a card bearing the name of "Mrs. Jackson." This would have been the oldest sister, Fanny Fern, who married Moses Jackson.

Cushing's assertion that John "did not even write back" carries the implication that he did, in fact, receive the letters. I believe that some correspondence did pass between Mary Ringo and the Texas Ringos. Certainly Mary and her daughters could not have addressed letters to random Texas towns in the hope that John just might pass through and drop by the local post offices. If John did not care enough to answer the letters, it is unlikely that he went out of his way to seek them.

I believe further that Mary Ringo and her daughters learned rather early of John's reckless prodigality in Texas and that they possessed information, probably letters or perhaps news-paper items, which they destroyed in their efforts to create a non-person of him, or at least a non-relative. On the one oc-casion of a personal visit with Charles in San Francisco, he told me several things that he did not wish, at the time, to commit to a letter. Enna Ringo, he said, apparently the most adamant of the sisters in their efforts to disassociate them-selves from John, destroyed anything and everything she could get her hands on that related to John's life in Texas and Arizona.[33] (One recalls Breakenridge's claim that Ringo had told him enough about his family for him to know that they were not aware Ringo was an outlaw.) Frank Cushing, who was alive when Charles and I talked, told Charles that he had written a number of letters at Enna's direction, warning of possible legal action against anyone who tried in any way to connect John with the California Ringos, including one threatening letter to a Florida relative (a Ringo) who wanted to publish an article on the family's outlaw. So determined was sister Enna to keep brother John's skeleton stuffed away in the closet that she proclaimed him a Texas Ranger when word filtered out that he was, indeed, in Texas,[34] an associa-tion she perhaps consciously made when she read or heard that John had been *arrested* by Texas Rangers.

Sometime during the 1930s Enna Ringo and Frank Cush-ing visited Tombstone and made discreet inquiries of the sheriff of Cochise County about John Ringo's time in Tomb-stone. The sheriff's knowledge, of course, like that of his contemporaries, was generally limited to Burns's *Tombstone* and Breakenridge's *Helldorado*, with an occasional old-timer tale probably tossed in.[35] The writings of Burns and Break-enridge, as we have seen, were highly flattering to John Ringo. If sister and nephew took any sort of comfort from what the sheriff had to tell them, it was not manifested in their later behavior. They persisted with righteous fervor in their efforts to proscribe John, and continued to do so for more than half a century after his death. He might have been Hamlet to Burns; to Enna and her sisters he was a cow-country Caliban, a chimerical manifestation who threatened to girdle the family tree. The sisters' obsession with disgrace tells us more about them, perhaps, than it does about John Ringo. They appear humorless and lacking in the introspective powers that might have taken fourteen-year-old John's wagon train experiences and vulnerability into consideration; and for people with a strong religious background (Methodist), they were sternly unforgiving. Most families, after nearly three-quarters of a century, would be intrigued, even amused, by a family rogue, especially if he were a cowboy rogue, a genuine western outlaw, unless, of course, he chanced to be a mass murderer (such as Quantrill or Colonel John Chivington) or had committed some particularly hideous crime. John Ringo was merely a relatively unknown and shadowy western outlaw with an equally unknown record. The sisters had conjured an apparition, then worked ceaselessly to exorcise it.

Nor could Ringo's sisters have developed strong or realistic feelings about John during the five years he lived with the family in San Jose. He left San Jose when Fanny was twelve, Enna nine, and Mattie seven. They saw him briefly and only once during the remaining thirteen years of his life. And the sisters, who seemed to believe themselves victimized by malign literary and domestic harassments, were only proxy voyagers, really, when it came to counting skeletons in the family closet. Colonel Coleman Younger, their uncle by marriage, was (as discussed in Chapter 6) a blood relative of three really notorious outlaws, the Younger brothers, one of whom bore his name. There is no evidence that Colonel Younger wasted time and energy in futile efforts to disown his nephews or that he experienced either embarrassment or disgrace because of them. "He was," Charles Ringo wrote, "a highly respected citizen of San Jose. He had 2 sons who were attorneys. Eval [sic] Younger—Atty-Gen of Calif—is of the same Younger family."[36]

Ironically, Enna Ringo's trip to Tombstone doubtless helped to enhance the mystery of John Ringo. However surreptitious her visit, word inevitably got out that John Ringo's sister had been in town. Before long, the popular imagination had transformed the angry, elderly, and reticent Enna into a beautiful and mysterious young woman, who, with two young boys to help her, exhumed John Ringo's body of a moonlit night and removed it to a quiet little Missouri River cemetery. That the notion of exhumation persisted in more than just romantic legend is verified in the old-age statement of Robert M. Boller, one of the men who had examined and identified the body, and who signed the coroner's report. "Later," Boller wrote, "Ringo's sister came down from California and took the body back with her."[37] Of course, she did not. Enna and Cushing did not even drive out to the Chiricahuas to visit John's grave.[38]

9
The Homecoming

WHATEVER IMPULSE or circumstances impelled him, John Ringo visited—or tried to visit—his sisters in San Jose, either in late 1881 or early 1882. Charles Ringo's account of the homecoming, which he heard from Frank Cushing, is garbled and conflicting. Charles wrote to Will that

> In 1881 he [John] came home and went back to sell his cattle and then *come back* [italics mine]. . . . When he sold his cattle he went on a terrible binge. The belief is that his partner killed him when he was drunk in order to get his money. He was *not* killed by Wyatt Earp.
>
> I have another story from a Mrs. Travis [identity unknown] whose husband was of that family, that the sisters would not let him in the house.* You will notice that the body was left in Arizona and not brought back." [1]

Later Charles wrote me:

> His family thought he was in the cattle business there [in Arizona]. He was[,] but of a different nature than his family

---

* Ringo relative May King offers further proof of the Ringo sisters' rejection of John. "One reason you never see any stories about his parentage," she wrote Joanna Green (who is, apparently, another Ringo researcher), "was because he never talked about his family who were ashamed of him. During the late '20's and '30's some of the [Ringo] family researchers wrote his sisters in San Jose, Ca. and they wouldn't admit that he was their brother" (May King to Joanna Green, September 18, 1982).

expected!!! In the early part of 1882 he decided to go home to San Jose and change his method of living. His family was very straight-laced and religious. When they found out what he had been doing they gave him a cold reception and refused to let him in the house. He did, however, get his picture taken which is in the hands of Frank Cushing. He went back to Arizona and either committed suicide, 'but by whose gun'?" [2]

Charles' two short statements, written two years apart, raise more questions than they answer. Did John Ringo go home in 1881 or 1882? The date is important. If he was, in fact, in San Jose in late 1881 and early 1882 he is clearly absolved of the shooting of Virgil Earp on December 28, 1881. Undercover Wells, Fargo agent Fred Dodge clears him of participation in that shooting, declaring the would-be assassin to have been Johnny Barnes, who was later wounded by Wyatt Earp in the shoot-out with Curly Bill at Iron Springs, and who later died of his wound. [3] Yet Ringo's near gunfight with Doc Holliday occurred on January 17, 1882. Of course he *could* have been in San Jose in late December and early January and in Tombstone by mid-January or earlier. The trains ran regularly between California and Arizona in 1881–1882. If he had chanced to visit San Jose in mid-March of 1882, then he is also exculpated in the murder of Morgan Earp on March 17, 1882. But this too would be cutting it close, since the *Epitaph* reported him in Tombstone on March 27, 1882.

We do not know how long he remained in San Jose, though one would theorize that it was not very long, if his sisters "would not let him in their house." Perhaps it was anger over their rejection that sent him back to Tombstone and to the near-fight with Holliday, but only perhaps. Charles' claim that he came home, then returned to Arizona to "sell his cattle," intending to "come back," but was diverted by one of those Homeric "binges" during which he was "killed by his partner," would put Ringo in Arizona in mid-1882; his body was found on July 14, 1882. Implicit in the statement of John Ringo's plans is his acceptance by his sisters, or why would he plan to "come back" to San Jose after the sale of his cattle? Are we to infer that the sisters thought John a legitimate cattleman right up to the moment of his visit, during which he might have unaccountably made the mistake of confessing his sins and been rejected rather than forgiven? What of the sisters' knowledge of his Texas outlawry, which led to the claim that he was a Texas Ranger? Who was Mrs. Travis, from whom Charles had the story of the sisters' refusal to let John in the house, and "whose husband was of that family." And to what family does Charles refer? I can find no Travis among the endless and repetitious genealogies Charles sent me.

I am of the inescapable opinion that Frank Cushing withheld information from Charles, partly, perhaps, owing to sisterly inculcation and habit, and quite possibly also to pecuniary considerations.[4] It is difficult to believe that during the long years the sisters and the complaisant Cushing were occupied in their efforts to beat back John Ringo's ghost that Cushing did not, at one time or another, learn the date of John's visit to San Jose and of the length of time he remained here. And certainly Cushing was under no obligation to reveal everything he knew to a "seventh cousin" whom he had met only once.

There is no doubt in my mind that John Ringo tried to come home. Nor do I doubt—if their later behavior is confirmation of anything at all—that the sisters "gave him a cold reception and refused to let him in the house." I believe, too, that John Ringo, rejected, had his photograph taken in San Jose and either delivered it to his sisters in person, perhaps as a peace offering, or had it sent to them as a farewell gesture. Perhaps John hoped that his photograph would, in time, produce a softening in his sisters. If so, he failed utterly to gauge their steel and their grim, single-minded resolve. One can only imagine the emotions of the young man as he returned to Arizona.

For still another reason, the date of his visit to San Jose is important. We know that John Ringo was in Arizona in March and part of April of 1882. He rode with Sheriff Behan's posse in pursuit of the Earp party during that time.[5] But we cannot account for him during late April, May, and June. The story that he, along with Ike Clanton and Pony Deal (a close friend and fellow outlaw) dropped below the border to avoid Wyatt Earp's dragnet after the killing of Curly Bill and the wounding of Johnny Barnes is without documentation; the killing of Curly Bill (in late March of 1882) could, however, have been a powerful and compelling argument for "going straight." It would have been as good a time as any to go home, for beyond Curly Bill were strewn the bodies of Indian Charlie, Frank Stilwell, Billy Clanton, Bill Leonard, Harry Head, Jim Crane, and the McLaury brothers. And Johnny Barnes lay dying. Old Man Clanton was dead. Once again Johnny was vulnerable. Could Curly Bill have conceivably been a father surrogate, who also deserted John Ringo through carelessness or clumsiness? Did Ringo see a parallel between his mother's (possible) dependence after the death of his father and that of the rustler gang, now looking to him for sustained leadership? (One recalls that Breakenridge said Ringo had great authority with the rustlers and that he often led the band on cattle raids, but that he kept to himself after they returned.) Figuratively speaking, did Johnny leave "home" again, that is, his outlaw "home"? And if so, could not his sisters' angry and unforgiving rejection, which, ironically, had sent him back to the outlaw world they deplored (a world which had now begun to crumble throughout the West in general) also be the ultimate cause of his death (probably by suicide)—a family tragedy come full circle?

Of course, all this is speculation. If John Ringo went to San Jose in late 1881, in November or December, it could have been in reaction to the O.K. Corral fight, which had resulted in the deaths of three of his friends and which had occurred on October 26, 1881; he would, then, have been absent from Tombstone when Virgil Earp was ambushed on

December 28, 1881. Efforts to place him in or out of Arizona at the times Virgil and Morgan Earp were shot are pointless; it can't be done. It is, however, possible to place him at least in Cochise County *roughly* at the time of both shootings, and both Stuart Lake and Josephine Earp declared Wyatt to have believed Ringo was involved in both. It is noteworthy that John Ringo was not named in the warrants issued for either shooting, and his presumed implication by Indian Charlie is probably as fictional as Lake's "uno, dos, tres" and "flashing Buntline" story (see Chapter 1).

Ringo was in Arizona in early August of 1881 (when he was arrested for holding up the card game in Galeyville),[6] and in early December (when he offered to sell the town of Galeyville all the mutton it could consume at "$1.00 per head"[7]). And he was likely involved in the killing of the Haslett brothers in June,[8] in retaliation for their killing of outlaws Bill Leonard and Harry Head (friends of John, both of whom had been accused of trying to hold up the Benson-Tombstone stage, during which attempt the driver, Budd Philpot, was killed, along with a passenger). There is no hard evidence to link Ringo to the killings, no eyewitness account. But the report that storekeepers Ike and Bill Haslett were shot down without warning, together with the revenge factor, offers an interesting parallel with the killings of Cheyney and Bader in Texas. Nor would it have mattered to Ringo and Curly Bill that Leonard and Head were reputedly trying to hold up their store when the Hasletts killed them.

Charles Ringo's statement that John "came home in 1881" and then went back to "sell his cattle," after which he went on a "terrific binge" and was killed or committed suicide, is simply an error. One would have to assume, since John died in mid-July of 1882, that it either took him nearly a year to sell his cattle (what cattle?) or, if he sold them shortly after he returned to Arizona, that it was, indeed, a "terrific binge" — one that lasted the better part of a year. Charles made a number of confusing errors, not the least of which involved careless sentence structure: "Mary Peters Ringo kept a diary which I have read," he wrote Gilchriese: "You can tell her grief in this until she arrived at San Jose. In the book at the end is the only picture known to exist of Johnny Ringo when he tried to come home to San Jose just before his death in 1883 [sic]. Johnny was only 14 years old at this time."[9] But the enigma of John Ringo comes far closer to solution in the misstatements and scrambled syntax of Charles than it does in the writings of those "professionals" who genuflected before that jealous old fraud, Billy Breakenridge, or before each other. Three representative quotes are ironically worthy of repetition at this point: Eugene Cunningham: "John Ringo— Ringgold was the family name in California, Breakenridge learned in later years—was the black sheep scion of an aristocratic family and well educated. . . . Men who knew him observed that he was more likely to go upon one of his wild sprees after receiving a letter from California addressed to him in feminine handwriting." John Myers: "He even received letters in a graceful feminine hand, and each one cast him adrift in despond for days thereafter." Walter Noble Burns: [Here Breakenridge rides towards Tombstone with Ringo. Ringo reads and re-reads a letter.] "He shook his head sadly as he held out the envelope to Breakenridge. 'Seems strange' he said, 'for a tough, no good fellow like me to get a letter like this.' 'Sweetheart?' queried Breakenridge, noting the superscription was in a woman's hand. 'My sister,' said Ringo solemnly. 'She writes to me regularly. Thinks I'm in the cattle business out here and doing fine. Doing fine. Humph! Dear little sister, I hope she never learns the truth.'"

One can imagine Enna Ringo, who doubtless read Burns's *Tombstone,* echoing at least one word of this little bit of contrived and mythic dialogue: *"Humph!"* And that persistent feminine theme, those famous "sprees" and days of despondency (which suggested at least a transcendent and mutual family love and which were triggered by letters from home in that "graceful, feminine hand") and often expressed further through an undocumented defense of womanhood in general, become, instead, palpable and brutal rejection at the hearth. One's vision of aristocratic, loving, and hoop-skirted sisters gliding about the old plantation or manor house, anxiously awaiting the prodigal's return, fades into an angry and sanctimonious spinster "school marm" and her sisters, who seem to have been driven by the very same furies for which their outlaw brother is celebrated. And with far less cause.

10

The Death of John Ringo

THE SULPHUR SPRINGS VALLEY runs roughly north to south, a long, broad and arid plain that separates the Dragoon and Chiricahua mountains. To the west is the South Pass of the Dragoons and through it runs the trail from Tombstone to Galeyville. To the east, the valley rises slowly against the foothill scrub to where the land flattens onto grassy tables before sweeping sharply upward in a visually synchronous whole to the coniferous peaks of the Chiricahuas. There were two ranches on the table lands, the B.F. Smith (or "Coyote" Smith) Ranch and the Will Sanders Ranch.[1] The ranches are separated by rocky-bottomed Turkey Creek, which flows out of Morse's Canyon and empties into Sulphur Springs Valley. Just back of the Sanders ranch house, in an umbrageous creek border of blackjack and live oak, stands a five-stemmed blackjack oak whose massive, canescent trunks ratoon from a single root, forming a protected semicircle around a deep, flat, interior bole.[2] John Ringo's body was found cradled in the bole, his head flung to the right, his .45 gripped in his right hand. He was shot through the right temple. To add to the mystery, he appeared to have been partially scalped. John Ringo was buried behind his tree. And his grave site, like his name, is eloquent of outlawry—a bouldered cairn in the heart of Apachería, hard by the banks of historic Turkey Creek and beside the Barfoot Trail, the old outlaw trail, facing west to the Dragoons and shadowed under the loom of the Chiricahuas.

Since the purpose of this chapter is to examine the various accounts and versions of how John Ringo died, I have included here a copy of the official statement for the coroner and sheriff of the county, so that comparative references can be quickly made when distinctions or conflicts occur, or appear to occur, between this statement and different individual stories and theories. John Ringo's death was the ultimate mystery in an almost consistently mysterious life. Everyone who was ever touched by John Ringo—either through personal and contemporary experience or from the historical and academic removes of a hundred years, or in imaginations grown creatively addled with time—subscribes to a posited theory or concept or yarn of how the rustler met his lonely death. Only one, if any, of these can be true. It should be borne in mind that the Statement for the Coroner and Sheriff seems to indicate rather generally that Ringo's death occurred by suicide.

Turkey or Morse's Hill Creek
14th July, 1882

Statement for the information of the Coroner and Sheriff of Cochise Co. A.T.*

There was found by the undersigned John Yoast the body of a man in a clump of Oak trees about 20 yards north from the road leading to Morse's mill and about a quarter of a mile west of the house of B.F. Smith. The undersigned viewed the body and found it in a sitting posture, facing west, the head inclined to the right.— There was a bullet hole in the right temple, the bullet coming out on the top of the head on the left side. There is apparently a part of

* Note that this statement was endorsed by the fourteen citizens on July 14, 1882, and was filed on November 13, 1882; the document has been reproduced here exactly as it appears in the records of the District Court of the First Judicial District, Cochise County, Arizona.

the scalp gone including a small portion of the forehead and part of the hair, this looks as if cut out by a knife. (These are the only marks of violence visible on the body. Several of the undersigned identify the body as that of John Ringo, well known in Tombstone. He was dressed in light hat, blue shirt, vest, pants and drawers, on his feet were a pair hose and undershirt torn up so as to protect his feet. He had evidently travelled but a short distance in this foot gear. His revolver he grasped in his right hand, his rifle rested against the tree close to him. He had on two cartridge belts, the belt for the revolver cartridges being buckled on upside down. The undernoted property were found with him and on his person.—

1   Colt's revolver Cal: 45 No. 222, —containing 5 cartridges
1   Winchester rifle octagon barrel Cal: 45 Model 1876 No. 21896, containing a cartridge in the breech and 10 in the magazine.
1   Cartridge belt containing 9 rifle cartridges.
1   Do   ---   ----   2 revolver Do
1   Silver watch of American Watch Co. No. 9339 with Silver Chain attached.
Two Dollars & Sixty cents ($2.60) in money.
6 pistol cartridges in his pocket.
5   shirt studs.
1   small pocket knife.
1   Tobacco pipe — 1 Comb
1   Block matches — 1 small piece tobacco

There is also a portion of a letter from Messrs. Hereford & I. Zabriskie, Attorneys at Law, Tucson to the deceased John Ringo.—

The above property is left in the possession of Frederick Ward, teamster between Morse Mill and Tombstone.

The body of the deceased was buried close to where it was found. When found deceased had been dead about 24 hours.

Thomas White	James Morgan
John Blake	Robert Boller
John W. Bradfield	Frank McKinney
B. F. Smith	W. J. Darnal
W. W. Smith	J. C. McGrager
A. E. Lewis	John Yoast
A. S. Neighbours	Fred Ward

"ENDORSED"
Statement by citizens in regard the death of
Jno Ringo
Filed Nov. 13/82
W. H. Seamans, Clk.
By Louis A. Souc, Depy.

There are a number of stories and theories about John Ringo's death; these theories—each to be considered in turn—involve either suicide or murder (by various contemporaries, including a tinhorn gambler named Johnny-Behind-the-Deuce, one-time lawman Wyatt Earp, Buckskin Frank Leslie, and a few other lesser-known characters).

ᛁᛪᛨᛧ

As with just about everything concerning Tombstone, the Earps, and John Ringo, one begins with Breakenridge, who seems never to have doubted that John Ringo committed suicide. It was his opinion, repeated by Burns and others, that Ringo, drunk, mounted, and out in the middle of nowhere, had removed his boots, hung them over the saddle horn and lain down to "sleep it off." The horse got thirsty and wandered away. Ringo awakened to find himself horseless and bootless and without water. He tore his undershirt into strips, wrapped the strips around his feet and socks, and walked in that condition to the tree where his body was found. He had sucked the lead from several cartridges "to get moisture in his mouth." Here, in detail, are the important parts of Breakenridge's story:

> As I was coming back from Sulphur Springs Valley, shortly after Sheriff Behan returned from his unsuccessful trip after the Earp crowd, I met John Ringo in the South Pass of the Dragoon Mountains. It was shortly after noon. Ringo was very drunk, reeling in the saddle, and said he was going to Galeyville. It was in the summer and a very hot day. He offered me a drink . . . of whiskey. . . . I tasted it and it was too hot to

drink. It burned my lips. Knowing he would have to ride all night [to] reach Galeyville, I tried to get him to go back with me to the Goodrich Ranch and wait until after sundown, but he was drunk and stubborn and went on his way. I think this was the last time he was seen alive. . . .

On the opposite side of the creek from Smith's house was a bunch of five black jack oaks growing up in a semicircle from one root, and in the center of them was a large flat rock which made a comfortable seat. Ringo was found sitting there with a bullet hole in his head.

His watch was still running, and his revolver was caught in his watch chain with only one shot discharged from it. . . .

His boots were gone and he had taken off his undershirt and torn it in two, and wrapped it around his feet, and when he was found the shirt was worn through, showing that he had walked for some distance. . . .

When Ringo awoke, he must have been crazed for water and started out afoot. He was within sound of running water when he became crazed with thirst and killed himself. . . . [Mrs. Smith, whose house was just across the creek, reputedly heard the shot] about two o'clock in the afternoon . . . the day after I met Ringo.[3]

Breakenridge's observations are inexplicable, the more so since no one seems to have analyzed them carefully. His claim that he met Ringo in the South Pass of the Dragoons "shortly after Sheriff Behan returned from his unsuccessful trip after the Earp crowd" has elicited no suspicion whatever to my knowledge. Breakenridge must have met Ringo on or about July 11 or 12, since Ringo's body was found on the 14th and, according to the Statement for the Coroner, by that date he had been dead for about twenty-four hours. The Earp "crowd" had left Cochise County in late April, two and a half months before Ringo died. Surely Behan and his posse could not have been chasing Wyatt Earp all that time. The county simply would not have borne the expense. And, in fact, Earp was known to be in Colorado on May 16,[4] just a week after the Tombstone *Nugget* reported him killed in a gun battle with

Behan's posse.[5] One is left to reflect on either a foggy memory or a deliberate distortion, and to puzzle over what Breakenridge meant by "shortly"—a week, a month, two months? It is worth noting, too, that Breakenridge refers to Behan's "trip" in the singular sense. Perhaps nothing much is to be made of the running together of events that were actually separated by several months. To the historian, however, admittedly quite possibly too concerned with specifics, such errors in time and place puzzle, particularly when one considers Eugene Cunningham's reference to Breakenridge's "steel trap mind."[6]

Breakenridge's positive belief that Ringo "was within sound of running water when he became crazed with thirst and killed himself" is not just puzzling, though, it is downright ludicrous to anyone who has examined the grave site. Ringo was, indeed, within sound of running water—and within sight of it, too, if Mrs. Smith heard the shot that killed him at 2:00 p.m. The Ringo Tree stands on the very brink of Turkey Creek—so close, in fact, that it will one day be toppled by the stream's undercutting action. Ringo had only to lunge forward from his seat in the tree's bole to sprawl head-first into the running water. And one must assume that if he possessed the capacity to draw his pistol and shoot himself he also possessed the capacity to fall forward into the stream—that is, unless the impulse for death, in his case, was stronger than the impulse for life. One also wonders how he managed to find the tree and take his seat (he seems to have deliberately sought it) since Breakenridge would have us believe that he could not locate the stream which flowed at the tree's very roots. The case for seeking the tree and its flat-rocked seat is stronger than the possibility of Ringo's stumbling onto it by chance, since it was reputedly a well-known nooning place for teamsters on the road to Morse's Mill. And since the "Ringo Tree" stands on the east bank of Turkey Creek, it is possible that Ringo actually crossed the stream in order to get to the tree. The other possibility, and a more remote one, it seems to me, is that he circled the mouth of Turkey Creek in the Sulphur Springs Valley and came up the east bank.

There are discrepancies, too, between the Statement for the Coroner and Breakenridge's story. Breakenridge claimed Ringo's pistol was "caught in his watch chain with only one shot discharged." The Statement for the Coroner clearly states that Ringo's gun was "grasped in his right hand" and refers to his "Colt" as "containing five cartridges." It says nothing about one cartridge having been discharged. It should be noted further that experts with the six-shooter reputedly kept an empty cylinder under the hammer to avoid an accidental discharge. (Some men—especially those who were constantly on the alert for danger—did load all six cylinders; it was, after all, an extra shot.) Breakenridge said that Ringo's socks and the torn shirt strips wrapped around his feet "showed that he had walked some distance," but the Statement for the Coroner declared flatly that "he had evidently travelled but a short distance in this foot gear."

Another item that is rarely mentioned adds significantly to the puzzle of John Ringo's death: his rifle. The rifle was found leaning against the tree next to his body. If, as Breakenridge contends, Ringo, crazed with thirst, could not locate the water that flowed at his feet, how could he have had the presence of mind to place his rifle carefully against the tree before sitting down? And why would Ringo have carelessly left his boots hanging on his saddle when he had thoughtfully pulled his rifle from its scabbard? He was supposed to have been befogged with booze. A man capable of making rational judgments and expecting danger keeps all weapons at hand. He also keeps his boots on unless, as the old saw goes, he hankered to "die with 'em off"; or unless they hurt his feet and were close to hand. One as "crazed with thirst" as Ringo presumably was would doubtless have dropped his rifle out on the desert. If he could not have seen a stream of water, he could not have seen to shoot. And in such painful, even desperate, circumstances, the rifle would have been an intolerable burden.

There are too many flaws in Breakenridge's story, flaws too obvious and flagrant to have been overlooked by a lawman who, from time to time, expressed a certain pride in his sleuthing abilities. One is left again with the inescapable feeling that something is very wrong here. Either what Cunningham called that "steel trap mind" had developed a weak spring or the old deputy failed to anticipate the continuing interest in Tombstone, the Earps, and John Ringo. Perhaps, too, it never occurred to him that anyone might study the topography of the death-and-grave site against his narrative. Inevitably, when one considers Breakenridge's antipathy towards the Earps and his provable distortions of other events, thoughts of some sort of cover-up occur, the possibility of which will be examined under the Wyatt Earp theory.

In a letter to the *Epitaph*, November 28, 1929, Judge J. C. Hancock, the creator of "Old Cack" (Curly Bill as the Montana candy-man), wrote that there is "no doubt but what he [Ringo] committed suicide, as I had a long talk with Robert M. Boller of Ajo, Arizona; and he was one of the men who was on the inquest and helped bury Ringo, he told me there was no question but what John had committed suicide." Hancock was an unreliable, if imaginative, source of information. Robert Boller, although he did serve on the inquest and helped to bury Ringo, was not much better. In a deposition to Mrs. George F. Kitt of the Arizona Pioneers Historical Society he claimed that he knew more about the law than Breakenridge, that he knew the Earps and Holliday in Dodge City (when he would have been thirteen or fourteen years old), that he theorized Ringo had the D.T.'s and thought he had "snakes in his boots" (why would one hang boots full of "snakes" over one's saddle horn?), and, finally, that Ringo's sister had removed his body to California.[7]

Joe Chisholm took Breakenridge's soporific account of Ringo's death and transformed it into a demise befitting a

robber baron of the border, a ten-hour, desert-crawling ordeal.
Unhorsed (by Chisholm's reasoning, at dawn), Ringo lurched
forward on

> bleeding [and] tortured feet, . . . rousing the desicated horn
> toads to swift flight across the Caliche, . . . setting locusts to
> . . . a vibrating clamor that assaulted his tympana. . . .
>
> The tongue swells until it completely fills the oral cavity
> ["mouth" is much too prosaic for this kind of death], which
> becomes as rough as sandpaper, grates against the equally
> harsh mouth-roof so that the victim can hear the scraping
> sound within his burning head. . . .
>
> The whole body becomes a pulsating furnace, even the
> eyeballs so heated and bloodshot that sight fails almost wholly,
> beholding only molten glare. . . .
>
> [Since Mrs. Smith did not hear the shot that ended Ringo's
> life until two o'clock in the afternoon], ten hours of scorching,
> suffocating travail in that incandescent semi-desert . . . surely
> had eliminated all the alcohol in his body; . . . literally it had
> been burned out of him. . . .
>
> Johnny Ringo had done the only thing possible to his suf-
> fering brain. And the irony of his terrible end is that he sat
> within sound of running water. Audible, that is, to a man
> whose senses had not been obliterated by ten hours of an-
> guish."[8]

As in Breakenridge's account, Ringo's gun is caught in his
watch chain. *Not* in Breakenridge's account—or in the Statement for the Coroner, either—is Chisholm's claim of Ringo's
brains "spattering the tree trunks" or of Robert Boller's "digging the slug out of the wood."[9]

Joe Chisholm's manuscript exemplifies the truly rotten
core of western writing. His account of Ringo's ten-hour ordeal on that "scorching," "suffocating," "blazing," "incandes-
cent semi-desert," as he struggles along on "tortured [and]
bleeding" feet is fiction *ad nauseum*. The Statement for the
Coroner does not mention bloody socks, a swollen tongue,
cracked lips, or other evidence of dehydration. But we are to

believe that, purged of all alcohol and all natural bodily juices, gazing at a world turned molten through blood-red eyeballs, John Ringo "had taken the only way out." [10] Somehow Ringo's valiant, ten-hour battle for life against the desert seems something of a contradiction, too, since Chisholm declared at the beginning of this childish little fiction that "the only woman he [Ringo] ever loved was Lady Death." [11] Why meet his "love" in such deplorable condition? He could have done it at rosy-fingered dawn when he awakened to find that his horse had run off.

One Chisholm seems to deserve another in the annals of Tombstone and Cochise County, and, of course, Daniel Fore (Texas Jim) Chisholm had *his* version of John Ringo's death: Charles Thomas (a member of the Curly Bill Gang), Ringo, Wes Fuller, and others were drinking heavily. Ringo became despondent, and he and Thomas headed for Galeyville (Breakenridge, it will be recalled, said he met Ringo riding alone):

> Finally, as he [Thomas] and Ringo were making their way through . . . Turkey Creek Canyon, Ringo chose a secluded, shady spot among some live-oak trees, dismounted and sat for a few moments. . . . Then, before Thomas realized what Ringo intended doing, the outlaw killer, who had once known BETTER days, pulled his six-gun, placed the muzzle against his temple and pulled the trigger.
>
> The spot where Ringo chose to "end it all," was not far from Skeleton Canyon, the place where he and his outlaw companions had murdered and robbed the Mexican smugglers. [12]

The bewildered Thomas carried no tools with which to dig a grave (as they always do in television westerns), and, fearing to be found near the body, he fled. Texas Jim, of course, got the story from Charles Thomas himself. This yarn is at least as plausible as Joe Chisholm's and at least Texas Jim made it up himself, even if he was a bit careless with his geography:

Ringo's death site is a long way from Skeleton Canyon, which runs from New Mexico's Animas Valley through the Peloncillo Mountains and on into Arizona's San Simon Valley, far east of Galeyville *and* the Chiricahuas.

The newspapers of the day concurred in the suicide theory: "King of the Cowboys Sends a Bullet Through his Brain," headlined the Tucson *Daily Star*.[13] "The circumstances of the case," observed the *Epitaph*, "hardly leave any room for doubt as to his self-destruction."[14]

ᕟᕐᖇᐃᕊᖇᐃ

One cannot imagine a nickname more regionally stereotyped, or to the popular magazine writers more redolent of the Old West, than "Johnny-Behind-the-Deuce." Johnny, whose real name was John O'Rourke, was one of those peripheral characters whose life touched briefly, but irrevocably, on two of Tombstone's most prominent figures: Wyatt Earp and John Ringo. Like Buckskin Frank Leslie, O'Rourke's origins and end are near blanks. Reputedly run out of another Arizona mining district, Johnny landed in Charleston, Arizona, where he was known as a tinhorn gambler and an "insignificant runt."[15] He was a suspect in the robbery of W. P. Schneider's cabin.[16] Schneider, a burly and somewhat arrogant man, was chief engineer of the Corbin Mill near Charleston. According to the *Epitaph*, Schneider did not care much for "one of his [Johnny's] character"[17] in general, and he was probably angry over Johnny's possible implication in the robbery of his cabin. Whatever their reasons, the *Epitaph* reported, the two men had words in a restaurant. When Schneider left the restaurant after eating his dinner, Johnny-Behind-the-Deuce (secreted behind something more substantial, one assumes), "with hell in his heart and death in his mind drew deadly aim and dropped his victim dead in his tracks."[18] Stuart Lake and William Breakenridge concur in the belief that the shooting took place in Quinn's Saloon, which may also have doubled as a restaurant. But Lake claimed that Schneider, a heavy loser in an all-night gambling spree and angered by one of Johnny's sarcastic allusions to his obvious lack of gambling talent, pulled a knife and Johnny shot him.[19] Breakenridge called it "cold-blooded murder."[20]

However it happened and in whatever establishment, Schneider was dead, and Charleston Constable George McKelvey put O'Rourke under arrest. In a short time a mob gathered and McKelvey was obliged to hustle Johnny off to Tombstone for protection, covering part of the distance on a commandeered thoroughbred mare.[21] And here one of the great stories of the Old West comes into bitter and angry debate: did Wyatt Earp closet Johnny-Behind-the-Deuce in Vogan's Saloon (sometimes referred to as a bowling alley) as his biographer, Stuart Lake, claimed, and with a double-barreled, sawed-off shotgun stand off a bloodthirsty Tombstone lynch mob? Or, as Frank Waters related in *The Earp Brothers of Tombstone*, was Johnny quietly protected from a merely curious, gathering crowd by city marshal Ben Sippy, who, without serious incident, hauled him off to jail in Tucson?

The Johnny-Behind-the-Deuce affair had further implications: although there is no documented proof of it, Lake claimed that John Ringo was one of the leaders of the lynch mob. And Johnny, gazing out at the mob in terror from behind the protective figure of Wyatt Earp, spotted Ringo. When the mob dispersed, Earp took Johnny to the Tucson jail. Some months later—the night of April 17, 1881, to be exact—Johnny escaped and was never seen again. But Lake wrote that Wells, Fargo agent Fred Dodge used the escaped Johnny as a scout or informer and claimed that when the little gambler, who had been camping in the Chiricahuas, "chanced on John Ringo, boiled drunk and sleeping it off under the oak trees along Turkey Creek, Johnny-Behind-the-Deuce played a sure thing and shot Ringo through the head."[22] Lake reasoned that Johnny thus settled two scores: revenge on John Ringo for trying to lynch him, and a rather conclusive expression of gratitude to Wyatt Earp for saving his life. Fred Dodge and western historian Phil Rasch concur in Lake's belief.

What gives this argument authority is Fred Dodge's flat statement to Stuart Lake. Lake apparently was pursuing the rumor (to be considered later in this chapter) that General Henry C. Hooker had hired Wyatt or a professional gunman to kill John Ringo:

> No, Wyatt did not kill John Ringo. You are right Wyatt had left Arizona some little time. . . .
>
> John Ringo was found dead sitting up with his back to a tree, where he had been placed. Johnny-Behind-the-Deuce murdered him. There was bad blood between the two and Johnny-Behind-the-Deuce was afraid of Ringo. Johnny was not in the same class as Ringo. So Johnny made a sure thing of it and murdered Ringo. This all worked through friends of both parties. Johnny went the same way. I did know H.C. Hooker, but do not know anything about his daughter-in-law, but I am willing to bet all the Cheap Pools that she never got the Ringo End from Wyatt."[23]

Undercover agent Dodge was on the scene. He was not only an able and indefatigable detective himself, he was also privy to almost everything that went on among the outlaws through his Charleston contact, J.B. Ayers (who was also a Wells, Fargo agent, according to Dodge). It was Dodge who heard from Ike Clanton that Wyatt Earp had killed Curly Bill at Iron Springs and had fatally wounded Johnny Barnes (Barnes, Dodge learned, was the one who had ambushed and crippled Virgil Earp). Dodge's statement then, direct and unequivocal as it is, would appear to be the final word on the death of John Ringo. And yet the statement raises questions: Ringo was not found with his "back to a tree where he had been placed." He was found sitting in the bole of the spreading blackjack, and there is no proof or even evidence to suggest that he was "placed" there. And since the tree was a known resting place (complete with a flat-rocked seat), whoever "placed" him there obviously intended that the body be found and declared a suicide. Would little Johnny-Behind-the-Deuce, who "was afraid of Ringo," have dared lug the big outlaw's body* to the tree (presumably after tossing him across the back of a horse), place the gun in his right hand, and then cast doubt on the probability of suicide by hacking off a gobbet of scalp—all within sound (and possibly sight) of the Smith home? And why was Johnny-Behind-the-Deuce, who had escaped from the Tucson jail in April of 1881, still in the Chiricahuas in mid-July of 1882, more than a year later? If there was "bad blood" between him and Ringo, any one of Ringo's friends or Ringo himself might have run onto him and killed him. In addition, he was wanted for murder and escape. The notion advanced that there was no warrant for him in Cochise County—that his crime had been committed when the area was Pima County—is absurd. A warrant could have been and would have been issued for him immediately upon his appearance or his discovery. He obviously knew that and so hid out—if, indeed, he was in the Chiricahuas at all. Had he been caught, he could have been hanged or consigned for life to one of those brutal rock cells hacked out of a cliff at the Yuma Territorial Prison. Common sense should have sent him galloping clear out of the country. The intimation, of course, is that he had been recruited by Fred Dodge (who helped him to "escape"?) to spy on the outlaws. Dodge, in turn, would have had to keep Johnny in supplies—for more than a year. (The little tinhorn would hardly have dared to shop in Galeyville.)

And why was there "bad blood" between O'Rourke and Ringo? Ostensibly the reference is to that lynch mob. But Ringo has never been clearly identified as even being a member of that mob, much less its leader. According to Stuart Lake, Johnny-Behind-the-Deuce told Wyatt Earp that the

* Ringo was reputedly six feet two or three inches tall and weighed one hundred ninety pounds, according to Charles R. Ringo. Enna Ringo was Charles' source for this physical description.

approaching Charleston mob was headed by "John Ringo and other cowboys . . . ,"[24] but (again according to Lake) Earp did not pinpoint Ringo in the mob; Lake quotes Earp as saying some fifty years later:

> The most dangerous mob in the world is a leaderless one, for the reason that there's no one on whom you can pin anything. The crowd that wanted to lynch Johnny-Behind-the-Deuce had shown no leader, so I picked one for them, and gave him a few assistants. There in the front row with a rifle in his hand was Dick Gird, multi-millionaire, employer of half the men at his back. . . . "Nice mob you've got, Mr. Gird." He swung his gun muzzle on the mine owner's belly. "If I have to get anyone, Mr. Gird . . . you're first. Three or four will go down with you." He named the men at Gird's right and left in the same matter-of-fact fashion.[25]

We are not told who the other men were, but Johnny-Behind-the-Deuce would seem to have had a better case against Dick Gird then against John Ringo.

Fred Dodge's succinct observation that Johnny-Behind-the-Deuce "went the same way" as Ringo is clarified to a certain extent in Lake's account. "Pony Deal and John Yoast," he wrote, "found Ringo's body. Deal, who was an outlaw friend of Ringo's, later hunted Johnny down and killed him. Ranchers who found and buried Johnny at the edge of Sulphur Springs Valley did not know they had planted the 'legendary' Johnny-Behind-the-Deuce." Pony Deal, Lake said, was killed soon afterward in a gunfight near Clifton, Arizona.[26] But Pony Deal's name does not appear on the Statement for the Coroner, and Yoast alone is stated to be the finder of Ringo's body. There is no record that Pony Deal (also spelled Diehl or Diel) was killed in a gunfight near Clifton; Deal, whose real name, according to Phil Rasch, seems to have been Charles Ray, apparently drifted into New Mexico, where he joined the Kinney rustler gang. He was arrested, tried in Las

Cruces in April of 1884, found guilty of rustling, and sentenced to prison.[27]

I am not sure what "all the Cheap Pools" were that Fred Dodge was willing to bet that General Hooker's daughter-in-law "did not get the Ringo End from Wyatt," but Dodge, who died in 1938, probably never learned that Wyatt did, indeed, claim to have killed John Ringo.

In his article "Johnny Ringo! The Elusive Man Behind the Myth," Jack DeMattos declares in his note section that Fred Dodge's account of John Ringo's death "naturally . . . does not add up (for reasons why, see note 15)."[28] Unfortunately, the note 15 to which we are directed cites Frank Waters's claim in *The Earp Brothers of Tombstone* that no lynch mob threatened Johnny-Behind-the-Deuce; there was only "a group of rubbernecking miners who had just knocked off from their shift."[29] Johnny thus had no reason to kill Ringo: no mob. Had DeMattos compared the full text of the *Epitaph's* coverage (January 17, 1881) of that mob scene to Waters's editing of it, he would have seen that there was, indeed, a mob out to lynch Johnny-Behind-the-Deuce (whether or not Ringo was part of it). Less excusable is DeMattos's flat assertion that "Wyatt Earp played no part in this situation at all."[30] To any Tombstone researcher, the *Epitaph, Nugget,* and William Breakenridge's *Helldorado* are the most immediate primary sources. One begins with them. Except for the 1976 publication of Josephine Earp's *I Married Wyatt Earp* and Fred Dodge's *Under Cover for Wells, Fargo* (1969), Breakenridge is the only participant in the Tombstone saga who left a full-length memoir.[31] And even though Breakenridge thoroughly disliked Wyatt Earp ("They [the Earps and Doc Holliday] got on my nerves, strutting because they had Wyatt behind them. Nobody else amounted to a thing")[32], on page 111 of *Helldorado* he not only refers to a "mob," he credits Wyatt Earp with "holding them off with a shotgun, and [daring] them to come and get him." Breakenridge does not mention Ringo as a member of the mob.

In an unpublished and undated typescript titled "The Mysterious Death of John Ringo," historian Phil Rasch offered the only semi-analytical approach to John Ringo's death. Rasch believed Johnny-Behind-the-Deuce was the killer; he based his conclusions on the wording of the Statement for the Information of the Coroner and Sheriff, which, he says, "suggests that none of the cartridges in Ringo's revolver had been fired."[33] (Rasch does not address the illogic of the Statement's general indication of suicide if there had *not* been an expended round in Ringo's pistol). That "suggestion," along with the removal of a small section of Ringo's scalp, persuades Rasch that Ringo did not commit suicide. "This," he theorizes, "suggests that someone removed a trophy after killing him."[34] Rasch does not question Ringo's presence in the lynch mob, but neither does he appear to be entirely convinced that O'Rourke deliberately selected Ringo for his singular act of retribution, nor does he wonder why the tinhorn hung out in the Chiricahuas for over a year after his escape from jail. "The supposition," he continues, "is that O'Rourke came upon Ringo asleep [while just wandering aimlessly about?] and saw his chance for vengeance upon one of the men who had so nearly succeeded in getting him lynched." Inferentially, O'Rourke would have shot *anyone* whom he had seen in that mob, had the opportunity so happily presented itself. "The truth of the matter," Rasch concluded, "will probably never be known. It is the writer's opinion that the theory that O'Rourke killed Ringo is the most plausible of those yet proposed—the only one which seems to account for all the facts."[35]

Rasch's brief analysis of John Ringo's death is an oversimplification. Too many questions remain unresolved or even unaddressed to justify Rasch's conclusion that Johnny-Behind-the-Deuce killed Ringo because that is the only theory that "seems to account for all the facts." Why, one wonders, if Ringo was just unlucky enough to be the one member of that mob that Johnny-Behind-the-Deuce caught napping did Fred Dodge say there was "bad blood between the two" and that "Johnny was afraid of Ringo?" Did something besides Ringo's presence in the mob cause that "bad blood"? If there is anything to Dodge's statement, the possibility of coincidence or happenstance in Johnny's "killing" of Ringo is largely eliminated. How do we know Johnny was actually still in the territory?* And if he was, would he have hung around after shooting Ringo, whose body had been left in a conspicuous spot, inviting quick revenge from Pony Deal or another of Ringo's friends, unless he *had* been recruited by Dodge—and promised protection—to keep tabs on Ringo or on the rustlers in general? And if so, why did Dodge fail to protect him?

Reasoning from that possibility both backward and forward, it is *possible* that Dodge arranged Johnny's "escape" from jail through the offices of Wells, Fargo. It is possible, too, that after the "killing" of Ringo Johnny's death and burial were faked. His disappearance was simply too vague and too tidy. Did Dodge, then, have a personal hand in the "killing"? And why did Johnny-Behind-the-Deuce wait for more than a year to take his revenge, if revenge was, indeed, a motive? Was Johnny a scapegoat, a sacrificial lamb? Or did John O'Rourke settle down peaceably in another territory or state, serene in his knowledge that Johnny-Behind-the-Deuce was "dead" and "buried"? We are left to puzzle over whether or not Johnny left the territory and returned, possibly by pre-arrangement with Dodge, or whether he actually hung out in the Chiricahuas for over a year, risking capture by the law or being killed by outlaws (or even by Apaches). John Ringo may very well have been killed, but the case for Johnny-Behind-the-Deuce as his killer is not a particularly convincing one. If Ringo was wanted badly enough to merit such intricate plotting—and there is no evidence that he was—Dodge could

---

* No corpus of Johnny-Behind-the-Deuce was ever produced; there are no details of his burial, nor of the "ranchers" who buried him, nor of the burial site, which was not marked.

simply have arrested him. And why pick a man to do the killing who was scared silly of his intended victim?

Frank Lockwood was the first person to my knowledge to reveal Wyatt Earp's claim to having killed John Ringo. Lockwood's research for *Pioneer Days in Arizona* seems to have consisted almost entirely of old-timer interviews and stories which he judged to be either "blunt, unadorned" accounts, as in the case of Breakenridge's *Helldorado*, or "suave and crafty dissimulations," as in the person of Wyatt Earp, whom he interviewed in Los Angeles shortly before Earp's death. Referring sarcastically to "transient writers seeking mere melodramatic effect . . . [who] elicit stories from old timers . . . [and] then *misdate,* erroneously locate, and embellish these stories to suit their own purpose," Lockwood then goes on to do a little erroneous misdating of his own. "Earp," Lockwood wrote, "told me in circumstantial detail of how he killed both Curly Bill and John Ringo. . . . It was during his hurried escape from Arizona that Wyatt Earp claims to have killed Curly Bill and John Ringo."[36] (One wonders why Wyatt claimed to have killed both of these men "during his hurried escape from Arizona," when it was a matter of record that Ringo was killed or committed suicide two and one-half months after the killing of Curly Bill—and, thus, long after Earp's "hurried escape." Earp presumably made the claim to Lockwood during the interview in Los Angeles, some forty years after the event.)

Wyatt Earp did, indeed, get Curly Bill during his "hurried escape from Arizona," and for reasons of his own he might have just tossed John Ringo in with the catch. But we know that Earp left Arizona in late April, 1882, and that Ringo was killed or committed suicide in mid-July, so the dates just don't work out. Lockwood, the historian, the imperious critic of those who write or embellish stories "to suit their own purpose[s]," did not take note of this two-and-one-half month discrepancy between Earp's departure and the "killing" of Ringo. It suited his purpose to believe entirely in Breakenridge. "Breakenridge," he wrote, "shows conclusively that Earp did not kill either of these men."[37] Quite possibly Lockwood was misled by Breakenridge's unfathomable claim to have met John Ringo on the day of his death and "shortly after Behan returned from his unsuccessful trip after the Earp Crowd." In *Helldorado* Breakenridge indicated the date of Ringo's death, but he ventured no comment on the date—or even the month—that the Earp party left Arizona. Lockwood obviously did not bother to check Breakenridge's stories against available newspaper accounts and records. Lockwood's reliance on a single, obviously prejudiced source is academically indefensible; it is the more inexcusable because of his sanctimonious condemnation of other writers.

Never one to quibble over words, Phil Rasch states bluntly that the story that "Ringo was killed by Wyatt Earp . . . rests on the unsupported word of Lockwood, who claimed that Earp himself related the story of the killing 'in circumstantial detail.' The weakness of this version was unwittingly exposed by Lockwood himself when he added that the murder occurred during Earp's 'hurried escape from Arizona.' Earp left Arizona late in April; Ringo was killed in mid-July."[38] Rasch is not quite accurate here. Lockwood did not *add* that the murder took place during Earp's escape from Arizona. He wrote that "it was during the hurried escape . . . that Wyatt Earp claims to have killed . . . John Ringo." Still, as an "embellisher," Lockwood was easily the equal of his fellow "transients"; and he seems to have been their superior in naiveté (Lockwood surely must have known that Ringo was a member of the Behan posse that chased Earp out of Arizona).

John D. Gilchriese is unquestionably an authority on Wyatt Earp. For decades he labored indefatigably in the mesquite vineyards of southeastern Arizona in single-minded resolve to separate the man from the myth. Cochise County and

Tombstone have become his private preserve, his patrimony. The legacy of his historical and literary progenitors, whose excesses and inaccuracies affronted his analytical mind and left him disillusioned, made him determined to bring forth the real man amid the forces, events, and landscapes that relentlessly shaped a strong and determined, if flawed, character. In 1986 Gilchriese's book on Wyatt Earp was nearing completion, a composite, one would hope, of a man and his time faithfully drawn from the objective distillation of this scholar's awesome knowledge of Earpana and from his collection of Earp memorabilia (which is so prodigious it was once housed in his personal museum in Tombstone). We need expect no hero or heel approach here; we shall certainly not be told, as C. L. Sonnichsen laments, tongue in cheek, that to some Wyatt Earp has become "a Christ figure in cowboy boots wielding the thunderbolts of the Almighty."[39]

I have known Gilchriese since my college days in the 1950s. We have had scores of conversations on our mutual interests and we exchanged a small avalanche of letters over the years. I always thought him to be the "document it" kind of historian, the somewhat cynical sort who had so often been misled that he subjected all data to a monumental and enduring exegesis. Gilchriese has long been in possession of a hand-drawn map sketched from memory by Wyatt Earp in his later years. The map, he says, is authentic, and it details the spot where Earp claimed to have killed Ringo and where he left the body in a sitting position against a tree. At the time Gilchriese showed the map to me I thought him to be skeptical of it; I certainly was. Yet in a 1964 feature article by Bob Thomas in the Arizona *Daily Star*, Gilchriese was quoted at length as making a formidable case for the killing of John Ringo by Wyatt Earp:

> I am convinced that Earp could have travelled from Colorado to the Chiricahuas, killed Ringo and travelled back again without being recognized. . . .

Earp could have taken the old Atlantic and Pacific Railroad (Santa Fe) through Raton Pass to East Las Vegas, New Mexico. That would be a day and a night by train. Then he could have ridden horseback from there to Roswell, N.M., skirting the Mescalero country and the western fringes of the Staked Plains.

From Roswell another horseback ride would take him to Lordsburg and from there he would ride straight to the Chiricahuas.

That means about six days by horse and one by train. It could be done.

Why would Wyatt, some 40 years after the killing, draw a map that was quite accurate . . . if he had not had some hand in the killing of Ringo?

[And why would Wyatt Earp undertake so arduous and dangerous a journey?] To avenge the death of Morgan and the maiming of Virgil.

[Then, largely in Wyatt's own words, Gilchriese dramatized the killing of John Ringo:]

Wyatt, on his feet, with his six-gun drawn and aimed, called, "Hello there, John."

Astonished, Ringo whirled and fired a wild shot at Earp. He then started running up a hill at an angle as Earp started blasting away.

"I fired two or three times at him. I think the second shot got him and I ended his career," Wyatt said succinctly.[40]

It would have been a spectacular odyssey, a supreme act of retribution, a test of endurance and determination and pinpoint timing, and all culminating in a cool and open, sure-enough shoot-out, rather than in a cowardly dry-gulching. It is the stuff of high drama and one can see it—*has* seen it—on the wide, wide screen: The steam-belching train, the ear-splitting whistle, a dizzying close-up of the turning wheels and, superimposed on them, the grim face of the passenger; the horseback ride across illimitable and breathtaking landscapes (making a wide, wide circle, of course, to include the carnelian buttes and spires of Monument Valley), the rider pausing to drink sparingly from his canteen in the *saguaroed* ambience of the Old Tucson movie set,* narrowed eyes gazing west as he methodically smacks the stopper back into the canteen with his palm. Giddap!

I think Wyatt Earp was quite capable of trying to do just that; I do not think he did it. First, such split-second timing allowed for no search for Ringo. Earp would have had to go directly to the site, kill his man, and get out. Even a one-day search (and Ringo might have been in Tombstone, Charleston, Galeyville, or even in Mexico) would have disrupted the six-day timetable. One would have to conclude that Earp either had an intricate network of spies along the way who kept him posted on Ringo's every movement (a very remote possibility, and one that his detractors would surely deny) or Ringo would have had to inform him ahead of time of where he would be waiting to get shot. The possibility of telegraph contact from Las Vegas, Roswell, and Lordsburg with sources in Tombstone, Charleston, or Wilcox is equally remote. If Ringo did not happen to be in town when Earp's "message" was received, the recipient could only have guessed at the outlaw's whereabouts. And Earp's timetable would not have permitted a "wait right there, Wyatt, and I'll have a look-see."

Second—and I am on shakier ground here because I am dependent upon a twenty-year-old recollection—Earp's map, as I recall, placed Ringo's body in San Simon, thus inserting the entire Chiricahua Mountain Range between where the body was actually found and where Earp said he left it. (I recall that Gilchriese and I discussed this at the time I saw the map.) One could probably make allowances for a memory lapse over the years, since Earp drew the map "some 40 years after" the event, but there is a difference between a memory lapse involving detailed places and events and the misplacing

---

* A permanent motion-picture set located near Tucson, Arizona.

of an entire mountain range. If Earp killed Ringo, it would have been a profound event in his kind of life, as significant, certainly, as the killing of Curly Bill—more so when one considers the planning, timing, and execution involved (one recalls that Wyatt stumbled onto Curly Bill only by accident). Along with the fight at the O.K. Corral and the fight at Iron Springs, Earp would not likely have forgotten such significant details of his "killing" of John Ringo.[41]

Third, Gilchriese's theory was offered in 1964, five years before the publication of Fred Dodge's *Undercover for Wells Fargo*. I do not know whether Dodge's blunt claim that Johnny-Behind-the-Deuce murdered Ringo or the fact that Earp did not know that Dodge was a Wells, Fargo agent has changed or altered Gilchriese's opinion or theory, but Dodge was no run-of-the-mill yarn spinner; he was a trusted agent, a seeker of anonymity rather than of notoriety, and his claim must be seriously considered. If Johnny-Behind-the-Deuce was a front man it was for Dodge, not for Wyatt Earp. And since Wyatt could not have gone directly to Ringo without assistance in Arizona, one can assume that the assistance did not come from Dodge, who would have been Wyatt's most logical contact. Finally, Earp would never have stalked and surprised Ringo with a six-shooter, an uncertain weapon even in the hands of an expert. Depending on the country, brushy or open, he would have used a shotgun or rifle, as he did with Curly Bill.

Almost as if to complicate the Earp story further, Wyatt, according to Josephine Earp, *named* his Arizona contacts or informants. The occasion arose upon the Earps' receipt of a copy of *Helldorado* and after William Breakenridge's visits to the Earp homes in Vidal (California) and Los Angeles. Wyatt had been reading (and presumably laughing over) Breakenridge's "steel-vest" story.[42] When he came to the section of the book where Ringo's body was found, he asked Josie to read that part. When she had finished, he asked:

"Do you know who Wells, Fargo paid to keep us posted on where we could find Johnny Ringo if he ever got to where he wasn't surrounded by his whole crowd?"

I shook my head in the negative.

"Two people," he said. "One was [Buckskin] Frank Leslie; the other was Billy Breakenridge. And Billy got the money."[43]

At the end of the statement editor Glen Boyer added an editorial comment: *"Do not miss the implication that Wyatt was bounty hunting when he got Ringo."*[44] There, of course, goes Wyatt's nobility of purpose (the avenging of Morgan and Virgil).

There is, obviously, a direct conflict here with Gilchriese's dramatic story of Wyatt's solo odyssey. In Josie's version, Wyatt refers to "us" and "we." Moreover, Gilchriese declared the killing to be an act of vengeance, while Boyer suggests revenge was sweetened by the prospects of a Wells, Fargo bounty. It is not clear, however, whether Breakenridge received the informants' pay *and* the bounty, or either; or if Wyatt Earp received the bounty.[45] And if Wells, Fargo had posted a bounty on John Ringo, would not Dodge have known about it? In fact, would he not have been the one to recommend it? It is illogical to assume that Wells, Fargo would undertake such a plot (assuming it *was* in the bounty business) without consulting its major operative in the area.

Because of their eagerness or determination to credit Wyatt Earp with the killing of John Ringo, John Gilchriese and Glenn Boyer overlooked several important points: both claimed the "killing" was at least partly an act of revenge for Ringo's supposed involvement in the shotgunning and maiming of Virgil and the later murder of Morgan. Yet Ringo's name does not appear on the arrest warrants issued in either case. Those named were Frank Stilwell, Florentino Cruz (alias Indian Charlie), Hank Swilling, Peter Spence, and [Jacob?] Freis. Second, Virgil was gunned down the night of December 28, 1881 (see Chapter 2 for details). Three weeks later, on January 17, 1882, John Ringo challenged Wyatt and Doc Holliday to that shoot-out in the middle of Tombstone's Allen Street. If Wyatt was, as Josephine Earp claimed, absolutely positive that Ringo was one of the men who had ambushed his brother Virgil (see Chapter 7), why didn't he accept the challenge, since he might have killed Ringo legitimately in self-defense? Or why didn't he take Ringo sometime during the two months that elapsed between Ringo's challenge and the killing of Morgan Earp in Tombstone on March 17, 1882? When one considers the single-minded determination and courage it would have taken to make the arduous sixteen-hundred-mile round trip from Colorado to Arizona to get his man, it is impossible not to believe that Wyatt would have killed Ringo before leaving Arizona. Ringo was provably in and out of Tombstone during the period between the shooting of Virgil and the murder of Morgan.

Boyer's suggestion that Wyatt was doing a spot of "bounty hunting" doesn't really seem to make sense. First of all, there is no record that Wells, Fargo ever posted a bounty for John Ringo. Second, if Wyatt was bounty hunting, why would he try to make the "killing" appear a suicide? Third, how could Wyatt have claimed a bounty for a declared suicide? And fourth, Wyatt did not claim the "kill" until more than twenty years after the event. The implication, of course, is that the bounty was offered (and probably paid) in secrecy. But how was the reward transmitted? Not through Dodge, who claimed that Wyatt did not know he was a Wells, Fargo agent, and who declared Johnny-Behind-the-Deuce to be Ringo's killer. In addition, it is inconceivable that Wells, Fargo would have contracted with Earp in Colorado to become a hired killer without working through Dodge—most especially since at this time Earp was himself a fugitive from the law in Arizona.

A further note on Breakenridge is in order here. Josie's charges are serious ones. In present-day parlance, she has declared that Wyatt said Breakenridge was the "finger" who betrayed his friend Ringo for the reward, with no risk either to his person or to his reputation. One could make a case for believing Josie. Breakenridge's story of Ringo's suicide, as we have seen, is unsupportable—the more so because he was a lawman and it bears the tone of a coverup. It should be remembered, too, that we have no record of what, if anything, Breakenridge said or thought of Ringo's death at the time it happened; we have only his story forty-six years after the fact. In addition, his "steel-vest" story, his attempts to prove Wyatt did not kill Curly Bill, his one-sided account of the O.K. Corral fight, his solicitation of the Earps' help and the use of their facilities in California at the time he was preparing to impugn Wyatt in *Helldorado*, reveal an ambivalence and dishonesty that is not difficult to relate to betrayal. Perhaps even his praise for John Ringo as college graduate, gentleman, and fearless gunfighter was merely a diversion. If Breakenridge did, in fact, "finger" John Ringo, his place in history is properly beside Bob Ford (who betrayed Jesse James) and Cock-Eyed Jack McCall (who murdered Wild Bill Hickok), rather than among the Old West's fearless lawmen. Fred Dodge detested him, considered *Helldorado* a fiction, and bluntly declared both Breakenridge and Sheriff John Behan to have been in league with the outlaw element. Throughout his long life Breakenridge maligned Wyatt Earp, suggesting again and again that the fight at O.K. Corral was premeditated murder.

Later writers and those who knew "Billy" in his great age adored him. Tombstone historian and old-timer Ethyl Macia told me at length (in personal conversations in 1956) what a fine and honest gentleman Billy was. Walter Noble Burns was immensely impressed by him. Frank Lockwood seems to have thought him infallible. Eugene Cunningham, reacting indignantly to the suggestion that Billy and Johnny Behan had acted to protect the outlaw element from the Earps, declared, "And that a man of Breakenridge's character . . . as it was made plain to Arizona during some sixty years of residence there . . . would have been willing to side even with Behan

in a shady trick . . . I do not, cannot, believe!"[46] Of course,
Cunningham's exclamatory declaration was purely an emotional one; it was not a historical statement. He was in no
position to judge an old man's youthful character. What a man
is at eighty is in no sense of the word conclusive evidence of
what he was at thirty. Nor could Cunningham presume to
speak for Arizona's view, if Arizona *had* a view, of Breakenridge over a sixty-year period. Tombstone's deputy, the white-
haired and bespectacled old Billy, the epitome of homespun
rectitude and incorruptibility who made "dusty facts twin-
kle," just might have been the "suavest and craftiest dissimulator" of them all.

Josephine Earp's full story of the killing of John Ringo by
Wyatt does not appear in either *I Married Wyatt Earp* (1976)
or in "Sinister Shadow from the Past," an article published in
True West (1975). Josie's editor, Glenn Boyer, chose to publish
the story in a 1974 edition of the Tombstone *Epitaph*. The
account is long and detailed (Josie obviously thought herself
something of a writer); the important highlights follow. Her
story begins with a 1937 visit to the Chiricahuas and to John
Ringo's grave. As she gave herself over to the "balsam fra-
grance" of those "enchanted mountains" whose pines bore
"spikes bristling like the spears of an army of giants," Josie
fell to reminiscing about "Ringo's passing" and her recollections of

> snatches of conversation between Wyatt and Doc at the Wind-
> sor Hotel in Denver during the eighties. . . . The words I
> recall were Doc's comment, "God, was old John ever surprised
> to see us drop in for supper." But who were "us"? The old
> names came back with difficulty. Wyatt and Doc, of course—
> Fred Dodge? I knew Fred was alive. I made a note to write
> him. That letter led to my visit to the Dodges in Texas[47]. . . .
> Other old names [came back] . . . Charlie Smith—Johnnie
> Green—John Meagher—and finally Doc's old friend from
> Texas, Harry Goober.[48] Seven of them. And in addition three
> informers were being paid [by whom?] to report to Fred

Dodge of the whereabouts of John Ringo—Buckskin Frank [Leslie] and Billy Breakenridge. The third was Johnny O'Rourke. Johnny owed Wyatt a favor. [He was] our old friend from Tombstone, Johnny-Behind-the-Deuce that Wyatt protected . . . from the lynch mob.[49]

The posse entered the country in ones and twos. Wyatt and Doc sporting beards to disguise their well-known features, traveled West on the Atlantic and Pacific R.R., then made their way south . . . by horse. The Hooker's Sierra Bonita Ranch was the rendezvous point, but they camped in the hills. . . .

By night rides Wyatt's little group shifted its camp to the Chiricahuas . . . north of the Galeyville trail.

[Josie then told how she got her story of the killing of John Ringo: Indirectly, generally by listening to conversations, but mostly by shrewd detective work:] . . . I am proud of my ability as a detective, which led me to suspect how Ringo got his. . . . One of my informants told me—I'd have made a good hard-boiled cop the way I sweated what I knew out of him—I'm not talking about Fred Dodge here—though he certainly was helpful and could have told me the whole story himself if he had desired. Fred, when he discovered that he wasn't protecting Wyatt any longer—talked quite freely to me. . . .

Breakenridge got word to Fred Dodge that Ringo was heading into the Chiricahuas, apparently for Galeyville. . . . [There follows an account of how Wyatt and his posse arrived too late to intercept Ringo and were forced to follow him. Wyatt found where John had left the trail and made his way up a secluded canyon, perhaps intending to make camp and sleep off his binge. Though it was getting late, Wyatt decided to stalk his prey, rather than wait for him to come back to the trail in the morning:]

The posse cautiously made its way up the canyon, keeping to the hillsides in order to be above . . . their quarry. Wyatt, Fred and John Meagher were on the west slope, Doc, Johnny Green and Charlie Smith on the east slope.[50]

By a stroke of luck, Wyatt's party spotted the licking

orange tongues of flame from a small fire. . . . The smoke was barely visible—Ringo was making coffee. . . . [Josie interrupted the manhunt at this point for an explication of the posse's intent: they intended to hang John Ringo—and in a conspicuous place. But something, perhaps a bird or his horse, warned Ringo, so] . . . They did not catch John, as they would have preferred, with his pants down, but they did catch him with his boots and shirt off. Sensing danger, John grabbed his pistol and belt [and left his rifle in its scabbard?] . . . and darted for the woods . . . ahead of Wyatt. The posse froze, . . . hoping to lull their quarry into believing he had been startled by a false alarm. There was a tense . . . five minutes. A rock . . . was dislodged by someone on the east slope. . . . Doc's group had kept moving, [and] . . . the passage of the rock to the bottom of the hill must have sounded to the taut-nerved listeners like a freight train.

[The stalk continued. It was growing dark. Ringo, Josie theorized, now wrapped his feet in his undershirt, hoping to escape in the night:] But it was the light colored foot coverings that revealed his movements to his stalkers. Wyatt drew a bead on the spot where he had seen John slip into a patch of brush, . . . holding his sights on the expected exit spot. At that point someone fired. All the posse later denied having fired a shot at all. . . . Ringo had to have fired that shot. Why did he do it? What did he shoot at? Did his thumb accidentally slip off a cocked . . . hammer? . . . Whatever happened, John broke from his cover . . . following the shot and . . . ran uphill. Wyatt took a quick careful lead on him with his rifle and fired. John fell heavily without a sound and lie [sic] still, never so much as jerking after he fell. . . .

So the last of the big bugs among the rustlers cashed in his checks.[51]

Josie went on to wonder if Ringo's upside-down cartridge belt reflected "Doc's sense of humor"; she also said that "the posse stayed to finish Ringo's pot of coffee, then packed John out of there."[52] Presumably they carried Ringo to the tree, where his body was certain to be found.[53] The only regret, apparently, that these casual coffee drinkers experienced was that they had not found and hanged Sheriff Behan. "What a sensational headline it would have made: . . . 'Sheriff Found Mysteriously Hung.'"[54] Josie was still smarting. Had she accompanied the posse and had Behan been caught, he might have got off with a simple gelding.[55]

If Josie's story has the ring of truth to it—and certainly it is at least as logical as John Gilchriese's version—possibly it is because that is the way Wyatt told it to her, at least in part. If she made the story up—and I believe her to have done just that—she was, indeed, an artful liar. But for one given to boasting about her clever detective work, Josie, ironically, relied entirely on Breakenridge, rather than on Wyatt or another posse-man, for her account of the physical evidence of John Ringo's death; in so doing she revealed a very limited reasoning capacity. Like Breakenridge, she took note of Ringo's upside-down cartridge belt, but added a dramatic and diverting touch by wondering if the belt reflected "Doc's sense of humor." Like Breakenridge, she did not mention the removal of a section of Ringo's scalp. And she repeated the bit about the revolver caught in the watch chain, though she was more explicit.*

Since Wyatt killed Ringo in a canyon, according to Josie (after Ringo had fired that mysterious shot, which was probably intended to account for the "exploded" round in his pistol, thus eliminating the possibility of suicide), and the posse lugged his body to the tree on Turkey Creek, who hung Ringo's revolver on his watch chain? It would have made absolutely no sense to do that, if the intent were to make Ringo's death appear to be a suicide, or unless we lay that, too, to Doc's "sense of humor." And if the hammer rested on a "fired cartridge" one would have to believe that the experienced,

---

* Josie stated that ". . . his [Ringo's] pistol was hung on his watch chain with one fired cartridge beneath the hammer. The watch chain was jammed under the uncocked hammer of his pistol so that the weapon was firmly held by it" (Tombstone *Epitaph*, December 20, 1974).

dangerous and fearless Ringo, he who braced both Wyatt and Doc on Tombstone's Allen Street, the man of "bulldog courage," not only panicked so badly at the appearance of Wyatt's posse as to get his revolver tangled in his watch chain when he fired that mysterious shot, he forgot to re-cock it as well, and just kept running with a heavy Army Colt dangling from his watch chain. If a posse-man hung the pistol on the watch chain, the hammer would most likely have rested on a *live* round, had the piece actually been fired, unless he thoughtfully raised the hammer so slightly as to slip the chain under it without rolling the cylinder.

Then there is the question of the shirt, socks, and undershirt. Josie wrote that while the posse would have "preferred to catch Ringo with his pants down, they did catch him with his boots and shirt off." But the Statement for the Information of the Coroner and Sheriff described Ringo as dressed in a "vest, blue shirt, pants and drawers." Did the posse dress his body in the vest and shirt (and then scalp him)? And if so, why? How did Josie know the "foot coverings" which "revealed Ringo's movements to his stalkers" were "light colored"? Presumably Wyatt or another posse member told her. There is no mention of the color of the foot wrappings in the Statement for the Coroner.

Josie simply tried, amateurishly and clumsily, to fit Breakenridge's story (which concluded that Ringo was a suicide) to her own story of Wyatt and his posse.* Had she seen the Statement for the Coroner, she might have spun a far more convincing yarn.

Josie's fiction is also eloquently refuted by both of Doc Holliday's biographers, by Colorado court records, by the unanticipated publication of Dodge's memoirs twenty-five years after her death, and by ballistics: for example, if Wyatt told Josie certain details of the killing—including the presence of

---

* And Wyatt, it will be recalled, told Frank Lockwood that he had killed Ringo during his "hurried escape from Arizona" (Lockwood, *Pioneer Days*, p. 285).

Doc Holliday in the posse—and if Josie, potentially "hard-boiled cop" that she was, "sweated" the whole story out of a Mr. Anonymous, she is still guilty of making up the statement by Holliday that she said she overheard in a conversation between Doc and Wyatt at the Windsor Hotel in Denver: "God, was old John ever surprised to see us drop in for supper." Both of Doc's biographers, John Myers and Pat Jahns, believe that Doc and the Earps split up for good after arriving in Colorado. Pat Jahns declared bluntly that "Doc . . . and Wyatt never saw each other again."[56] And even if the two had got together before and after the killing of Ringo and if there is simply no record of those meetings, Doc still could not have been with the Earp posse in the Tombstone area on July 14, 1882, because the records of the District Court of Pueblo County, Colorado, show that Holliday himself, not just his lawyer, was present in court on July 11, 14, and 18, 1882, as the respondent in a preliminary hearing in a larceny charge against him.[57] Coincidentally, Ringo was killed about the time Doc was making his court appearance.

Josie's little fantasy is just as seriously refuted by Fred Dodge as it is by Colorado court records. Dodge, as we have seen, emphatically denied to Stuart Lake that Wyatt Earp killed Ringo. Yet Josie actually placed him in the Earp posse which hunted Ringo down. Someone lied—and logic, the evidence, and the facts point to Josie. In *Undercover for Wells, Fargo*, Fred Dodge claimed that no one in Tombstone knew he was an agent, not even Wyatt Earp, whom he liked and admired. Why, then, as Josie declared, would William Breakenridge, (whom Dodge believed to be in league with the outlaws), know that Dodge was a Wells, Fargo agent and notify him that Ringo was heading for the Chiricahua Mountains? Dodge could not have risked letting Breakenridge, of all people, know his identity. And, of course, if the Wells, Fargo agent had really wanted Ringo, why not just take him at gunpoint in Tombstone? Ringo had been arrested on a number of occasions in both Texas and Arizona. There is no record of his resisting arrest. He was not hiding out. Why all the intricate planning? Why wait until he was in the mountains, where he might have escaped—if that was his intent—for good?

Finally, there is the question of ballistics and the weapon Wyatt used in the "killing" of Ringo: Josie has him dropping Ringo with a single "cool and skillful" rifle shot. If Wyatt shot Ringo with a rifle and from some distance, the head wound would have been significantly different than the one described in the Statement to the Coroner. The flat trajectory of a .44-40 or .45-70 slug (the rifle calibers most favored in 1882) would tend to slow over the distance and would have begun a slight wobble, or waffle, due in part to slowdown, in part to imperfect rifling. The slug would have flattened on impact, quite probably blowing away half of Ringo's head. The same kind of wound would have been inflicted had Wyatt used a six-gun, a .44 or .45, firing from a distance as Ringo ran (John Gilchriese's version).

The Statement for the Coroner does not mention powder burns or embedded powder grains, but the clean entering wound and the upward course of the bullet clearly indicate that the wound was either self-inflicted or fired by another party who was in a position to press the muzzle against Ringo's head.* Almost invariably a self-inflicted head wound results in an upward passage of the slug. This would be particularly true if the person were using a gun the size of Ringo's. In order to bring a Colt .45 with a seven-and-one-half-inch barrel to bear against the temple (the spot where Ringo was shot), one would have to extend the arm out full length, with elbow crooked and wrist twisted; in such a position, the muzzle would point slightly upward. Had Ringo been shot while

---

* The wound was on the right side of the head, and, according to Ringo's sister Fanny Fern, John was right handed. This information was given to Fanny's nephew, Frank Cushing, who mentioned it to Charles Ringo in discussions the two men had about John's death (Charles Ringo, conversation with author, January, 1972).

sleeping, the assassin, standing, would have fired downward, inflicting an altogether different kind of wound. And because of the all-encompassing nature of the five-trunked tree where Ringo's body was found, the killer would not have been able to get a shot at the right temple unless he had literally stood in Turkey Creek, on Ringo's right, and poked the gun between the trunks. Had Ringo's head been inclined to the left while sleeping, he could have received a wound in the right temple, but the shot would have had to be fired from above, and so the course of the bullet logically would have been downward.

Josie Earp was an enormously conceited and strong-willed woman who might have thought of herself as a writer rather than as a loyal defender of her husband and teller of his story. It is possible she consciously used Wyatt to advance her literary ambitions, rationalizing her exploitation through the heroics she claimed Wyatt demonstrated in leading his posse and in firing the fatal shot. (This was some shot, incidentally—a temple hit on a man who was "running rapidly uphill," at some distance, and in the dim evening light.) Wyatt possibly told her something of the story. She might have learned of it from John H. Flood, a long-time friend of Wyatt's during the old lawman's later years and who, with Wyatt's unenthusiastic collaboration, was preparing his own manuscript on the life and times of Wyatt Earp.[58] However she came by the story and whatever prompted or motivated her to write it, Josie might have got by with it had not Doc—obviously unknown to her—got himself arrested for larceny at such an inopportune time and date (further proof that she and Wyatt had no contact with Doc after they split up in Colorado) and had Fred Dodge's memoirs not been posthumously published.

If one rejects Josie's story, one must also reconsider her description of Breakenridge's role as stool pigeon or "finger" man in the killing of John Ringo. Along with heroizing Wyatt and demonstrating her own literary talents, Josie doubtless saw the chance to discredit "Billy-Blab"* for his own attempt to discredit Wyatt in *Helldorado*. But Billy was half a dozen years beyond retribution when Josie wrote her piece ("Gone," as Eugene Cunningham put it in the old deputy's obituary, ". . . on that trail where the pony tracks point all one way. . .).[59] But if Breakenridge cannot be accused of being a stool pigeon in this particular instance, it is not, in my opinion, because of any sturdy code of frontier ethics or values he bore. He might not have betrayed John Ringo (there is no record, at least, of his receiving the reward and Dodge would never have used him as an informer); that he had his price, however, is all too obvious in his exploitation of Wyatt Earp for the greater sales of *Helldorado*. And exculpation in the peripheral and treacherous role Josie assigned to him with her mythic posse does not in any way explain his own unacceptable story of John Ringo's death.

According to the official record, Nashville "Buckskin Frank" Leslie killed two men in Tombstone: Mike Killeen—a bartender whose widow he later married and whom he immortalized among the tall tales of the Old West by reputedly etching her live silhouette against their bedroom wall with bullet holes—and Billy "The Kid" Claiborne ("The Kid" part was self-proclaimed)—former cowboy for John Slaughter, worshipful hanger-on around the outlaws and a pot-valiant little would-be gunfighter who went to the O.K. Corral with the Clantons and McLaurys, and sprinted off (even ahead of Ike Clanton) when the shooting began. Leslie's third kill was a woman, his common-law wife, Mollie.

Leslie reputedly admitted the killing of John Ringo to Yuma Penetentiary guard Frank King,[60] when he was

---

* According to Glenn Boyer, editor of *I Married Wyatt Earp*, Josie often referred to Billy Breakenridge as "Billy Blab," and she believed that his "latter-day reputation as Tombstone's deputy was self-generated" (p. 71).

incarcerated there after killing Mollie. In *Tombstone*, Walter Noble Burns upped Buckskin Frank's man-tally to fourteen (pp. 266–267) and dramatized a story of Leslie as he was seen by William Sanders, Sr., galloping hard on Ringo's last trail (p. 277): Ringo had been drinking with Buckskin Frank Leslie and Billy Claiborne. The drinking led to the shooting of Ringo by Leslie, which act was witnessed by Claiborne, who later challenged Buckskin Frank (presumably after much brooding over the "murder of Ringo") and was killed.* Claiborne's reputed last words accused Leslie of murdering Ringo, but the story seems to be another of Tombstone's tall tales. Of Breakenridge, Behan, and Dodge, none considered Leslie a possibility in the death of John Ringo, and it is probable that Leslie hatched the story himself while in Yuma, hoping that his claim, if taken seriously, might earn him a reduction of sentence. It was not, and did not. Breakenridge believed that Leslie made up the story in an effort to "curry favor with the Earp sympathizers, . . . but the evidence proved this to be a lie. We all know Leslie would not care to tackle him [Ringo] even when he was drunk."[61]

As usual, Breakenridge's statement calls up questions which receive no clarification from him: why would Leslie try to "curry favor" with the "Earp sympathizers"? The Earps were gone. They were no longer a power in Tombstone or in Cochise County, not to mention Yuma Penitentiary. What possible benefits could such "currying" have brought his way? That "evidence" which proved Leslie's claim a "lie" (presumably the inquest evidence) also, as we have seen, proved Breakenridge a liar, as attested by a quick comparison of the Statement for the Coroner with Breakenridge's story. And Breakenridge's declaration that Leslie would not "tackle" Ringo "even when he was drunk" is unconvincing. Buckskin

---

* Of Billy Claiborne's death, the Tombstone *Epitaph* of November 19, 1882, headlined: "'Billy the Kid' Takes a Shot of 'Buckskin Frank' The Latter Promptly Replied and the Former Quietly Turns His Toes Up to the Daisies."

Frank Leslie was a gunman and killer. He did not hesitate to step outside with a pistol and confront Claiborne, who was using a rifle. Leslie had a known record. Ringo had none, at least no record so intimidating that a man like Leslie would be afraid to shoot him when he was dead drunk. If Fred Dodge believed that timid little Johnny-Behind-the-Deuce could pot a drunken Ringo, why would Breakenridge think Leslie would be afraid to do the same thing? And Ringo had not exactly proven himself the soul of inebriated dexterity and accuracy in his clumsy effort to shoot Louis Hancock. The notion that a man like Frank Leslie would be afraid to shoot a drunken Ringo is, of course, absurd. The note of contempt for Leslie in Breakenridge's statement leads on to suspect the deputy of withholding information, possibly because Leslie's claim conflicted with his own story of Ringo's suicide.

For one who claimed to know so much about Ringo and who lived so near the death site, it is odd that the name of William Sanders (Sr.) does not appear in the Report for the Coroner (which mentions only the Smith ranch). However, if Sanders did see Frank Leslie riding hard on Ringo's trail into the Chiricahuas, it is possible that he did kill the outlaw. Sander's claim is more plausible than Josephine Earp's. He was at least on the scene, not eight hundred miles away in Colorado. And his claim is not burdened with geographical and physical contradictions and errors, as Josie's and Breakenridge's stories are. It is a flat claim, without elaboration and difficult to prove or refute. However, I suspect it received a certain credibility on the part of Walter Noble Burns, who may or may not have heard the story from Sanders. *

In any case, Burns's account of Ringo's death is so riddled with errors as to be useless. He wrote that Ringo's "brains were scattered over the tree trunks"; the Statement for the Coroner mentions no such thing. He declared Jim Morgan to be the finder of Ringo's body; the Statement of the Coroner

---

* The Sanders house was built in 1885, and it is very unlikely that Henry Sanders saw Ringo's body.

names John Yoast. He repeats Breakenridge's story of Ringo's gun being caught in his watch chain; the Statement for the Coroner said "His revolver he grasped in his right hand." Finally, Burns wrote that "Jim Morgan, Theodore White, and Bill Knott, acting as a Coroner's jury, decided the death was suicide----"[62] Fourteen men actually made that indirect determination and signed the Statement for the Coroner, including James Morgan and *Thomas* White; the name of Bill Knott is not among them. It should be noted here that Burns once told Ethyl Macia that he "was not writing the history of Tombstone, but a story *based on* the history of Tombstone."[63]

One final claimant—or rather, one for whom the claim was made—to the killing of John Ringo remains the most shadowy of all of Tombstone's notorious, or near-notorious, figures. His name was Lou Cooley,* and he was a rider, perhaps a hired gunman, for General Henry C. Hooker. Hooker's Sierra Bonita Ranch had been heavily rustled by the Curly Bill–Ringo gang, and it was Hooker who refused to give the Behan outlaw posse any help in its pursuit of the Earps (see Chapter 2). Hooker, it was rumored, although there is no documentation of it, had hired Wyatt Earp to kill Curly Bill, and Earp was paid for the killing when he passed through the Sierra Bonita Ranch on his way out of Arizona. That left John Ringo unaccounted for and the job fell to Cooley. At least one old-timer thought Cooley did the job. His name is Ed J. Cornelison and here is his story:

> . . . Ringo was found dead about three months after Curly [Bill]. He was found in a remote canyon. He had been scalped and shot in the brain. If it was Apaches they would have taken his gun and ammunition and everything else. The Coroner

* No relation to Scott Cooley of Texas, who figured prominently in the Hoodoo War.

said it was suicide but nobody believed that [it] was. Some said Buckskin Frank Leslie had killed him as they had been on bad terms for some time and had argued quite a lot and did not like each other. But many said it was done by Hooker's men who had a ranch in that area. A quick man named Cooly [Lou Cooley] was kept on by Hooker to deal with such things. Later Jim Earp* had this job. Ringo and Curly had not kept to Mexicans but had robbed anyone for years and Hooker had decided to end it all. It was known all over that Hooker had paid Wyatt Earp a lot of money to kill Curly. Why else should Earp have killed Curly? Curly was not one of the people who shot Virgil and Morgan Earp. Curly had always been a friend of the Earps before this. Ringo went into Mexico as soon as he heard of Curly's death but Cooly was watching out. After Ringo's death [some] cattlemen, and Hooker and Cooly were in Tombstone and they said it was good that Curly and Ringo were killed and they laughed. After this the local rustling all stopped. But Hooker and the Vales (Vail) were powerful but it was better to say nothing even though many people knew it was Cooly. . . .[64]

Cornelison's story, like so many other old-timer tales, has a ring of plausibility to it, and it perpetuates the faint but persistent rumor that Ringo was killed by a cowboy. It is possible that Hooker did decide to take action against the outlaws and that he hired a gunman. Certainly he would not have been the first rancher to do so. His contempt for Behan and his posse when they arrived at his ranch in pursuit of the Earp posse was so forcefully expressed it nearly led to a shooting. And, too, Wyatt Earp, whose posse had passed through Hooker's ranch a day or so earlier, had doubtless told the rancher he had killed Curly Bill and that he was leaving Arizona. Hooker might well have reasoned that with the Earps gone and with Behan galloping into his ranch yard at the head

---

* Jim Earp was Wyatt's oldest brother; actually the reference here should be to Warren Earp, Wyatt's youngest brother.

of a posse which included, among others, Ike and Phin Clanton and John Ringo himself, it was time to take the law into his own hands.

Cooley, however, never emerges as a figure in his own right. We know nothing of him—of his "triggernometry," Gene Cunningham would have said—or of the special abilities he would have had to have to hunt down and kill a man like John Ringo. But what really discredits Cornelison's statement is his claim that "it was known all over that Hooker had paid Wyatt Earp a lot of money to kill Curly," that "Curly was always a friend of the Earps"—"why else should Earp have killed Curly? Curly was not one of the people who shot Virgil and Morgan Earp."

There is no proof that Hooker paid Earp anything. And the Earps were not friends of Curly Bill, most particularly after the rustler-chief killed Tombstone marshal Fred White and Wyatt cracked his skull with a six-gun barrel and threw him in jail (see Chapter 2). Earp did not just ride out and pot Curly for the bounty. He stumbled onto him at Iron Springs and they shot it out. And how would Cornelison have known that "Curly [Bill] was not one of the people who shot Virgil and Morgan?"

I am persuaded that John Ringo committed suicide, that the evidence, when considered step by step, leads rather conclusively in that direction. First of all, the kill-claims of and for Wyatt Earp can logically be dismissed for the reasons considered in this chapter. So, I think, can the boast of Buckskin Frank Leslie and the claim made for Lou Cooley and divers other cowhands.[65] Fred Dodge's blunt statement that Johnny-Behind-the-Deuce "murdered" Ringo is quite another matter and must be seriously reconsidered. In considering the possibility of Johnny-Behind-the-Deuce as the killer, I have concluded that the case made by Dodge was not a particularly strong one. I believe that if O'Rourke was involved at all he was a diversion, with Johnny-Behind-the-Deuce becoming an Ace-in-the-Hole: Dodge and Wells, Fargo could have, as I have indicated, arranged for his escape from jail and—in the event Ringo's death was declared to be murder—for O'Rourke's "death" and a new identity: Johnny-Behind-the-Deuce could take the blame and disappear. In short, if Ringo *was* murdered, I think Dodge either did the killing himself or arranged for a professional to do it, *perhaps* a Lou Cooley. But since the death was generally believed to be a suicide there was no need for Dodge to say anything about O'Rourke as the "killer." Dodge did not—significantly, it seems to me— dispute the Statement for the Coroner at the time it was rendered, nor did he, as far as we know, ever mention O'Rourke's name until Stuart Lake queried him about Wyatt Earp's claim to killing Ringo. Dodge wrote Lake that he did not believe that Earp had made the claim. O'Rourke, as the deal *might* have been struck, would be permitted to "die" before the guns of Pony Deal, rather than being returned to prison (an event he would not likely have hung around for). But since Ringo was declared a suicide, why would it have been necessary to "kill off" O'Rourke unless, of course, it was the agreed pay-off against prison for whatever peripheral role the tinhorn might have played?

John Ringo was a rustler, not a "road agent." There is no record of his being accused of, or indicted for, stage robbery in Arizona, the only reason for which Wells, Fargo could possibly have been interested in him. Wells, Fargo's chief detective James B. Hume's *Robbers Record — 1871–1884*, does not contain Ringo's name, though Hume lists all stage robbers, dead or alive, during that period.[66] And in its July 22, 1882, story of Ringo's death, the *Epitaph* unequivocally declared that "while undoubtedly reckless, he was far from being a desperado. . . . Friends and foes are unanimous in the opinion that he was a strictly honorable man in all his dealings and that his word was as good as his bond" (rustling Mexican cattle did not stain one's honor—stage robbery would have!). Yet, unless. Dodge was working independently of Wells, Fargo (a most unlikely possibility), his correspondence with Stuart Lake justifies the assumption that the express company not only wanted Ringo (and perhaps other gang members), but wanted him badly enough to have *possibly* arranged O'Rourke's "escape" from jail (and, as Glenn Boyer claims, offered the bounty that brought Wyatt Earp on the shoot), so that Dodge could use him as a spy and informer. Dodge would not have had the authority to secure the release of the tinhorn on his own, and certainly not without revealing himself as a Wells, Fargo agent. Had O'Rourke escaped from jail by himself he would have been under no obligation to Dodge *or* Wells, Fargo; he would, doubtless, have headed straight for the Mexican border, which is precisely what I believe he did.

The Johnny-Behind-the-Deuce theory simply does not make sense, unless Fred Dodge thought he was covering for Wyatt Earp, or perhaps for himself. Johnny was a tinhorn, a thief, a coward, and a murderer. It burdens credibility that Wells, Fargo and Dodge—who must have been a reasonably good judge of character—would have put enough trust in such a person as to spring him from jail (in the expectation that he would serve faithfully in whatever capacity they had in mind), stash him away in the wilderness of the Chiricahua Mountains, and keep him supplied (he could not have survived otherwise)—all to spy on and perhaps kill John Ringo, who was not even wanted for stage robbery. The possibility that O'Rourke was keeping tabs on other members of the gang and stumbled onto Ringo, drunk and asleep in the tree bole (the Stuart Lake version), is equally remote, because the only gang members ever accused of, or indicted for, stage robbery (Jim Crane, Harry Head, Bill Leonard, and Frank Stilwell) were dead. Stuart Lake was the only one to accuse Curly Bill of stage robbery (James Hume considered him only a possibility), and Curly was dead, too.

Most improbable of all is the notion that Johnny-Behind-the-Deuce actually hung out in the rugged Chiricahuas for

fifteen months—risking both outlaws and Apaches and enduring loneliness, probable hunger, and other serious hard-
ships—because he felt an obligation to Fred Dodge or because he was nursing a burning desire for revenge through a
freezing Chiricahua winter. Such action would have been an
honorable and daring gamble completely beyond the character or resources of Johnny-Behind-the-Deuce.

It was never definitely proved that John Ringo was a member of the mob that tried to lynch Johnny-Behind-the-Deuce
(the *Epitaph,* for example, did not even mention him). Fred
Dodge said, without elaboration, that there was "bad blood"
between Ringo and O'Rourke and that the little tinhorn was
"afraid" of the outlaw. But Wyatt Earp, as we have seen,
pinpointed mining engineer Dick Gird as the mob's leader,
not John Ringo. Ringo reputedly immersed himself in drinking and gambling between rustling raids, withdrawing, according to Breakenridge, almost monastically from the gang,
and regarding the world about him with sullen insouciance.
Why should he have cared if a tinhorn shot a mining engineer,
or cared enough, at least, to ride the six miles from Charleston
to Tombstone at the head of a mob? Ringo was a lone rider, a
man apart, and one who did not like to lead, according to
Breakenridge and to others who knew him. Participation in a
mob action would have been out of character. If Ringo was
not in the mob, then (or only another face in it), Johnny-
Behind-the-Deuce was without motive—at least one strong
enough for him to risk selecting a man reputed to be "the
most dangerous gunman of them all" for a singular act of
revenge.

The Statement for the Coroner seems to reflect the opinion of the fourteen men who signed it: suicide. One of the
signers, Robert Boller, as we have seen, believed that Ringo
had the "D.T.s" and had shucked his boots because he
thought there were "snakes in them." It should be borne in
mind, though, that the members of that hastily formed panel
were not especially articulate or verbal men; nor were they

trained in law enforcement techniques, in the necessity to protect the death site, or to comment on and record in precise detail all their findings, all evidence and possibilities. They were more interested in inventory than in details. They meticulously recorded every item found on Ringo's person, but they omitted vital particulars: they noted that Ringo's Colt "contained 5 cartridges," but they did not, tantalizingly, say whether one of the five rounds had been fired or if a sixth, exploded cartridge lay under the hammer. Proponents of the murder theory argue that professional gunmen always kept an empty chamber under the hammer to avoid accidents (a "thumb slip") and conclude, therefore, that none of the five rounds had been fired; they also argue that on the frontier "cartridge" meant a live round, not a casing. But if the pistol had not been fired, by what rationale did the panel seem to find for suicide? And it did not always hold that expert gunmen kept an empty chamber. Curly Bill, for example, had six rounds in his revolver the night he killed marshal Fred White. And no less a figure than Wyatt Earp himself carried a sixth round under the hammer (despite his later claim to the contrary): one night in Wichita, according to the Wichita *Beacon*, when "policeman Erp" (*sic*) was sitting in a saloon back room, "his revolver slipped from his holster . . . causing a discharge of one of the barrels [rounds]."[67] Tombstone pundit Lorenzo Walters declared that one shot had been fired from Ringo's revolver, but he went on to nullify his credibility by claiming that Ringo's body had been found "seated on a rock between two small trees, away out in the San Simon Valley, with a bullet hole between his eyes."[68] (In *Billy King's Tombstone*, C. L. Sonnichsen also declared "there was a bullet hole between his [Ringo's] eyes."[69]) And, for whatever it is worth, William Breakenridge said that "one shot had been fired from it [Ringo's gun]."[70]

There is no mention in the Statement for the Coroner of powder burns about the wound or of grains of powder embedded in the flesh. It is possible, however, that if the muzzle had been pressed tightly against the skull, burns and grain flecks would have been minimal and not particularly noticeable to untrained examiners, especially if the wound was covered with a carapace of dried blood. The Statement for the Coroner describes Ringo's clothing and the torn undershirt wrappings around his feet, but it raises no questions about the missing boots, nor does it even mention the boots. No apparent study was made of the terrain about the death site, since there is no mention of horse tracks or of reasonably fresh droppings. (Had Ringo been killed elsewhere, as Josie Earp claimed, and his body had been hauled to the tree, there should have been sign: seven horses would have left tracks all over the place.) The serial number of Ringo's rifle was carefully recorded, but no panel member seemed to wonder why Ringo pulled his rifle from the saddle scabbard and left his boots looped over the saddle horn.[71] The Statement offers no word of dehydration, of sunburn, of cracked and swollen lips, or of a distended and swollen tongue.

The two most baffling aspects of Ringo's death are, of course, the removal of a portion of the scalp and the pistol belt that was buckled on upside down, with the latter nearly as puzzling as the former. Here again, one is frustrated by the failure of the citizens' Statement for the Coroner to describe the scalp wound adequately: "A part of the scalp [was] gone including a small portion of the forehead and part of the hair," which "looks as if cut out by a knife." No measurement of the wound is offered—not the length, the width, or even the general size of it. One could envision either a long, narrow strip of flesh removed (a furrow) or a round patch that inexplicably took part of the forehead. If Ringo was, indeed, scalped—if, as Phil Rasch theorized, "someone removed a trophy"—it was a badly botched job and a gruesome choice of trophy. I suggest the possibility that the scalp wound was made by an animal—rodents or, perhaps, a hawk, owl, or buzzard. Ringo was estimated to have been dead for "about 24 hours," which was long enough in that mid-July heat for putrefaction to have set in; that and the bloodied head would surely have drawn such creatures. The real question that comes to mind, of course, is: why would the killer take such pains to make the death appear a suicide, by placing Ringo's pistol in his hand, and then destroy—or at least cast doubt on—this effect by a senseless removal of a section of the scalp?

Ultimately, the answer to the question of murder or suicide hinges largely on whether there was a discharged round in Ringo's pistol. If a killer had used *his own pistol* to shoot Ringo, then placed the outlaw's gun in his hand, he surely would have fired a round from Ringo's gun, too. One does not shoot oneself and collapse with a fully loaded weapon in hand. But at her nearby ranch, Mrs. Smith, according to Breakenridge, heard only one shot at around two o'clock in the afternoon (Gilchriese's story has Earp firing "two or three times at him"). The fatal shot was fired from a pistol that was almost certainly pressed against the skull. Would a frightened Johnny-Behind-the-Deuce have got that close to Ringo (drunk, sleeping, or not)? Surely he would not have risked removing the sleeping outlaw's pistol from its holster in order to shoot him with his own gun. And why even try to make it look like suicide? There was no method in those days of tracing a killer through ballistics[72] and no one (except Fred Dodge) even knew that O'Rourke was in the Chiricahuas (if, indeed, he was). For that matter, why would Wyatt Earp, known to have been in Colorado, rig the death to appear a suicide, then boast of the killing later?

The buckled-upside-down pistol belt is puzzling. More than anything else, it appears to suggest a certain disorientation or confusion, perhaps the confusion of a mind already preoccupied with thoughts of suicide or, just possibly, of a man who was drunk or suffering from a monumental hangover. The panel members said there were "2 revolver cartridges in the cartridge belt." They did not say whether they picked up any loose cartridges about the site, although they noted that there were "6 pistol cartridges in his pocket." But the careful leaning of his rifle against the tree does not bespeak the actions of a man whose mind was so disordered, whether from alcohol, from heat and thirst, or from acute depression, or from all of these, that he stumbled into the tree's bole (by accident) and could not locate the stream that flowed noisily at his feet.

I believe that John Ringo's mind was reasonably clear, that he was capable of forming judgments, and that he sought the seat in the tree bole by the stream. Moreover, I believe it entirely possible that he rode his horse directly to the site where his body was found and that the horse "spooked" and ran off when the shot was fired and it smelled fresh blood. Trained cow ponies with the reins thrown down just did not wander off. I place no great importance on the missing boots. And the panel itself concluded that he had walked "but a short distance" in his socks and torn strips of undershirt. The boots, which reputedly turned up later, still looped over the saddle horn, were never, to my knowledge, examined. It is possible they were brand new or too small or that they hurt his feet and that he intended to soak his feet in Turkey Creek. This was not a man stumbling blindly for miles across a desert with his "bleeding" feet swathed in strips of cloth. He knew he had no great distance to walk. He wrapped his feet against whatever walking he intended to do, slid his rifle from its scabbard and walked to the tree where he rested it and took his seat.

I believe that John Ringo committed suicide. First, the nature of his wound indicates self-infliction. If the panel failed to state whether the pistol had been fired, it could just as easily have failed to report powder grains and burns, and the upward angle of the path of the bullet clearly supports self-infliction. Second, to have held the muzzle of the revolver against his temple, Ringo would have had to crook his arm and wrist at an awkward angle. It is true that this angle, along with the jump of a discharged .45, would probably have caused the gun to fall free of his body had his grasp not tightened in instant death over the grip. (There is no mention of whether or not the gun had to be forcibly removed from Ringo's hand.) It is equally true that (although the gun clasped in his hand *could* have been planted) many suicides who have done themselves in with guns have been found with the weapons clasped in their hands.

One thing about the gun that does not make sense is the claim (by William Breakenridge and Josephine Earp) that Ringo's pistol was caught in his watch chain. There would have been, in my judgment, less than one chance in a thousand that that could have happened. And for it to be caught in the watch chain *by its hammer* would be virtually impossible, since the hammer would have had to drop on the exploded cartridge. Only if the hammer had dropped *over* the chain could it have caught and held.

As important as the physical clues was John Ringo's probable state of mind. He has been repeatedly described as gloomy and suicidal.[73] Alcohol to him seems to have been a serious depressant. And there is an embarrassment of psychological extensions and symbols here if one chooses to use them: the deep, all-embracing tree bole with its spreading trunks as beckoning womb; the gurgle of the stream, evocative of the ebb of life sending soothing, dream-like diapasons of sound rolling through the troubled mind; thoughts of his father's useless death (and his own useless life) in that Wyoming desert, now possibly refracted through the shimmering similarity of landscape; the vision of his father's mutilated head with "the brains blown in all directions,"[74] and of the stillborn child who "looked just like father did;" perhaps, by thought association or extension, he saw a similar vision of himself. There was also the death of his outlaw friends, the rejection by his sisters, and no place, now, for Johnny to run, no escape from himself. Or was it all of these, overwhelming and engulfing, that led to a sudden compulsion to run no farther?[75]

What we know for certain is that John Ringo was barely thirty-two years old, that he wore a vest, blue shirt, and a "good-guy" white hat, that he died, contrary to predictions—including his own—with his boots off (which may also be the reason he had removed them), and that he is buried under a rock cairn just behind the tree where he died. For the record, his man-tally stands at one: himself.

Epilog

BECAUSE OF THE Ringo family's preoccupation with shame and disgrace, which must be considered obsessive even by nineteenth-century Victorian standards, and because of their determination to destroy or conceal all information or material that connected the outlaw son and brother to the Ringo family in San Jose, virtually everything that has been written about John Ringo is inaccurate or grossly exaggerated. We know some basic facts of his adult life; we know nothing of his childhood. History catches its first glimpse of him at fourteen, through Mary Ringo's *Journal,* but only as a fleeting presence, not as a personality. And of his five years in San Jose we learn from his nephew, Frank Cushing, only that John was a grammar-school dropout and a drunkard.

John Ringo has no real record to commend him to western history. No one, not even his acquaintances, seemed to have known him, except in the vaguest of terms. What emerges from a synthesis of all credible accounts are the faint outlines of a Jekyll-Hyde personality: the polite, likable, even erudite companion when sober, and the homicidal psychopath when drunk. Nearly every writer concerned with John Ringo credits him—inaccurately—with killing Louis Hancock in a barroom brawl, but in his obituary the Tombstone *Epitaph* stated that no crime had been charged to him in Arizona.

I have no doubt, however, that John Ringo was a vicious

killer, that he probably, if not provably, was involved in the killings of Charley Bader and a Mason gambler named Cheyney during the Hoodoo War in Texas and in the killing of the Haslett brothers in Huachita, New Mexico. Texas newspapers indicate that Ringo was at least present at the killings of Cheyney and Bader, and he was indicted for the killing of Cheyney. Only rumor and supposition tie him, along with Curly Bill, to the killing of the Hasletts.[1] The kill-pattern, however, was certainly the same: like Cheyney and Bader, the Hasletts were shot down without warning. As far as the *record* stands, then, a far better case can be made for John Ringo's cowardice than for bulldog courage. Weighed against Ringo's involvement in the Texas and New Mexico murders, along with the clumsy attempt on Louis Hancock and the gang shooting of Cowboy Dick Lloyd,* we have only the possibility that, if he had not been stopped by the police, he *might* have shot it out, face-to-face, with Doc Holliday on Tombstone's Allen Street.

Was Ringo, then, a coward? Almost certainly not, if he inherited any of the courage at all that carried his pregnant mother on to Nevada and California after the shocking death of her husband to raise five children on her own. It is far more likely that John Ringo simply followed the classic pattern of such gunmen as Wes Hardin, Bill Longley, Billy The Kid, Clay Allison, and Ben Thompson: he probably did not care one whit whether his target was a man's back or whether his man was facing him and shooting.

What of the myth of Ringo's fast draw and marksmanship? There is no record or account of a fast draw, and even Stuart Lake and Walter Noble Burns said he held his guns hidden in his pockets when he faced Doc Holliday. Breakenridge did say that Ringo was a good shot, but he offered no examples. A. M. Franklin, who claimed that Ringo saved him from a

* Cowboy Dick Lloyd was shot dead by the entire Curly Bill–Ringo gang when he rode his horse into a saloon at Fort Thomas, Arizona Territory (Breakenridge, *Helldorado*, pp. 113–15; Burns, *Tombstone*, pp. 79–82).

gunfight (see Chapter 3), declared Ringo to be "admittedly the best pistol shot in the country"; pistol in "each hand," [he] shot the "necks off beer bottles" and even placed two out of five shots into the "open necks of the bottle"—and this after giving each gun a "three-quarter" spin.[2] Franklin's bottle-busting story is suspect (in fact, I consider his entire deposition suspect), especially since ambidexterity, or shooting accurately with both hands, was rare, if not unknown, on the frontier. And it hardly squares with nearly missing Hancock at point-blank range.

With so meager a record, then, why has John Ringo become a major figure in the pantheon of western outlaws and gunmen? The legend, I am convinced, began with Walter Noble Burns and his creation of a Hamlet-like figure driven by personal agonies and furies, and in whom was embodied the classic struggle between good and evil, the quintessentially honorable outlaw and killer unable to come to terms with either his early reputable past or his disreputable present. Burns fired the imaginations of countless other writers who created their own versions of Ringo, often endowing him with qualities that merely revealed personal and largely inaccurate perceptions of what an outlaw and gunman ought to be.

Many writers, in fact, have seemed to prefer the Ringo myth to the truth. *The Shooters*, for example, by Leon Metz, was published in 1976, with the claim that it presented "Historical and True Stories of Notorious Gunmen." In this book, however, Metz wrote ". . . the strangest and most dangerous man who ever strapped on a six-shooter [was] John Ringo. . . . He gave the appearance of a good education and is said to have quoted freely by memory from the bards of yore. But if John kept a little poetry in his soul, he kept rot whiskey by the gallon in his stomach, . . . [and] when a saloon drunk made an unkind remark about a lady currently plying her trade in the street, . . . the sullen Ringo bashed the drunk over the head with his six-shooter, and then shot him through the throat. A funeral took place on the following day at Row 8 on Boot Hill."[3] (Ringo simply *must* be credited with a "kill"!) The dust jacket for this book proclaims that "through the author's intensive research combined with his whimsical humor, the shooters and gunmen appear as realities rather than the figments of fiction and fantasy." If Metz's research was anything even approaching "intensive," then he saw the newspaper accounts of the Ringo-Hancock shooting, which have been on file at the Arizona Pioneers Historical Society for fifty years or more. I first saw them in 1958. Metz, of course, did see these accounts: Ringo did, for example, strike Hancock over the head with his six-shooter—this is the only factual statement in Metz's yarn; to assume that Metz guessed at the head-bashing places too heavy a burden on coincidence. But by substituting "saloon drunk" for Hancock's name, by laying the affair to one of those celebrated defenses of womanhood rather than to Hancock's preference of beer to whiskey, by failure to name the town where the fracas occurred, and by authoritatively tossing in that phony Boot Hill row number, Metz, counting on the innocence or ignorance of his readers, appears to chalk up a genuine "kill." And thus he helps to embellish the Ringo myth.

William Breakenridge followed Burns's *Tombstone* with his *Helldorado,* in which he conferred a college degree on Ringo and set Ringo up as Wyatt Earp's antagonist, a theme that was later amplified and intensified in Eugene Cunningham's widely read and quoted *Triggernometry.* Breakenridge did succeed in creating a "bad guy" image for Wyatt Earp. And I never fail to be amazed that Ringo is almost invariably the "good guy." When the records of both men, such as they are, come under the honest gaze of history, Wyatt Earp, that "cold blooded killer," killed for the first time *of record* at the O.K. Corral—and then in self-defense. His later killings were acts of revenge and, if not particularly honorable (Curly Bill excepted), they are at least understandable, when one considers the cowardly ambushing of his brothers. Ringo's purported killings—if, indeed, he was involved—were plain, back-shooting murders. Ironically, we probably never would have heard of John Ringo—or of Curly Bill, John Behan, and the Clantons, of Breakenridge himself, or even much about Tombstone—if it had not been for the Earps and Doc Holliday and the O.K. Corral.

Although John Ringo was always depicted as the soul of abiding mystery, the silent, brooding, Byronic figure, apotheosized as a gallant in torment whose life was beyond redemption, I am of the belief that those celebrated Ringo "furies" are reducible to the bullying self-indulgence and self-pity of a vicious and dangerous drunk. John Ringo's image was created for him by the inaccuracies of innumerable writers, and I believe that he remains a western figure largely because of the mellifluous tonal quality of his name.

In Chapter 4 I listed a cross-section of theatrical, musical, and literary uses made of his name over the years. In 1980 a new novel popped up, titled *Ruby Sweetwater and the Ringo Kid*.[4] It has nothing to do with John Ringo. I am reminded of the first time I saw John Ringo's grave. As I stood looking at the bouldered cairn directly behind the death-tree, an old, nineteenth-century western song, "I've Got No Use for the Wimin," came to my mind. The song's theme was the betrayal of "an honest young puncher" by a girl named "Lou." The puncher became a "hard-shooting gunman" who was finally trailed out onto the prairie and killed by Texas Rangers. Dying, he was concerned only with his burial:

> *Wrap me up in my blanket,*
> *Bury me deep 'neath the ground.*
> *Cover me over with boulders*
> *Of granite, gray and round.*

And as I looked from the boulder-heaped grave to the waiting, five-armed blackjack, out to the dust-deviled Sul-

phur Springs Valley, and back up to the darkly shadowed
Chiricahuas, the dominant feeling was that all external things
here, along with a pervasive spirit of place, were embodied
and unified in the name:

Ringo!

A name of its place and time and calling.

A name that rings like a bell.

Notes to Chapters

Introduction

1. C. L. Sonnichsen, *Ten Texas Feuds* (Albuquerque: University of New Mexico Press, 1957), p. 90.

2. Jo Jo James, quoted in *The Hero in America,* by Dixon Wecter (Ann Arbor: University of Michigan Press), 1963, p. 352.

3. Bernard De Voto, quoted in *Great Western Short Stories,* edited by J. Golden Taylor (Palo Alto, California: The American West Publishing Company, 1967), p. xi.

1. Ringo!

1. Walter Noble Burns, *Tombstone—An Iliad of the Southwest* (New York: Doubleday and Company, 1927), p. 46.

2. Ibid., p. 135.

3. Ibid., p. 134–35.

4. Joseph Millard, "Johnny Ringo—Cultured Killer," *True Western Adventures* (August, 1960): 65.

5. Burns, p. 134.

6. Burns, pp. 134–35.

7. The Austin *Weekly Statesman,* January 6, 1876; The Austin *Daily Statesman,* October 17, 1875; *The San Antonio Express,* October 6, 1875.

8. William M. Breakenridge, *Helldorado—Bringing the Law to the Mesquite* (Boston and New York: Houghton Mifflin Company, 1928), p. 134. *Helldorado* was written with the assistance of western novelist William MacLeod Raine.

9. Frank C. Lockwood, *Pioneer Days in Arizona* (New York: The Macmillan Company, 1932), pp. 281–282. I have visited these sites and locations and all others described in this book many times.

10. Jack Burrows, "Ringo," *The American West* 7, No. 1 (January, 1970): 17.

11. Burns, *Tombstone*, p. 133.

12. Breakenridge, *Helldorado*, p. 134.

13. Ibid., p. 136.

14. Ibid.

15. The *Tucson Star,* December 14, 1879; The *Arizona Miner,* December 14, 1879.

16. Breakenridge, *Helldorado*, p. 135. The Tombstone *Nugget*, August 11, 1881.

17. Breakenridge, *Helldorado*, p. 135.

18. Ibid., p. 136.

19. Burns, *Tombstone*, p. 134.

20. Breakenridge, *Helldorado*, p. 135.

21. Ibid., p. 136.

22. Ibid., p. 137. Ringo actually skipped bail, though he later returned to Tombstone and was again freed on bail. In the April, 1985, issue of *Real West* (vol. 28, no. 202), Jack De Mattos is in error in claiming (p. 41) that Ringo "skipped town" because he was under indictment for the January 6, 1882, holdup of the Bisbee stage.

23. The Tombstone *Epitaph*, August 19, 1881.

2. The Tombstone Situation and the Earp-Clanton Feud

1. The Tombstone *Epitaph*, May 3, 1882. (The President was Chester A. Arthur.)

2. Besides the Earp brothers and Doc Holliday, there were the Clantons (Billy was killed at the O.K. Corral), Tom and Frank McLaury (also killed at the O.K. Corral), Curly Bill, John Ringo, "Buckskin" Frank Leslie, Charlie Storms, Luke Short, William B. "Bat" Masterson, William "Billy the Kid" Claiborne, Frank Stilwell, sheriffs John Behan and, later, John Slaughter, Wm. M. "Billy" Breakenridge, editor John Clum, and Johnny-Behind-the-Deuce O'Rourke. All are referred to in books on Western Americana; most have figured in motion pictures. Wyatt Earp, Bat Masterson, John Ringo, John Clum, and John Slaughter have been featured in weekly television series. During a portion of the period 1879–1882, John C. Frémont was territorial governor.

3. James E. Serven, "The Buntline Special—Fact or Fiction?", *The American Rifleman* 115, No. 3 (March, 1967): 18–20. A.E.Z. Judson, alias Ned Buntline, the creator of Buffalo Bill and one of the fathers of the dime novel, was supposed to have had five of the super-barrelled Colt revolvers made. One went to Wyatt Earp, the others to peace officers Neal Brown, Charlie Bassett, Bat Masterson, and Bill Tilghman. Colt

Firearms has no record of such a transaction or gifting. Jay Monoghan (*The Great Rascal: The Exploits of the Amazing Ned Buntline* [Boston: Little, Brown and Company, 1952] refers to the presentation of the guns on pp. 258–259, but he quotes Stuart Lake. See also William B. Shillingberg, *Wyatt Earp and the "Buntline Special" Myth* (Tucson, Arizona: Blaine Publishing Company, 1976).

4. Stuart N. Lake, *Wyatt Earp: Frontier Marshal* (Boston and New York: Houghton Mifflin Company, 1931), pp. 145–146.

5. Ibid., p. 235.

6. Douglas D. Martin, *Tombstone's Epitaph* (Albuquerque: The University of New Mexico Press, 1951), p. 168.

7. Tombstone *Epitaph*, October 20, 1880; *Nugget*, November 12, 1880.

8. *Tucson Star,* September 23, 1881.

9. Doc Holliday has become as famous as Wyatt Earp and more so than John Ringo. He has been the subject of at least two biographies and dozens of articles. He has also been represented in a number of motion pictures and countless television westerns.

10. Josephine Sarah Marcus Earp, *I Married Wyatt Earp: The Recollections of Josephine Sarah Marcus Earp,* collected and edited by Glenn G. Boyer (Tucson: The University of Arizona Press, 1976), p. 16, note 1.

11. Lockwood, *Pioneer Days*, p. 283.

12. Martin, *Tombstone's Epitaph*, p. 10; Lockwood, *Pioneer Days*, p. 283.

13. Martin, *Tombstone's Epitaph*, p. 10.

14. Lockwood, *Pioneer Days*, p. 284.

15. Ibid., p. 283.

16. Martin, *Tombstone's Epitaph*, p. 11.

17. Conversation with Will Sanders at John Ringo's grave site at Sanders's Turkey Creek Canyon Ranch, Sulphur Springs Valley, in southeastern Arizona, August 20, 1956. For another interview with Sanders, see a staff-authored travel article in *Sunset Magazine* (June, 1956): pp. 24–31. The article (which carries a photo of Sanders seated in the tree forks where Ringo's body was found) quotes Sanders as saying his father found Ringo's body.

18. Breakenridge, *Helldorado*, p. 179.

19. Sol Israel to Stuart N. Lake, September 21, 1928. Lake Collection, Huntington Library, Los Angeles, California.

20. Martin, *Tombstone's Epitaph*, p. 167.

21. *Epitaph*, October 28, 1880.

22. Ibid., October 29, 1880.

23. Eugene Cunningham, *Triggernometry: A Gallery of Gunfighters* (Caldwell, Idaho: The Caxton Printers, Ltd., 1947), p. 115.

24. Ibid., pp. 99–100, p. 119.

25. Eugene Cunningham to author, May 28, 1953.

26. Burns, *Tombstone*, pp. 139–41; Breakenridge, *Helldorado*, pp. 135–36; The Tombstone *Daily Nugget*, August 11, 1881; Cunningham, *Triggernometry*, pp. 100–102.

27. Eugene Cunningham to author, August 10, 1953; *Triggernometry*, p. 119.

28. Burns, *Tombstone*, p. 138; Lake, *Wyatt Earp*, p. 307.

29. Breakenridge, *Helldorado*, p. 157.

30. Cunningham, *Triggernometry*, p. 119; Burns, *Tombstone*, pp. 137–38.

31. *Epitaph*, December 29, 1881, March 20, 1882; Frank Waters, *The Earp Brothers of Tombstone: The Story of Mrs. Virgil Earp* (New York: Clarkson N. Potter, Inc., 1960), p. 191.

32. *Epitaph*, October 27, 1881.

33. Waters, *Earp Brothers*, pp. 186–87.

34. Breakenridge, *Helldorado*, p. 157.

35. Ibid., pp. 157–58. In his efforts to romanticize Ringo, Breakenridge does not mention that Earp, Doc, and Ringo were arrested the day after the encounter at the order of Police Court Judge A. O. Wallace for carrying concealed weapons. Wyatt was discharged because he was a deputy U.S. marshal. Doc and Ringo were fined thirty dollars each. Earp and Holliday were arrested by Dave Neagle, who was later to become Tombstone's police chief, and Ringo was arrested by James Flynn. Neagle had just defeated Flynn for the office of chief of police. *Epitaph*, March 18, 1882.

36. Burns, *Tombstone*, p. 138.

37. Joe Chisholm, "Tombstone's Tale: The Truth of Helldorado," undated manuscript, pp. 1–3.

38. Lake, *Wyatt Earp*, p. 307.

39. Ibid., pp. 307–308.

40. George Whitwell Parsons, *The Private Journal of George Whitwell Parsons* (Phoenix, Arizona: Statewide Archival and Records Project, 1:286, November, 1939). Lake, *Wyatt Earp*, p. 306.

41. Lake, *Wyatt Earp*, pp. 234–35.

42. Martin, *Tombstone's Epitaph*, pp. 210–11; The *Tucson Citizen*, March 26, 1882.

43. *Epitaph*, March 21, 1882.

44. Apparently the Earp party did constitute a posse. On January 24, 1882, Tombstone Mayor John Carr (John Clum had been defeated for reelection on January 3, 1882) issued a proclamation informing the people of Tombstone that "Wyatt Earp had warrants for the arrest of divers persons charged with criminal offenses. I request the public within the city to abstain with any interference with the execution of said warrants." The

warrants had been issued, presumably, by Judge William M. Stilwell of the District Court of the First Judicial District of Cochise County. The warrants apparently bore no expiration date, since they still obtained on March 24, 1882. *Epitaph*, March 24, 1882.

45. Lake, *Wyatt Earp*, pp. 333–37.

46. Ibid., p. 231; *Epitaph*, March 20, 1882.

47. *Epitaph*, March 23, 1882.

48. Lake, *Wyatt Earp*, p. 138. Martin, *Tombstone's Epitaph*, p. 241. *Epitaph* March 27, 1882.

49. Lake, *Wyatt Earp*, pp. 340–41. In a story to the San Francisco *Examiner* (August 2, 1896), Earp referred to Curly Bill's gun as "a Winchester." It could have been a Winchester shotgun.

50. *Epitaph*, October 28, 1881. See also: Letter to Stuart N. Lake from Fred Dodge, October 28, 1928, in Dodge's *Under Cover for Wells, Fargo: The Unvarnished Recollections of Fred Dodge*, edited by Carolyn Lake (Boston: Houghton Mifflin Company, 1969), pp. 234–35. If anyone qualifies for the oft repeated claim that he was "the real thing," it would seem to be the late Fred Dodge. An undercover agent for Wells, Fargo, Dodge arrived in Tombstone in 1879 and remained there nearly ten years. From the moment he got off the stage in Tombstone he became a close friend of the Earps, especially since he was a look-alike for Morgan. Dodge worked closely with Wyatt Earp during Earp's stay in Tombstone and without ever revealing himself to be a Wells, Fargo agent. Dodge practically revered Wyatt Earp, commenting again and again on his bravery, coolness, and devotion to the law. Dodge died in 1938 at the age of eighty-four, after having cooperated in every way with Stuart Lake in his writing of *Wyatt Earp—Frontier Marshal* (but only after receiving assurances from Wyatt Earp himself that Lake's efforts were sanctified). He wanted to help his friend Wyatt Earp in any way possible. When Wyatt died, Dodge continued to assist Lake and gave his final approval of the published book.

Lake died in 1964 while engaged in the writing of a history of Wells, Fargo. His daughter, Carolyn Lake, born during the Dodge-Lake collaboration, has gathered together Dodge's story and, with the most skillful editing, produced this valuable piece of Western Americana thirty years after Dodge's death.

From the above citation (pp. 234–35), here is what Fred Dodge wrote to Lake about the confrontation at Iron Springs:

> You asked for information about the death of Curley (sic) Bill. By reason of my connection with Wells, Fargo and Co., and also because of my association with Wyatt Earp and others of his party, I had full information concerning the fight at Iron Springs in which Wyatt Earp and party were ambushed by Curly Bill and party.

Immediately after this fight I intrusted myself in ascertaining the true facts about the death of Curly Bill. J. B. Ayers, a saloon keeper [who also worked for Wells, Fargo] of Charleston, where the outlaws and rustlers head-quartered, told me that the men who were in the fight told him that Wyatt Earp killed Curley Bill and that they took the body that night and . . . buried him on [Frank] Patterson's ranch, on the Babocomari [Creek]. Johnny Barnes, who was in the fight and was badly wounded, and was one of the Curly Bill party, told me that they opened up on the Earp party just as Wyatt swung off his horse . . . and they thought they had hit Wyatt but it was the horn of the saddle that was struck. That Wyatt throwed down on Curley Bill right across his horse and killed him. . . . Sometime after this Ike Clanton himself told me that Wyatt had killed Curley Bill.

51. Breakenridge, *Helldorado*, p. 177.

52. Ibid., pp. 177–78.

53. *Epitaph*, November 28, 1929.

54. Ibid.

55. Breakenridge, *Helldorado*, p. 178.

56. Ibid., pp. 178–79. According to Lake, who does not cite his source(s), other well-known outlaws were: Hank Swilling, Frank Patterson, Pony Deal, Rattlesnake Bill Johnson, Jim Hughes, Ed and Johnny Lyle. Lake, *Wyatt Earp*, p. 346. He does not mention Johnny Barnes, who Dodge said was wounded in the fight with Curly Bill and later died from his wounds.

57. *Epitaph*, April 14, 1882.

58. Ibid. Lake (*Wyatt Earp*) identified the offensive posseman as Ike Clanton—probably an educated guess, since Ike did a lot of talking and threatening when he felt it was safe to do so. Almost certainly it was not John Ringo. Breakenridge (*Helldorado*) omits the incident altogether.

59. *Epitaph*, April 14, 1882.

60. Josephine Earp, *I Married Wyatt Earp*, p. 66.

61. Tucson *Daily Star*, July 18, 1882, and June 7, 1938.

62. Pop Church, quoted in Eugene Cunningham to author, May 23, 1953.

63. Eugene Cunningham to author, August 12, 1954.

64. John Ringo to Sheriff Charles Shibell, March 3, 1880. The original letter is in the collection of the late historian researcher, and writer, Robert N. Mullin.

3. Ringo, Doc, Wyatt, and the Writers

1. Burns, *Tombstone*, p. 7 of section on sources.

2. Frederick R. Bechdolt, *When the West Was Young* (New York: The Century Company, 1922), p. 151.

3. Ibid., pp. 154–55.

4. "Statement for the Information of the Coroner and Sheriff of Cochise Co. A.T. Turkey or Morses' Hill Creek, 14th July, 1882." This Statement of citizens in regard to the death of John Ringo, filed November 13, 1882, with the District Court of the First Judicial District, Cochise County, Arizona, confirms this description.

5. Sara Grace Bakarich, *Gunsmoke—The True Story of Old Tombstone* (Tombstone, Arizona: Tombstone Press, 1954), pp. 95–97.

6. Ibid., p. 97.

7. Ibid., pp. 103–104.

8. John Myers Myers, *Doc Holliday* (Boston and Toronto: Little, Brown and Company, 1955), pp. 127–28.

9. Ibid., p. 128.

10. Ibid., p. 187.

11. Pat Jahns, *The Frontier World of Doc Holliday—Faro Dealer from Dallas to Deadwood* (New York: Hastings House, 1957), p. 152.

12. Ibid., pp. 222–23.

13. Chisholm, "Tombstone's Tale," pp. 5–6, 9.

14. Ibid., p. 9.

15. Ibid., p. 106.

16. Louise and Fullen Artrip, *Memoirs of (the Late) Daniel Fore (Jim) Chisholm and the Chisholm Trail* (Yermo, California: Artrip Publications, 1959), p. 6.

17. According to Walter Noble Burns, nineteen Mexicans were killed in this encounter, or ambush, and $75,000 in Mexican silver were taken (Burns, *Tombstone*, p. 106). According to the *Epitaph* four Mexicans were killed and the silver amounted to $4,000 (*Epitaph*, August 5, 1881).

18. Artrip and Artrip, *Memoirs*, p. 7. One name puzzles in Chisholm's narrative: "Tap Duncan." Chisholm mentions Duncan only as a cowboy, but Tap Duncan was an alias for Harvey Logan, the notorious Kid Curry of Butch Cassidy's Wild Bunch. Logan was going by the name Tap Duncan when he was killed. See Robert West Howard, *This is the West* (New York: The New American Library [Signet Book], 1957), p. 119.

19. Artrip and Artrip, *Memoirs*, p. 99.

20. Ibid., p. 100.

21. Ibid., pp. 101–102.

22. Ibid., p. 104.

23. Ibid., p. 105.

24. Ibid., p. 159.

25. Ibid., p. 109.

26. Ibid., p. 111.

27. Cunningham, *Triggernometry*, pp. 99–100.

28. Ibid., p. 119.

29. Eugene Cunningham to author, August 20, 1953.

30. William Breakenridge, quoted in a letter from Eugene Cunningham to author, May 28, 1953.

31. Eugene Cunningham to author, October 11, 1953.

32. Ray Hogan, *The Life and Death of Johnny Ringo* (New York: Signet Books, 1963), pp. 27–28.

33. Tony Goodstone, ed., *The Pulps* (New York: Chelsea House, 1970), pp. 57–85, *passim*.

34. Gary L. Roberts, "The West's Gunmen: II," *The American West* 8, No. 2 (March, 1971): 20.

35. Dave Markson, "Ringo," *Men—True Adventures* 6, No. 3 (March, 1957): 24–25.

36. Ibid., p. 25.

37. Ibid., p. 37.

38. Ibid.

39. Ibid.

40. Howard N. Monnett, "General Jo Shelby and Johnny Ringo," publication unknown (1971?:27).

41. Ibid.

42. Ibid., pp. 27–28.

43. Ibid., p. 28.

44. "Ringo Gets a Tombstone," The San Jose (California) *Mercury-News*, February 17, 1974.

45. Monnett, "General Jo Shelby," p. 28.

46. Robert M. Boller to Mrs. George F. Kitt, Arizona Pioneers Historical Society, Tucson, Arizona. I have no date for the letter, but it was probably written before 1932, the year Breakenridge died, since Boller appears to refer to Breakenridge as if he were still living.

47. "Statement for the Information of the Coroner and Sheriff," np.

48. A. M. Franklin, penciled account, no date. Document is on file at the Arizona Pioneers Historical Society, Tucson, Arizona.

49. "Reminiscences of a Stage Driver, Clifton, Arizona, to Lordsburg, New Mexico, in the 1880's," July 29, 1927. Arizona Pioneers Historical Society, Tucson, Arizona.

50. Judge J. C. Hancock, letter to the *Epitaph*, November 28, 1929 (quoted in part before with respect to Wyatt Earp and Curly Bill—see Chapter 2, notes 53 and 54). For further confirmation of Earp's arrest of Curly Bill, see Dodge, *Under Cover*, pp. 236, 241–42.

51. Conversations with John G. Gilchriese, Summer 1977. Gilchriese's

story is not recorded in J. Evetts Haley's adulatory biography, *Jeff Milton: A Good Man with a Gun.* Eugene Cunningham wrote me that both Break-enridge and Capt. John Hughes of the Texas Rangers had told him that, though Milton was "nervy," he was also mean and a bully. Eugene Cunningham to author, August 14, 1957.

52. *Tucson Star,* July 18, 1882.

53. *Epitaph,* July 22, 1882.

54. *Tucson Star,* June 7, 1938.

55. Tombstone, *Nugget,* August 11, 1881.

4. A Summary and That Magic Name

1. Hogan, *The Life and Death of Johnny Ringo,* Foreword, vi.

2. Ray Hogan, *Marshal Without a Badge,* (Greenwich, Conn.: Fawcett Publications [Gold Medal Book], 1959), pp. 21–24.

3. For an especially well-written and meticulously researched psycho-biography, see Michael Paul Rogin, *Fathers and Children: Andrew Jackson and the Subjugation of the American Indian* (New York: Alfred A. Knopf, 1975). Rogin, it seems to me, never convincingly establishes the oral-anal-mammary connection between Jackson's "rages" and his treatment of Indians.

4. There has been some agreement with the name-quality concept. McNeal Bourne observed that Ringo's name "has a built-in gunslinger sound to it" (*Tombstone Epitaph,* National Edition, May 1977, p. 18). Jack DeMattos wondered ". . . just what Ringo did—other than possessing a mellifluous name—that has so endeared him to the hearts of generations of western buffs" ("Johnny Ringo! The Elusive Man Behind the Myth," *Quarterly of the National Association and Center for Outlaw and Lawman History* 3, No. 2 [Autumn, 1977], p. 4).

5. Burrows, "Ringo," p. 21.

6. Dixon Wecter, *The Hero in America* (Ann Arbor: University of Michigan Press, 1963), p. 87.

7. Ibid., p. 86.

8. Helen F. Moore, "What's in a Name?", cited in Wecter, *The Hero in America,* p. 86.

9. From "Ringo" © 1970, Don Robertson Music Corporation.

10. The London *Evening News,* June 18, 1966. The strip was sent to me by the late Edna G. Landin, President of Tombstone's Chamber of Commerce, who worked hard to preserve Tombstone's storied past, and whose efforts, it seemed to me, were never fully appreciated.

11. Burrows, "Ringo," p. 19.

5. "Two-Gun Charlie" Ringo

1. *Ringo Reunion in Print* 1, 1 (October 1, 1934). This 4-page periodical was published in Covington, Kentucky, by the Society of Ringo Descendants in America. (All Ringo materials cited in this book came to me from Charles R. Ringo and remain in my collection.)

2. May King to Charles R. Ringo, June 6, 1970.

3. David Lear Ringo to Charles R. Ringo, July 13, 1970.

4. David Lear Ringo, "Chart of the Ringo Family, in *The First Five Generations of the Ringo Family in America*, Vol. 2 of the Ringo Family History Series (Alhambra, California: Freeborn Family Organization, 1982). The chart, tracing the male line only, was originally presented at a meeting of the Hunterdon County Historical Society, Ringoes, N. J. October 21, 1967.

5. Ibid.

6. Charles R. Ringo to author, January 28,1972.

7. I have had some correspondence with Erwin and he has confirmed ownership of the items mentioned. He has prepared his own manuscript on John Ringo. For some years he attempted to collaborate with Frank Cushing, got to know Cushing well, and certain arrangements were made. Their efforts, it would seem, were never consummated. Erwin was bitter over his dealings with Cushing, who seems to have played cat and mouse with him. David Lear Ringo, however, reached a tentative agreement with Erwin to collaborate on a television series. But when David could not reach a "reasonable" agreement with Erwin and learned that actor Dick Powell had done a pilot film for a series on John Ringo, David "called the whole thing off" and asked Erwin to return papers dealing with Martin Ringo's Mexican-War experiences. Erwin did not respond to David's letters, nor did he ever return the papers. David Lear Ringo to Charles R. Ringo, September 15, 1970.

8. Charles R. Ringo to author, January 28, 1972.

9. Ibid., June 24, 1970.

10. I made another effort to contact Frank Cushing in 1977. I received a letter from the attorney handling Cushing's estate for his nephew, William Warren Batchelder. Cushing had died on May 18, 1977. In my letter I had again suggested collaboration, and included a copy of John Ringo's letter to Sheriff Charles Shibell, cited earlier in this book. The attorney wrote that he had "forwarded [the] letter to Mr. Batchelder and perhaps you will hear from him if he has any information on John Ringo." Batchelder did not reply. Russell G. Behrens, Atty., to author, August 30, 1977.

11. Frank M. Cushing to Dr. William K. Hall, November 11, 1969. I am at a loss to explain how Cushing printed copies of Mary Ringo's Journal

if it was in the possession of Allen Erwin. Either Erwin lent it to Cushing, or Cushing borrowed it from the Ringo family, returned it, and it was later given to Erwin.

12. Frank M. Cushing to Dr. William K. Hall, January 27, 1970. Fanny Fern Ringo married Frank Moses Jackson. Their son was Frank Ringo Jackson, and it was his daughter who gave the gun, journal, and pot to Erwin. I have been unable to learn how John Ringo's pistol and rifle were returned to the family. The rifle was lost in the San Francisco earthquake.

13. Frank M. Cushing to Charles R. Ringo, August 12, 1970.

14. Appended handwritten note by Charles Ringo to author on copy of the letter from Frank M. Cushing to Charles R. Ringo (August 12, 1970).

15. Frank M. Cushing to Charles R. Ringo, August 12, 1970.

16. Charles R. Ringo to Will (Ringo?) May 9, 1970. I have not been able to determine who "Will" is. I assume he is a nephew (the son of David L. Ringo). Charles never clarified his observations. Clarification often came through repetition, but not in the case of "Will."

17. Charles R. Ringo to May King, June 12, 1970. May King is considered an authority on her branch of the Ringo family. Dr. William K. Hall to Charles Ringo, June 20, 1970, confirms this genealogy.

18. Ibid.

19. Charles R. Ringo to Will, May 9, 1970.

20. Charles R. Ringo to May King, June 12, 1970. Daniel Ringo was, indeed, Chief Justice of the Supreme Court of Arkansas from 1836 to 1844. From 1849 to 1861 he was United States District Judge. After the Civil War he practiced law in Little Rock. He is of John Ringo's side of the family tree. "Graves of Eminent Men," *Arkansas Historical Association* 2 (1908): 286.

To David L. Ringo, Charles spoke of his own line of descent from Samuel H. Ringo, 1761–1835. Among the distinguished professionals were Dr. R. B. Ellis—graduate of Transylvania University of Lexington, Kentucky, and Medical College in Pennsylvania—who was a delegate to the convention that nominated Democrat James K. Polk for president. In 1850 he captained a wagon train to California, and he was a friend of Mark Twain.

Dr. John W. Ringo, son of Samuel A. Ringo(?), was a physician in Parkville, Missouri. Two other sons were Richard A. Ringo, merchant, and Charles S. Ringo, educated at William and Jewell College, Liberty, Missouri, Baptist minister, President of Baptist Seminary, Arrow Rock, Missouri. Later, in California, he, too, was a friend of Mark Twain. (Charles R. Ringo to Dave, May, Claude, Will, et al., June 21, 1972.)

21. Edward G. Quick, *John Ringo and His Gold* (n.p.: May, 1964, revised 1971), 7-page booklet.

22. Charles R. Ringo to David Lear Ringo, February 18, 1972.

23. Charles R. Ringo to author, June 24, 1970.

24. Ibid., December 15, 1972.
25. Charles R. Ringo to Will, May 9, 1970.
26. Charles R. Ringo to author, September 7, 1970.

6. The Journal of Mary Peters Ringo

1. David Lear Ringo, *"Chart of the Ringo Family."*
2. Charles R. Ringo to author, January 28, 1972.
3. Ibid.; John Ringo's sister Mattie confirms that their father had been in the Mexican War and that he had contracted tuberculosis while stationed in Sacramento ("Foreword," by Mattie Rell [Ringo] Cushing, to Mary Peters Ringo, *The Journal of Mrs. Mary Ringo* [Santa Ana, California: privately printed by Frank Myrle Cushing, 1956]). The journal itself is hereafter referred to as *Journal of Mary Ringo*.

Although Martin Ringo saw no action in California, he did see some service with Colonel A. W. Doniphan's Mounted Missourians; I have not had access to his record, which is among the papers that were not returned by Allen Erwin to David Lear Ringo (David L. Ringo to Charles R. Ringo, September 15, 1970).

4. Charles R. Ringo to author, January 28, 1972.
5. Ibid.; Mattie Bell Ringo Cushing's reference to her own age and to that of her brothers and sisters confirms the years of their births (*Journal of Mary Ringo*, "Foreword," n.p.).
6. Burns also made a hero of Billy the Kid (Walter Noble Burns, *The Saga of Billy the Kid* [1926]). See also Charles A. Siringo, *A Lone Star Cowboy* (Santa Fe: 1919).
7. *Joural of Mary Ringo*, Foreword, n.p.
8. *Journal of Mary Ringo*, p. 1.
9. Ibid., p. 4.
10. Ibid.
11. Ibid., p. 6.
12. Ibid., p. 8.
13. Ibid., p. 9.
14. Ibid., p. 10.
15. Ibid., p. 15.
16. Ibid., p. 16.
17. Ibid., p. 18.
18. Ibid., p. 19.
19. Ibid.
20. Ibid., pp. 20–21.
21. *Liberty* [Missouri] *Tribune*, August 26, 1864, and September 16, 1864.
22. Charles R. Ringo to Will, May 9, 1970.

23. *Journal of Mary Ringo*, p. 21.

24. Ibid.

25. Ibid., p. 22.

26. Ibid., p. 24.

27. Ibid., p. 25.

28. Ibid., p. 26.

29. Ibid., p. 28.

30. Ibid., p. 29.

31. Ibid., p. 31.

32. Ibid., p. 36.

33. Ibid.

34. Mattie Bell Ringo Cushing (In Conclusion) pp. 37–38.

35. Charles R. Ringo to Dave (David L. Ringo), Mary (Ringo), et al. June 21, 1972.

36. Charles R. Ringo to author, January 28, 1972.

37. Frank Cushing quoted in Charles R. Ringo to Will, May 9, 1970.

7. The Graduate

1. Monnett, *General Jo Shelby*, pp. 27–28.

2. Chisholm, "Tombstone's Tale," pp. 9, 36–37.

3. Artrip and Artrip, *Memoirs*, p. 102.

4. Charles R. Ringo to Will, May 9, 1970.

5. Eugene Cunningham to author, August 20, 1953.

6. San Jose, California, City Directory, 1897, p. 355.

7. Charles R. Ringo to Dave, et al., June 2, 1972.

8. Ibid.; Charles R. Ringo to author, January 28, 1972; Charles R. Ringo to Will, May 9, 1970.

9. Burns, *Tombstone*, p. 134.

10. Josephine Earp, *I Married Wyatt Earp*, p. 66.

11. Ibid., pp. 66–68.

12. J. Marvin Hunter and Noah H. Rose, *The Album of Gunfighters* (Helotes, Texas: Warren Hunter, 1951). Photos of dead men appear on pp. 7 (Jesse James), 17, 31–32 (The Daltons), 35 (Bill Doolin), 60 (Ned Christie), 83 (Ben Kilpatrick), 125 (John Wesley Hardin).

13. Henry Nash Smith, *Virgin Land: The American West as Symbol and Myth* (Cambridge: Harvard University Press, 1970), p. 103.

8. The Hoodoo War and Those Dear Little Sisters

1. Charles R. Ringo to Will, May 9, 1970.

2. Ibid.

3. Although Cushing referred to the plural—"sisters"—it seems

unlikely that Mary corresponded with Augusta Younger while both were living in San Jose, unless, of course, Augusta had moved east. Reference must have been to a third sister (not named in the material I received from Charles Ringo), who resided in the East.

4. David Lear Ringo to Charles R. Ringo, July 13, 1970.

5. Ibid.

6. C. L. Sonnichsen, *Ten Texas Feuds* (Albuquerque: University of New Mexico Press, 1957), pp. 90–91.

7. Claude Elliott, "Union Sentiment in Texas," *Southwestern Historical Quarterly* (April, 1947): 401–407.

8. Sonnichsen, *Ten Texas Feuds*, p. 90.

9. Ibid.

10. Austin *Daily Statesman*, November 18, 1875.

11. Sonnichsen, *Ten Texas Feuds*, p. 90. Sonnichsen's chapter on the Hoodoo War sparkles with color and wit. A longtime "feud collector," Sonnichsen is probably the foremost authority on Texas feuds.

12. Ibid., p. 91. With Clark already a sheriff and Hoerster a cattle inspector, it is unclear what the "office" was to which they were "elected."

13. Austin *Daily Statesman*, November 18, 1875.

14. Sonnichsen, *Ten Texas Feuds*, p. 92.

15. Ibid.

16. Ibid.; Thomas W. Gamel, *The Life of Thomas W. Gamel* (Mason, Texas: privately printed, n.d.), pp. 27–32.

17. Sonnichsen, *Ten Texas Feuds*, pp. 92–93.

18. Ibid., p. 93.

19. San Antonio *Herald*, August 30, 1875.

20. Sonnichsen, *Ten Texas Feuds*, pp. 95–96; May King to Charles R. Ringo, June 6, 1970.

21. James B. Gillett, *Six Years with the Texas Rangers* (Austin, Texas: Von Boeckmann–Jones, Co., 1921), p. 74; Sonnichsen, *Ten Texas Feuds*, p. 94.

22. San Antonio *Herald*, August 17, 1875.

23. San Antonio *Herald*, September 20, 1875; Austin *Daily Statesman*, October 17, 1875.

24. Gamel, The Life of Thomas W. Gamel, p. 27. Gamel also wrote (p. 32) that "a man" later told him that the had found "Ringoe's" body in the "roots" of a tree "in Mexico."

25. The State of Texas vs. John Ringo, George Gladden and others, November, 1876. The indictment, signed by William Kooch, Foreman of the Grand Jury, is on file at the District Court, County of Mason, Texas.

26. Austin *Weekly Statesman*, November 9, December 7, 1876. C. L. Sonnichsen, *Billy King's Tombstone* (Caldwell, Idaho: The Caxton Printers, 1942), pp. 30–32; May King to Charles R. Ringo, June 6, 1970.

27. Dora Neill Raymond, *Captain Lee Hall of Texas* (Norman: University of Oklahoma Press, 1940), pp. 131–32; *Galveston* [Texas] *News*, August 25, 1877.

28. Wayne Gard, *Frontier Justice* (Norman: University of Oklahoma Press, 1949), pp. 55–56.

29. Frank A. Tinker, "No One Called Him Johnny," *The Tucson Citizens' Magazine*, October 30, 1982, pp. 12–13.

30. Official Election Register 259–269, Texas State Library, Austin, Texas.

31. Sonnichsen, *Ten Texas Feuds*, p. 98.

32. Charles R. Ringo to Will, May 9, 1970.

33. Conversation with Charles R. Ringo, March 5, 1971.

34. Ibid.; Allen A. Erwin to author, January 7, 1978.

35. Conversations with Mrs. J. H. Ethyl Macia, August, 1957 (Mrs. Macia was a Tombstone old-timer, an educated woman who knew Tombstone's history). The sheriffs of Cochise County in the 1930s were: George Henshaw, 1927–1930; Fred A. Kenney, 1931–1932; Tom A. Voelker, 1933–1934, I. V. Pruitt, 1932–1935, 1935–1952 (Ellen M. Young, Clerk of Superior Court, County of Cochise, Bisbee, Arizona, to author, July 30, 1979). I have been unable to determine which of these sheriffs Enna Ringo and Frank Cushing contacted. In a private conversation Charles Ringo told me that Cushing had intimated that Enna had visited Wyatt Earp in Los Angeles after Earp made his claim to killing John Ringo, but that Wyatt was noncommital. The date of this visit was believed to have been between 1910 and 1912.

36. Charles R. Ringo to John D. Gilchriese, January 28, 1972. John D. Gilchriese is an authority on Tombstone and Wyatt Earp.

37. Robert M. Boller to Mrs. George F. Kitt. Arizona Pioneers Historical Society, Tucson, Arizona. Date of letter is unknown, but is probably before 1932 (see Chapter 3, note 46).

38. Conversation with Charles R. Ringo, March 5, 1971; this information was confirmed in Allen A. Erwin to author, January 7, 1978.

9. The Homecoming

1. Charles R. Ringo to Will, May 9, 1970.

2. Charles R. Ringo to author, January 28, 1972.

3. Dodge, *Under Cover*, p. 24.

4. Conversation with Charles R. Ringo, March 5, 1971. Charles said Cushing mentioned potential book sales.

5. *Epitaph*, March 27, 1882; Breakenridge, *Helldorado*, pp. 178–79.

6. *Nugget*, August 11, 1881.

7. *Epitaph*, December 9, 1881.

8. *Arizona Daily Star,* June 23, 1881.

9. Charles R. Ringo to Gilchriese, January 28, 1972. Charles, in turn, was misquoted by others. In the *Tombstone Epitaph National Edition*, May, 1977, p. 18, Alford E. Turner wrote: "The Ringo Family genealogy . . . compiled by Charles R. Ringo, indicates that John Peter [*sic*] Ringo . . . was born in Missouri on May 3, 1850. . . . According to family records, court records, and his own word [John Ringo's?] the name was John Peter Ringo." I cannot imagine that this information came from Charles. The only correct statement here is the date of John Ringo's birth.

10. The Death of John Ringo

1. The Statement for the Information of the Coroner and Sheriff of Cochise County, A.T., (1882) mentions only the Smith Ranch in its description of the death of John Ringo. But Will Sanders told me that the ranch was there when Ringo's body was found and that his father knew John Ringo (conversation with Will Sanders, August 20, 1956.) Sanders made the same claim to *Sunset Magazine* (June, 1956: 31).

2. William Breakenridge and others claimed there was a flat rock in the bole that formed a comfortable seat. There was no rock at the time of my first visit in 1956.

3. Breakenridge, *Helldorado,* pp. 187–89.

4. Lake, *Wyatt Earp,* p. 355; *Tucson Star,* May 16, 1882; Breakenridge, *Helldorado,* p. 179; *Epitaph,* April 14, 1882.

5. *Tombstone Nugget,* May 10, 1882.

6. Eugene Cunningham to author, May 31, 1954. In this same letter Cunningham also stated that Breakenridge was inordinately jealous of Wyatt Earp ("He thoroughly disliked him and all the Earps") and that at every opportunity in his conversations with Cunningham, Breakenridge suggested that Wyatt Earp was afraid of Ringo.

7. Robert Boller to Mrs. George F. Kitt.

8. Chisholm, "Tombstone's Tale," pp. 153–55.

9. Ibid., p. 156.

10. Ibid., p. 155.

11. Ibid., p. 5. Chisholm also claimed that Ringo was a friend of his father (a justice of the peace in Bisbee) and that Ringo was a frequent visitor to the Chisholm home, where, as a "college graduate," he and the elder Chisholm discussed such recondite subjects as archaeology, Mexican poetry, and social science (p. 36).

12. Artrip and Artrip, *Memoirs,* pp. 112–13. Daniel Chisholm and Joe Chisholm were not related, though both shared a common talent for yarn spinning.

13. Tucson *Daily Star,* July 18, 1882.

14. *Epitaph*, July 22, 1882.

15. Lake, *Wyatt Earp*, p. 246.

16. *Epitaph*, January 17, 1881.

17. Ibid.

18. Ibid.

19. Lake, *Wyatt Earp*, p. 246.

20. Breakenridge, *Helldorado*, pp. 111–112.

21. Some accounts have Jack McCann, proprietor of the Last Chance Saloon, which was located between Charleston and Tombstone, taking O'Rourke to Tombstone on his blooded mare, Molly McCarthy (Burns, *Tombstone*, p. 68). Lake claims it was "Virgil Earp, riding Dick Naylor, a thoroughbred belonging to Wyatt," (*Wyatt Earp*, p. 247). The *Epitaph* mentions neither. Referring to the ride, the *Epitaph* observed: "However . . . it is certain that he [O'Rourke] came in [to Tombstone] ahead, his horse reeking sweat, and dismounting in front of Vogan's Saloon asked for protection" (*Epitaph*, January 17, 1881). Dodge (*Under Cover*, p. 11) corroborates Lake.

22. Lake, *Wyatt Earp*, p. 357; Dodge, *Under Cover*, p. 239. Dodge (p. 241) confirmed his use or attempted use of Johnny-Behind-the-Deuce as an informer.

23. Fred Dodge to Stuart Lake, cited in Dodge, *Under Cover*, p. 239.

24. Lake, *Wyatt Earp*, p. 247.

25. Ibid., pp. 249–50.

26. Ibid., pp. 257–58.

27. *Las Vegas* [New Mexico] *Daily Optic*, April 7, 1884; Phil Rasch, "The Resurrection of Pony Diehl," Los Angeles Westerners *Branding Iron*, December 1957. Lorenzo D. Walters claims that Pony Deal (or Diehl) was wounded in a gunfight with outlaws Joel Fowler and John Burns, trailed to a house whose owner he killed, and was himself burned to death in the house when Fowler and Burns set fire to it; the event occurred near Clifton, Arizona. Lorenzo D. Walters, *Tombstone's Yesterday* (Tucson, Arizona: Acme Printing Company, 1928), pp. 258–59. Walter's book, which is shot through with errors of fact and place, may be Lake's source for his claim that Deal was killed in a gunfight.

28. Jack DeMattos, "Johnny Ringo!" p. 10, fn. 28.

29. Ibid., p. 8, fn. 15; Waters, *Earp Brothers*, pp. 114–15.

30. DeMattos, "Johnny Ringo!", p. 10. In a later article, DeMattos declared that Ringo "was trying to *save* Johnny-Behind-the-Deuce, not lynch him." He ofers no verification for this revelation (Jack DeMattos, "Gunfighters of the Real West: Johnny Ringo," *Real West* 28, No. 202 [April, 1985]: 41).

31. Former Tombstone mayor (1880–1882), John Clum, wrote a short

piece titled "It All Happened in Tombstone," published in the *Arizona Historical Quarterly* in October, 1929. The rest of the primary materials consist of documents, newspapers, court records, letters, and depositions, along with secondary materials.

32. Eugene Cunningham (quoting William Breakenridge) to author, August 10, 1953, July 11, 1957.

33. Phil Rasch, *The Mysterious Death of John Ringo*, undated typescript, 3 pp. The fact that Rasch makes no mention of Dodge's *Undercover for Wells, Fargo* would seem to place the writing of the article before 1969.

34. Ibid., pp. 1–2.

35. Ibid., p. 2.

36. Lockwood, *Pioneer Days*, pp. 283, 285.

37. Ibid.; "Breakenridge," Douglas D. Martin once wrote me (June 5, 1953), "was a pipsqueak and completely unreliable as a source of information."

38. Rasch, "Mysterious Death," p. 1.

39. C. L. Sonnichsen, *From Hopalong to Hud: Thoughts on Western Fiction* (College Station: Texas A & M University Press, 1978), pp. 23–24.

40. *The Arizona Daily Star,* January 26, 1964 (feature article by Bob Thomas).

41. Interviewed by Denver newspapers in 1900 (Dawson Scrapbook, June copy, Colorado Historical Society, Denver), Wyatt had said, "We missed Jack Ringo." Glenn Boyer has pointed out that at that time Wyatt was in "some danger of prosecution." (Just what Wyatt was in "danger of prosecution" for in 1900 is puzzling: it could not have been for the O.K. Corral fight, which had occurred nineteen years before, and for which the statute of limitations had long passed, and certainly it could not have been for killing John Ringo, whose death had been largely regarded a suicide in 1882.) At any rate, Wyatt made the kill-claim much later, first to Frank Lockwood, then to Stuart Lake; later, in his own *Autobiography* (published in a limited edition on October 26, 1981, by Glenn G. Boyer), which was dictated to long-time friend John Flood, Wyatt placed his killing of Ringo in the "Swiss Elm" (Swisshelm) Mountains, a spur of the Chiricahuas (Glenn G. Boyer to author, March 19, 1981). That, of course, was not where the body was found, either. Boyer, however, is convinced that Wyatt killed Ringo. See Glenn G. Boyer, "Welcome to Earp Country," *Arizona Highways* 58, No. 11 (November, 1982): 13.

42. Breakenridge, *Helldorado*, pp. 175–77. Breakenridge's story was of two outlaws, Pink Truly and Alex Arnold, who claimed to have been at Iron Springs when Wyatt reputedly killed Curly Bill. Curly Bill, according

to the outlaws, was not at the springs. Earp fired on Truly and Arnold, who returned the fire. Earp wore a "white shirt" and made a "splendid target." Arnold "drew a fine bead on Wyatt and fired." Wyatt turned and staggered off, saved by a "steel vest" under his shirt. Later, an unnamed deputy, peeking out from a crack in a barn, noted that "Earp's overcoat had a bullet hole through each side of the front of it" and heard someone say "the steel saved you that time." Earp must have been wearing that "white shirt" *over* his "overcoat".

43. Josephine Earp and Glenn G. Boyer, "Sinister Shadow from the Past," *True West* 23, No. 1, Whole No. 131 (September–October, 1975): 23.

44. Ibid.

45. James B. Hume (Wells, Fargo chief detective), "Wells, Fargo & Co.'s Express Robbers Record, 1871–1884." Hume does not mention John Ringo, though he lists robbers both dead and alive during that period. Obviously Ringo was not wanted by Wells, Fargo. And the company has no record or reference to bounties paid to either Breakenridge or Earp. Joan W. Salz (curator, Wells, Fargo Bank History Room, San Francisco, California) to author, July 23, 1979.

46. Cunningham to author, September 23, 1956. This view is also reflected in Cunningham's *Triggernometry*, p. 113.

47. Josie had visited Fred Dodge in 1932; the story of Ringo's death was written in 1937, five years *after* her visit with Dodge. Glenn G. Boyer to author, March 19, 1981.

48. "Harry Goober" is a *nom de gun*. Whoever he was, he preferred anonymity.

49. There is no evidence of a friendship between the Earps and O'Rourke.

50. The mysterious Harry Goober apparently remained with the horses.

51. The *Tombstone Epitaph* 95, No. 34 (December 20, 1974).

52. Ibid.

53. In the newspaper article cited above (note 51), Josie's description of the death site and scene, like Breakenridge's, does not match that given in the citizens' Statement for the Information of the Coroner and Sheriff.

54. The *Tombstone Epitaph* 95, No. 34 (December 20, 1975). For the opposite view of Wyatt as possible or potential "hangman," see Alford E. Turner, *The Earps Talk* (College Station, Texas: Creative Publishing Company, Early West Series, 1980). Turner's book has an introduction by Glenn G. Boyer.

55. Josie was the inamorata of Sheriff John H. Behan when she first

came to Tombstone. (Behan was believed to have been overly friendly to the outlaw element in Tombstone and Cochise County [*Epitaph*, August 19, 1881]). Wyatt Earp, though "married" (no record), wooed her away from the sheriff. Glenn G. Boyer's excellent editing of Josie's *I Married Wyatt Earp* tells the story of this historic triangle, which, as much as anything else, heightened tensions among Earp, the sheriff, the outlaw faction, and the law-and-order people. In his biography of Earp, Stuart Lake ignored Josie at her insistence. Privately he referred to her as "a regular old gorgon" (Robert N. Mullin to author, December 12, 1979).

56. Pat Jahns, *The Frontier World*, p. 239.

57. *Minutes of the District Court of Pueblo County, Colorado* (Vol. 5, pp. 354–355), "Case No. 1851, the People vs. J. H. Holliday for larceny," July 11, 1882. After this hearing, Doc was not brought to trial (The *Pueblo* [Colorado] *Chieftan*, July 19, 1882). The *Chieftan* dates Holliday's court appearance on July 19, a probable reference to the continuance of his case.

58. Josephine Earp, *I Married Wyatt Earp*, p. 248. John Gilchriese acquired some of the Flood material, including the map showing the location of the killing of Ringo. I have seen the chapter in Earp's *Autobiography* that deals with the "killing" of John Ringo. Titled "Where There's Smoke," the chapter features a totally false account of Ringo's killing. Earp, at the head of a posse, picked Ringo off with a rifle shot, after Ringo had emptied his own rifle. Boyer believes William S. Hart, who was mining Wyatt for information relative to making a motion picture of the incident, might have "encouraged" or "assisted" Flood, to whom Wyatt "dictated" his memoirs. Glenn G. Boyer to author, April 29, 1981 (included also a copy of Chapter 14, "Where There's Smoke," pp. 321–25, from Earp's *Autobiography*).

59. Cunningham, *Triggernometry*, p. 128.

60. Frank M. King, *Mavericks* (Pasadena, California: n.p., 1947).

61. Breakenridge, *Helldorado*, p. 189.

62. Burns, *Tombstone*, pp. 264–65.

63. Conversations with Mrs. J. H. Ethyl Macia, June 1953.

64. Ed. J. Cornelison, as told to Henry G. Conrad, unpublished manuscript, 1934. David H. Cruickshanks Collection, London, England.

65. One captivating yarn by a self-proclaimed writer of "Western stories for over thirty years," caps the absolute extremes of writing about John Ringo and about the American West. This one is in the form of a letter to *Frontier Times* which was later reprinted in the El Paso *Southwesterner*. The writer was Jack Mills of Albuquerque, New Mexico:

> Ringo was shot by a cowboy. Johnny's horse was lame and he wanted to
> trade horses with a cowpoke. Tempers flared in the deal and Ringo was

shot. His body was shipped to Tucson, Arizona, and was buried on a friend's ranch about five miles north of the Mexican border. The fellow who owned the ranch was one of his handy gunmen. I could give you the names of all of his gunmen and also give you the location of the ranch, but 10,000 writers would call me a damned liar.

Ringo's killer lived as a neighbor to me in Colorado, dying there in 1934 at the age of ninety-one. He had the newspaper clippings to prove his story, picture and all. My grandfather was well acquainted with Johnny Ringo and his parents. Grandfather said that Ringo was a lousy shot, although he did have a hot temper with a mighty low boiling point. . . .

I have been writing Western stories for over thirty years, but never considered Ringo . . . worth writing about.

66. See also Larry D. Ball, *The United States Marshals of New Mexico and Arizona Territories, 1846–1912* (Albuquerque: University of New Mexico Press, 1978), p. 116.

67. The Wichita (Kansas) *Beacon*, January 12, 1876.

68. Walters, *Tombstone's Yesterday*, p. 99.

69. Sonnichsen, *Billy King's Tombstone*, p. 31.

70. Breakenridge, *Helldorado*, p. 188.

71. The boots were found looped over the saddle horn when the horse later wandered into the Chiricahua Cattle Company Ranch. The horse was also reported stolen from a Mexican. Another story has it that only one boot was found; another that a horse's skeleton was found bearing a saddle with the initials J.R.. The Tucson *Weekly Citizen*, July 30, 1882, reported that the son of B. F. Smith found Ringo's "1,000 lb. Bay" wandering some two miles from the death site, still saddled.

72. Colonel Calvin Goddard invented the Comparison Microscope for judging ballistics evidence in 1927.

73. *Epitaph*, July 22, 1882.

74. The *Liberty* [Missouri] *Tribune*, August 26, 1864, September 16, 1864.

75. An Ohio University study found that "more than a third of the emergency-room suicide patients tried to kill themselves on impulse, not as a result of chronic depression." *The San Francisco Chronicle*, July 23, 1983.

Epilog

1. The *Arizona Daily Star*, June 23, 1881, reported that the Hasletts were killed in a running fight with outlaws led by Jim Crane. Curly Bill and John Ringo might have been in the fight, but neither was mentioned.

2. A. M. Franklin, penciled account, no date (Arizona Pioneers Historical Society, Tucson, Arizona). Other than this account by Franklin

(who claimed to be a cattleman), and his account in the depositions (see Chapter 3), there seems to be no record of him.

3. Leon Claire Metz, *The Shooters* (El Paso, Texas: Mangan Books, 1976), pp. 250–51, 279.

4. *The San Francisco Chronicle Review,* December 28, 1980, p. 8. The story includes such historical figures as Butch Cassidy and The Sundance Kid, Tom Horn, and others; but the "Kid" is not John Ringo.

References Cited

Archives

Arizona Pioneers Historical Society, Tucson, Arizona.

Burrows Collection. Jack Burrows, San Jose, California.

Cochise County, Arizona. Records of the District Court of the First Judicial District.

Colorado Historical Society, Denver, Colorado. Dawson Scrapbook (citing 1900 Denver newspapers).

Cruikshanks Collection. David H. Cruikshanks, London, England.

Mullin Collection. Robert N. Mullin.

Mason County, Texas. District Court Records.

Pima County, Arizona. Pima County District Court Records.

———. Pima County Recorder's Office, Tucson, Arizona.

Pueblo County, Colorado. Minutes of the District Court.

Wells, Fargo Bank History Room, San Francisco, California.

Books and Magazines

Artrip, Louise, and Fullen Artrip. *Memoirs of (the Late) Daniel Fore (Jim) Chisholm and the Chisholm Trail.* Yermo, California: Artrip Publications, 1959.

Bakarich, Sara Grace. *Gunsmoke—The True Story of Old Tombstone.* Tombstone, Arizona: Tombstone Press, 1954.

Bechdolt, Frederick R. *When the West Was Young.* New York: The Century Company, 1922.

Boyer, Glenn G. "Welcome to Earp Country." *Arizona Highways* 58, No. 11 (November, 1982): 13.

Breakenridge, William M. *Helldorado—Bringing the Law to the Mesquite.* Boston and New York: Houghton Mifflin Company, 1928.

Burns, Walter Noble. *The Saga of Billy the Kid.* n.p.: 1926.

———. *Tombstone—An Iliad of the Southwest.* New York: Doubleday & Company, 1927.

Burrows, Jack. "Ringo." *The American West,* 7, No. 1 (January 1970): 17.

Clum, John. "It All Happened in Tombstone." *Arizona Historical Quarterly,* October 1929.

Cunningham, Eugene. *Triggernometry: A Gallery of Gunfighters.* Caldwell, Idaho: The Caxton Printers, Ltd., 1947.

DeMattos, Jack. "Johnny Ringo! The Elusive Man Behind the Myth." *Quarterly of the National Association and Center for Outlaw and Lawman History* 3, No. 2 (Autumn 1977): p. 4.

———. "Gunfighters of the Real West: Johnny Ringo." *Real West* 28, No. 202 (April, 1985): 41.

Dodge, Fred. *Under Cover for Wells, Fargo: The Unvarnished Recollections of Fred Dodge.* Edited by Carolyn Lake. Boston: Houghton Mifflin Company, 1969.

Earp, Josephine Sarah Marcus. *I Married Wyatt Earp: The Recollections of Josephine Sarah Marcus Earp.* Collected and edited by Glenn G. Boyer. Tucson: The University of Arizona Press, 1976.

Earp, Josephine, and Glenn G. Boyer. "Sinister Shadow from the Past." *True West* 23, No. 1, Whole No. 131 (September–October, 1975): 23.

Earp, Wyatt. *"Where There's Smoke,"* in *Autobiography.* Published in a limited edition by Glenn Boyer, 1981.

Elliott, Claude. "Union Sentiment in Texas." *Southwestern Historical Quarterly* (April, 1947): 401–407.

Gamel, Thomas W. *The Life of Thomas W. Gamel.* Mason, Texas: privately printed, n.d.

Gard, Wayne. *Frontier Justice.* Norman: University of Oklahoma Press, 1949.

Gillett, James B. *Six Years with the Texas Rangers.* Austin, Texas: Von Boeckmann–Jones Company, 1921.

Goodstone, Tony, ed. *The Pulps.* New York: Chelsea House, 1970.

"Graves of Eminent Men." *Arkansas Historical Association* 2, 1908.

Hogan, Ray. *The Life and Death of Johnny Ringo*. New York: Signet Books, 1963.

————. *Marshal Without a Badge*. Greenwich, Connecticut: Fawcett Publications (Gold Medal Book), 1959.

Howard, Robert West. *This is the West*. New York: The New American Library (Signet Book), 1957.

Hunter, J. Marvin, and Noah H. Rose. *The Album of Gunfighters*. Helotes, Texas: Warren Hunter, 1951.

Jahns, Pat. *The Frontier World of Doc Holliday—Faro Dealer from Dallas to Deadwood*. New York: Hastings House, 1957.

King, Frank M. *Mavericks*. Pasadena, California: n.p., 1947.

Lake, Stuart N. *Wyatt Earp: Frontier Marshal*. Boston and New York: Houghton Mifflin Company, 1931.

Lockwood, Frank C. *Pioneer Days in Arizona*. New York: The Macmillan Company, 1932.

Markson, Dave. "Ringo." *Men—True Adventures* 6, No. 3 (March, 1957): 24–25.

Martin, Douglas D. *Tombstone's Epitaph*. Albuquerque: The University of New Mexico Press, 1951.

Metz, Leon Claire. *The Shooters*. El Paso, Texas: Mangan Books, 1976.

Millard, Joseph. "Johnny Ringo—Cultured Killer." *True Western Adventures* (August 1960): 65.

Monnett, Howard N. "General Jo Shelby and Johnny Ringo." Publication unknown: 1971?: 27.

Myers, John Myers. *Doc Holliday*. Boston and Toronto: Little, Brown and Company, 1955.

Parsons, George Whitwell. *The Private Journal of George Whitwell Parsons*. Phoenix, Arizona: Statewide Archival and Records Project, 1:286 (November 1939).

Pueblo County, Colorado. *Minutes of the District Court of Pueblo County, Colorado*. "Case No. 1851, the People vs. J. H. Holliday for Larceny." Vol. 5, pp. 354–355, July 11, 1882.

Quick, Edward G. *John Ringo and His Gold*. N.p., 1964. Revised 1971. 7-page booklet.

Rasch, Phil. "The Resurrection of Pony Diehl." Los Angeles Westerners *Branding Iron*, December 1957.

Raymond, Dora Neill. *Captain Lee Hall of Texas*. Norman: University of Oklahoma Press, 1940.

Ringo, David Lear. "Chart of the Ringo Family," in *The First Five*

Generations of the Ringo Family in America. Vol. 2 of the Ringo Family History Series. Alhambra, California: Freeborn Family Organization, 1982. The chart, tracing the male line only, was originally presented at a meeting of the Hunterdon County Historical Society, in Ringoes, N. J., on October 21, 1967.

Ringo, Mary Peters. *The Journal of Mrs. Mary Ringo*. Santa Ana, California: privately printed by Frank Myrle Cushing, 1956.

Ringo Reunion in Print 1, 1 (October 1, 1934). This 4-page periodical was published in Covington, Kentucky, by the Society of Ringo Descendants in America.

Roberts, Gary L. "The West's Gunmen: II." *The American West* 8, No. 2 (March, 1971): 20.

Rogin, Michael Paul. *Fathers and Children: Andrew Jackson and the Subjugation of the American Indian*. New York: Alfred A. Knopf, 1975.

Serven, James E. "The Buntline Special—Fact or Fiction?" *The American Rifleman* 115, No. 3 (March, 1967): 18–20.

Siringo, Charles A. *A Lone Star Cowboy*. Santa Fe: n.p., 1919.

Smith, Henry Nash. *Virgin Land: The American West as Symbol and Myth*. Cambridge: Harvard University Press, 1970.

Sonnichsen, C. L. *Billy King's Tombstone*. Caldwell, Idaho: The Caxton Printers, 1942. Reissued by The University of Arizona Press, Tucson, 1972.

———. *From Hopalong to Hud: Thoughts on Western Fiction*. College Station: Texas A & M University Press, 1978.

———. *Ten Texas Feuds*. Albuquerque: University of New Mexico Press, 1957.

Sunset Magazine (June 1956): 24–31.

Taylor, J. Golden, ed. *Great Western Short Stories*. Palo Alto, California: The American West Publishing Company, 1967.

Turner, Alford E. *The Earps Talk*. College Station, Texas: Creative Publishing Company, Early West Series, 1980.

Wagoner, J. J. "History of the Cattle Industry in Southern Arizona, 1540–1940." *University of Arizona Bulletin* 22, No. 2 (April 1, 1952): 105.

Walters, Lorenzo D. *Tombstone's Yesterday*. Tucson, Arizona: Acme Printing Company, 1928.

Waters, Frank. *The Earp Brothers of Tombstone: The Story of Mrs. Virgil Earp*. New York: Clarkson N. Potter, Inc., 1960.

Wecter, Dixon. *The Hero in America*. Ann Arbor: University of Michigan Press, 1963.

Newspapers

Arizona Daily Star, June 23, 1881; Jan. 26, 1964.
Arizona Miner, Dec. 14, 1879.
Beacon [Wichita, Kansas], Jan. 12, 1876.
Daily Nugget [Tombstone], Aug. 11, 1881.
Daily Star [Tucson], July 18, 1882; June 7, 1938.
Daily Statesman [Austin], Oct. 17, 1875; Nov. 18, 1875.
Epitaph [Tombstone], Oct. 20, 1880; Oct. 28, 1880; Oct. 29, 1880; Jan. 17, 1881; Aug. 5, 1881; Aug. 19, 1881; Oct. 27, 1881; Oct. 28, 1881; Nov. 17, 1881; Dec. 9, 1881; Dec. 29, 1881; Mar. 18, 1882; Mar. 20, 1882; Mar. 21, 1882; Mar. 23, 1882; Mar. 24, 1882; Mar. 27, 1882; Apr. 14, 1882; May 3, 1882; July 22, 1882; Nov. 19, 1882; Nov. 28, 1929; Dec. 20, 1974.
Evening News [London], June 18, 1966.
Galveston [Texas] *News,* Aug. 25, 1877.
Herald [San Antonio], Aug. 30, 1875; Sept. 20, 1875; Aug. 17, 1875.
Las Vegas [New Mexico] *Daily Optic,* Apr. 7, 1884.
Liberty [Missouri] *Tribune,* Aug. 26, 1864; Sept. 16, 1864.
Mercury-News [San Jose, California], Feb. 17, 1974.
Nugget [Tombstone], Nov. 12, 1880; Aug. 11, 1881.
Pueblo [Colorado] *Chieftan,* July 19, 1882.
San Antonio Express, Oct. 6, 1875.
San Francisco Chronicle, July 23, 1983; February 11, 1984.
San Francisco Chronicle Review, Dec. 28, 1980, p. 8.
Tombstone Epitaph, National Edition, Dec. 20, 1974; May 1977, p. 18.
Tombstone Nugget, May 10, 1882.
Tucson Citizen, Mar. 26, 1882.
Tucson Star, Dec. 14, 1879; Sept. 23, 1881; Sept. 28, 1881; May 16, 1882; July 18, 1882; June 7, 1938.
Weekly Citizen [Tucson], July 30, 1882
Weekly Statesman [Austin], Oct. 17, 1875; Jan. 6, 1876; Nov. 9, 1876; Dec. 7, 1876.

Manuscripts, Depositions, Letters

Boller, Robert M. to Mrs. George Kitt. Date unknown (probably before 1932). Arizona Pioneers Historical Society Collection.

Chisholm, Joe. "Tombstone's Tale: The Truth of Helldorado." Manuscript, n.d. Gilchriese Collection.

Cornelison, Ed J., as told to Henry G. Conrad, 1934. Manuscript. Cruikshanks Collection.

Cunningham, Eugene. Letters, 1952–1957. Burrows Collection.

Franklin, A. M. Penciled account, no date. Arizona Pioneers Historical Society Collection.

Hume, James B. "Wells, Fargo & Co.'s Express Robbers Record, 1871–1884." Wells, Fargo Bank History Room Collection.

Martin, Douglas D., to author, June 5, 1953. Burrows Collection.

Rasch, Phil. "The Mysterious Death of John Ringo." Undated typescript, 3 pages. Mullin Collection.

"Reminiscences of a Stage Driver, Clifton, Arizona to Lordsburg, New Mexico, in the 1880's," July 29, 1927. Arizona Pioneers Historical Society Collection.

Ringo, Charles. Letters, 1970–1973. Burrows Collection.

Ringo, John, to Sheriff Charles Shibell, March 3, 1880. Mullin Collection.

Salz, Joan W. (curator, Wells, Fargo Bank History Room, San Francisco, California) to author, July 23, 1979. Burrows Collection.

Statement for the Information of the Coroner and Sheriff of Cochise Co., A. T., Turkey or Morse's Hill Creek, 14th July, 1882. This document, an endorsed statement made by fourteen citizens in regard to the death of John Ringo, was made on July 14, 1882, and filed on November 13, 1882. Records of the District Court of the First Judicial District, Cochise County, Arizona.

Index